Labour: a party fit for imperialism

ROBERT CLOUGH

SECOND EDITION

IMPERIALISM

COUNTERATTACK Nº 2

First published 1992
Second edition 2014

Larkin Publications
BCM Box 5909 London WC1N 3XX

British Library Cataloguing in Publication Data
A catalogue record for this book is available from the British Library

ISBN 978-0-905400-27-3

Cover photograph: Focus E15 campaign supporters on the march through Newham, 5 July 2014

Typeset in Bembo and Univers
by Boldface

Printed and bound by CPI Group (UK) Ltd, Croydon, CR0 4YY

Contents

In memory of

TERRY O'HALLORAN

comrade and friend

Acknowledgements

This book would not have been written without the collective support of my comrades of the Revolutionary Communist Group. I have borrowed unashamedly from articles they have written in the newspaper *Fight Racism! Fight Imperialism!*; a small group of comrades have read and re-read successive drafts, removing the wilder formulations and helping me to tighten the main arguments that it puts forward. I would like to mention in particular David Reed, for his relentlessness; the advice and comments of Eddie Abrahams, Carol Brickley, Andy Higginbottom and Maxine Williams, and the organisational work of Nicki Rensten.

RC

Second edition:

Particular thanks are due to Jim Craven for writing Part 6.9 From New Realism to New Labour and Part 7 Labour in government 1997–2010. Without the effort that he put in during 2009–10, the task of producing this edition would have been a daunting challenge.

Thanks are also due also to David Yaffe and Carol Brickley for editing the new material; to Carol additionally for the typesetting, and to Nicki Rensten for proof reading the final version.

RC

Orgreave June 1984 – British police in action against striking miners

Preface to the second edition

The first edition of *Labour: a party fit for imperialism* took the history of the Labour Party up to its defeat at the 1992 election. This new edition brings it up to date and includes a revised and extended Part 6, a new Part 7 which covers the Labour Governments from 1997 to 2010, and a new conclusion in Part 8. There are minor revisions to earlier parts.

RC SEPTEMBER 2014

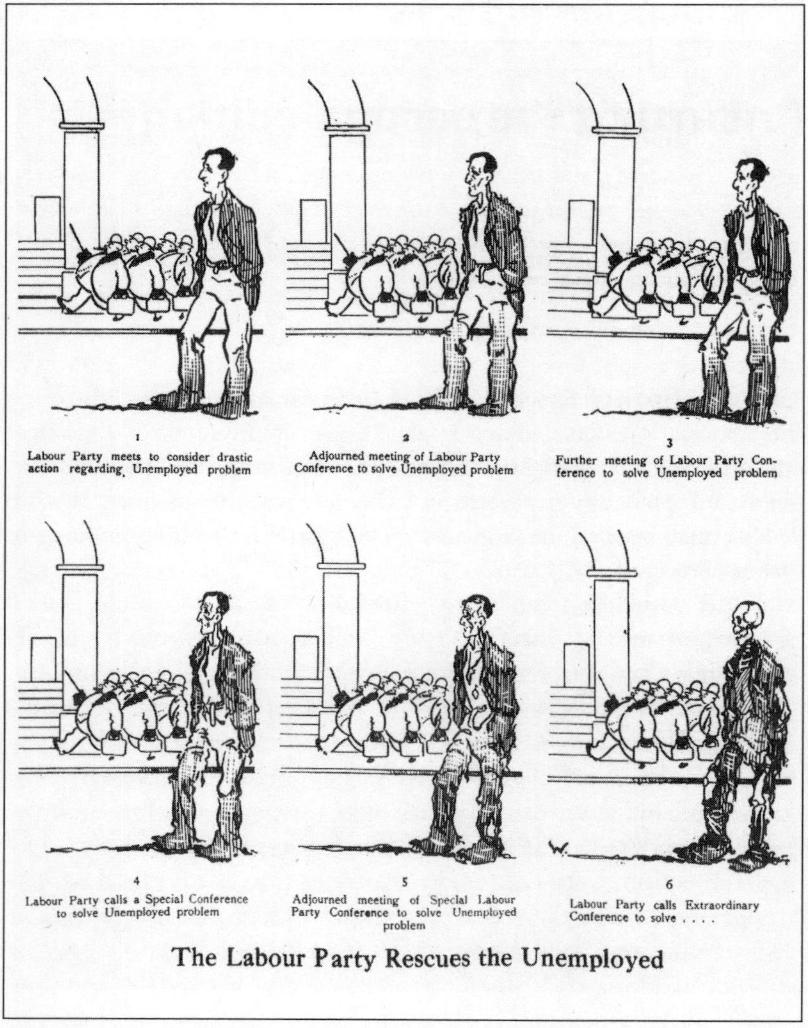

Cartoon from The Communist 1921–22

INTRODUCTION to the first edition 1992

Labour's impasse

There are two conclusions to draw from Labour's fourth successive general election defeat. The first is that only under very exceptional conditions has it ever been able to form a government with a significant majority on its own account. The second is that today, such exceptional conditions would require the political and electoral fragmentation of the Tory Party.

Labour's failure has given rise to much debate on its future. Should it reduce or sever its links with the trade unions? Should it support some kind of proportional representation? If so, should it also establish an electoral agreement with the Liberal Democrats to achieve this end? Should it end its commitment to universal benefits? Such questions have filled the left with dismay, since it regards it as an unquestionable axiom that Labour is a workers' party, and that the links with the trade unions express this class basis. In its view, to sever the connection would leave the working class without any independent representation, and would therefore be a historic setback. It has therefore responded with a deluge of articles to the effect that since the working class is still a majority of the population, the issue should not be whether to break with the unions, but how better to represent them.

This book has a very different perspective. It shows that the Labour Party was created by a small, privileged stratum of the working class in alliance with a radical section of the middle class for the purpose of defending their political interests, and that it is not, never has been, and never will be, a party of the working class. The narrowness of this social base amongst the better-off sections of the working class forces it to appeal for the votes of the mass of the rest of the working class so that it can present itself as a credible parliamentary force. But this does not make it a working class party, and in any case, the votes of the working class are not enough for it to win an election outright. For that, it needs the votes of a much broader section of the middle class, and only twice has this ever happened: in 1945 and 1966. Every other time it has formed a government, it has either been as a minority party or held the barest of majorities.

This different perspective exists because this book presents a different starting point to that of the rest of the left: that throughout Labour's existence, Britain has been a major imperialist power, and that this has been decisive in determining Labour's political development. The narrow stratum of the working class that formed the Labour Party, an aristocracy of labour made up overwhelmingly of skilled craftsmen, arose during the period of Britain's world industrial monopoly following the defeat of Chartism. During the last quarter of the 19th century, as Britain's ascendancy was steadily eroded by US and German competition, the privileged position of the labour aristocracy depended more and more on crumbs it received from Britain's colonial monopoly. As this too came under challenge, so did the position of the labour aristocracy, and from a force it had hitherto regarded as its ally: the Liberal Party. To defend its interests in these conditions, it needed separate parliamentary representation, and to obtain it, it founded the Labour Party in alliance with a section of the radical middle class. Since the privileged conditions of these better-off sections of the population depended on the maintenance of the British Empire, Labour could not defend the one without supporting the other. It was therefore from the outset an imperialist party.

The left critics of Labour, however, either implicitly or explicitly deny the imperialist character of British capitalism, and as a consequence dismiss any suggestion of a split within the working class. It is the theoretical basis on which they can sustain the myth of

Labour as a working class party, and it is consistent with the role the left generally plays as a protector of the Labour Party when political conditions demand. An example of this was the 1992 general election campaign, when the left almost without exception campaigned for a Labour vote despite the fact that the policy differences between Labour and Tory were quite insignificant.

As we shall see, even though Labour was to become a major parliamentary force after the 1918 Representation of the People Act enfranchised the mass of the working class – though excluding women under 30 - these additional votes were insufficient for Labour to win a working Parliamentary majority. For this, it would need to be able to reconcile the interests of the mass of the working class with those of both its privileged upper layers and a broad section of the middle class; only in the exceptional conditions of the post-war boom would this prove possible [prior to 1997]. This social-democratic or Keynesian consensus of interests was achieved through the establishment of the welfare state. The end of Keynesianism in the 1970s was recognition that the basis for guaranteeing the privileged conditions of the aristocracy of labour and the middle class whilst simultaneously sustaining adequate living standards for the mass of the working class had disappeared. The relative affluence of the former could now only be maintained at the direct expense of the latter. The current discussion within the Labour Party on 'targeting' benefits reflects this new reality.

Since the turn of the 20th century, the form of British imperialism has undoubtedly changed, although not its substance. With it, the labour aristocracy has also changed, although the division within the working class remains as craft workers have given way to trade union and labour functionaries, skilled white collar workers and administrators, particularly in the public sector. The prevailing political culture of this stratum is completely corrupt. By corrupt, we mean it is indifferent to the destitution and oppression both at home and abroad that is the necessary condition for its privileged and parasitic existence. It is completely undemocratic and slavish in spirit, even when political necessity impels it to proclaim the opposite. This philistinism has become the hallmark of Labourism; no fitter illustration of its consequence is the fact that our democratic and political rights are so poor that appeals for their improvement make up the majority of the work of the European Court. The left too, drawn as it is particularly from the more affluent sections of public sector workers whose numbers expanded so greatly through the boom after the Second World War, have succumbed to this dominant culture, and have become no less corrupt than those they seek to replace: their privileged social position has also determined their political standpoint.

The structure of this book reflects its aims. The first section deals with the rise of the labour aristocracy and its relationship to the mass of the working class, the conditions which forced to seek independent parliamentary representation, and the early years of its existence until the adoption of its 1918 Constitution. The second, third and fourth parts show how Labour has made the defence of the Empire and British imperialism the cornerstone of its political standpoint. The relative length of these sections is necessary because no other history of the Labour Party has recorded it. From the standpoint of the oppressed masses of the world, however, this was the true face of Labour and its commitment to 'democracy' and 'equality'; what Labour has achieved in defending British imperial interests is of far greater historical significance than any of its paltry domestic accomplishments. The last part then examines the relationship of the Labour Party to the mass of the British working class since 1918, showing how Labour has consistently attempted to exclude the latter from political life, and, when workers have attempted to defend themselves, attacked them without compunction using all the resources at its disposal.

The 1992 election took place against the backdrop of an accelerating industrial, financial and political decline of British imperialism. From being the world's largest creditor nation with net overseas assets worth over £100 billion in 1986, its assets were worth a net £16 billion in 1991 after recovering from being a net debtor in 1990. Tokyo has overtaken London as the world's financial centre.

North Sea oil revenues are a fraction of their peak in the mid-1980s. Manufacturing output in 1992 is at most 1 per cent above its 1979 level, and manufacturing investment below. The result is an unprecedented peacetime balance of trade deficit on manufactured goods, in the midst of the longest recession since the 1930s. The Public Sector Borrowing Requirement, currently £34 billion, is being constantly revised upwards, whilst services constantly deteriorate through cuts in real spending.

Despite this, or more accurately because of it, Labour proved unelectable. It could not persuade the middle class and better-off sections of the working class to shift their support from the Tories, nor could it offer anything meaningful to the mass of the working class, particularly its more impoverished sections. Indeed, Labour ignored them throughout the election and its aftermath; they now only feature as objects of pity or fear, dismissed as an 'underclass'. However, this so-called 'underclass' is rapidly expanding: 47 per cent of all employees now earn less than the European Decency Threshold. The 'underclass' with its connotation of 'unorganisable rabble', the 'people of the abyss' has in fact become a euphemism for the working class, and expresses how far it has been excluded from normal political life. The Los Angeles riots in 1992 show that an impoverished working class will only accept so much. The issue then becomes: who will represent their interests? Labour certainly will not.

ROBERT CLOUGH JUNE 1992

British marines in action, Malaya 1950
(Photo Marx Memorial Library)

PART ONE

The foundation of the Labour Party

1.1 *The rise of the labour aristocracy*

The final defeat of Chartism in 1848 ushered in a period during which British capitalism held unchallenged sway throughout the world. From 1850-75 British capitalism, with the markets of the world under its domination, rapidly expanded and was able to relax the extreme pressure which had been ever present in the 1830s and 1840s. Wages rose and conditions improved especially for the skilled craftsmen who more and more assumed the leadership of the working class. These privileged workers turned aside from Chartism to build up their craft trade unions and co-operative societies. 'The spirit of rebellion died and proposals for radical reconstruction of society were brushed aside.'[1]

During this third quarter of the century, annual rates of industrial expansion averaged 2 to 3 per cent, although the increase in productivity was much greater. So, while wages as a share of national income declined, real wages rose substantially – perhaps by as much as a third. By far the greater part of these increases accrued to a privileged stratum of skilled workers and craftsmen – the labour aristocracy. This stratum, some 10 to 15 per cent of the working class, earned a weekly

1. GDH Cole, *Chartist Portraits*, Macmillan, 1965, p338. This section is drawn from D Reed, 'Marx and Engels on the labour aristocracy, opportunism and the British labour movement', *Fight Racism! Fight Imperialism!* No 27, March 1983.

wage approximately double that of unskilled workers. It organised itself into unions which for the first time had a trained staff of full time officials, with high subscriptions providing for a range of friendly benefits such as unemployment and sickness benefit. Such unions carried out trade practices which hinged on preventing unskilled workers from getting into the trade.

The co-operative societies developed alongside the craft unions. Those who joined them received a 'dividend in purchase', as well as interest on share capital. Whatever the claims of those skilled workers and others who sponsored such societies, the fact that shares were in the region of £1 each would rule out any benefits for the millions of workers earning 15 shillings or less per week. The labour aristocracy was building for itself a stake within the capitalist system; a fact which soon found a political expression. Already in 1858, Engels was noting that the:

> '... English proletariat is actually becoming more and more bourgeois, so that this most bourgeois of all nations is apparently aiming ultimately at the possession of a bourgeois aristocracy and a bourgeois proletariat alongside the bourgeoisie. For a nation which exploits the whole world this is of course to a certain extent justifiable.'[2]

Although sections of the trade union leadership played a significant role alongside Marx and Engels in the establishment of the First International, they were often at loggerheads. The International was a major influence behind the Reform League, which was formed in 1865 to agitate on two demands of the Charter – universal male suffrage and vote by secret ballot. Its standing committee of 12 consisted of six middle class radicals and six workers, of whom three, Cremer, Odger and Howell, were members of the General Council of the First International. However, the influence of Marx and Engels was insufficient to prevent the trade union leaders from compromis-

2. F Engels, *Letter to K Marx*, 7 October 1858, in *Marx & Engels Selected Correspondence*, Progress Publishers, nd, p132.

ing with the radical bourgeoisie. In 1866 and 1867, Liberal politicians and manufacturers made substantial donations to the League. In return, the League qualified its demand for male suffrage with the phrase 'registered and residential', thus deliberately excluding the large mass of labourers, casual workers and unemployed. Marx wrote at the time 'Cremer and Odger have both betrayed us in the Reform League where, against our wishes, they have made compromises with the bourgeoisie.'[3]

After the passage of the 1867 electoral Reform Act, the English trade union leaders in the League worked secretly in exchange for payments and Home Office bribes to mobilise the working class vote behind the Liberals in the 1868 general election; two leaders, Cremer and Howell were paid electioneering expenses and £10 each to canvass for the Liberals, leading Marx to comment on the 'so-called leaders of the English workers' who 'are more or less bribed by the bourgeoisie and government.'[4]

The conflict also emerged over the Irish question, when Marx defended the Fenian movement within the International in 1869 and attacked Gladstone for his brutal policies and his hypocrisy. English trade union leaders including Odger objected strongly and defended Gladstone, while three unions left the International altogether. Despite these defections, the International was able to organise massive demonstrations in support of Fenian prisoners. As Engels said later, 'the masses are for the Irish. The organisations and labour aristocracy in general follow Gladstone and the liberal bourgeoisie'.[5]

The strength of British capitalism allowed the bourgeoisie to make concessions to the working class without threatening its economic or political power, and the labour aristocracy was only too happy to accept. In 1874, Engels summarised the development:

'Wherever the workers lately took part in general politics in

3. K Marx, *Letter to Becker,* 31 August 1866.

4. K Marx, in *Minutes and Documents of the Hague Congress of the First International*, Progress Publishers, 1976, p124.

5. F Engels, in *Marx and Engels on Ireland,* Progress Publishers, 1978, p460.

particular organisations they did so almost exclusively as the extreme left wing of the "great Liberal Party"... In order to get into Parliament the "Labour leaders" had recourse, in the first place, to the votes and money of the bourgeoisie and only in the second place to the votes of the workers themselves. But by doing so they ceased to be workers' candidates and turned themselves into bourgeois candidates.'[6]

1.2 *British imperialism under challenge*

'Advocacy of class collaboration; abandonment of the idea of socialist revolution and revolutionary methods of struggle; adaptation to bourgeois nationalism; losing sight of the fact that the borderlines of nationality and country are historically transient; making a fetish of bourgeois legality; renunciation of the class viewpoint and the class struggle for fear of repelling the "broad masses of the population" (meaning the petty bourgeoisie) – such, doubtlessly, are the ideological foundations of opportunism.'[7]

Opportunism in England consolidated itself in the last quarter of the century. Although by the end of the period, Britain's monopoly industrial position had disappeared for ever in the face of the rising challenge from Germany, the US and France, it possessed a vast Empire, to which major additions were made in the 1880s and 1890s. The plunder from this Empire was to act as a cushion protecting British capitalism from the full impact of the new competition.

The relative decline of British industry was evident in nearly every branch. Whereas industrial output had grown by 39 per cent in the 1850s, and 33 per cent in the 1860s, the average for the three subsequent decades was to fall to 20 per cent. Productivity, which had risen annually by 1–2 per cent now increased by 0.5 per cent in the

6. F Engels, *The English Elections*, in *Marx and Engels on Britain*, Progress Publishers 1971, pp369-70.

7. VI Lenin, *The Position and Tasks of the Socialist International*, *Collected Works* (CW) vol 21, Progress Publishers, p35.

1880s and a mere 0.2 per cent in the 1890s. Individual branches reflected this change: British coal production as a percentage of world production fell from 51.5 per cent to 29.2 per cent, and of pig iron from 40.5 per cent to 22.1 per cent in the period 1870 to 1900. Pig iron production may have increased by 50 per cent during the period, but German output rose 330 per cent and US output 630 per cent. Steel production told a similar story: British production rose from 1.29 million tons in 1880 (31 per cent of the world total) to 4.9 million tons in 1900 (17.6 per cent); however, in the same period, German production rose from 0.69 million tons to 6.36 million tons, and US production from 1.25 million tons to 10.19 million tons.

The increasing lack of competitiveness of British industry expressed itself in a falling domestic rate of profit; hence profitable investment had to be sought abroad, in the Empire, both formal and informal (see Table 1). The result was an immense accumulation of capital overseas (Table 2).

Such figures if anything underestimate the tendency: GDCF includes investment in housing and public building. It would seem that in the years just before the war, perhaps 80 per cent of capital issues on the London market were destined for overseas. Accumulated

Table 1[8]

	Gross Domestic Capital Formation (GDCF) as % GNP	Foreign Investment as % GDCF	Foreign Investment as % GNP	Total Capital Formation as % GNP
1870–9	10.5	44.0	4.6	15.1
1880–9	9.2	62.1	5.7	14.9
1890–9	9.7	36.7	3.6	13.3
1900–9	10.6	41.6	4.4	15.0
1904–13	9.4	75.6	7.2	16.6

8. DH Aldcroft and HW Richardson, *The British Economy 1870–1939*, Macmillan, 1969, p120.

Table 2 Accumulated capital abroad[9] (£000,000)

1870	692	1900	2,397
1880	1,189	1910	3,371
1890	1,935	1913	3,990

overseas investment rose as a percentage of GNP from 73 per cent in 1870 to 139 per cent in 1890, and 164 per cent in 1910, by which time it amounted to about a third of domestic capital investment;[10] again, almost certainly, official figures underestimate this proportion. Nabudere estimates that the years 1870 to 1913 saw a capital export of £2,400 million yielding a net income of £4,100 million, and that Britain was able to finance new overseas investment out of the return on old investment.[11]

Quite apart from attracting a higher rate of profit, such overseas investment had other benefits, both direct and indirect. First, it facilitated increased capital exports: £600 million invested in overseas railway building between 1907 and 1914 created a monopoly market for iron, steel and rolling stock; secondly, the consequent improvement in means of communications cheapened the costs of transport and therefore of raw materials and foods.

In addition to its colonial monopoly, British imperialism maintained a maritime monopoly, and a monopoly in the finance and insurance of world trade. The former was reflected in its continued domination of the world shipbuilding industry (see Table 3); the construction of larger ships with improved propulsion systems together with the introduction of refrigeration contributed as much as improved land communications to the cheapening of imported raw materials and foods.

9. D Nabudere, *The Political Economy of Imperialism*, Zed Press, 1975, pp113-115.
10. *ibid*, p64.
11. *ibid*.

Table 3 Shipbuilding – tonnage launched[12] (000s of tons)

Year	UK	Germany	US	World
1895	951	88	85	1,218
1900	1,442	204	333	2,304
1905	1,623	255	303	2,515
1910	1,143	159	331	1,958

Its financial and insurance monopoly expressed itself in a steady increase in invisible overseas earnings other than from investment (see Table 4 overleaf).

Total invisible earnings from abroad rose from 9.3 per cent of GNP in 1870 to 11.5 per cent in 1890 and 13.6 per cent in 1913, a year when gross private trading profits amounted to only 14.2 per cent of GNP. Throughout this period, the balance of payments deficit on visible trade was more than made up by the rising surplus on the so-called invisibles. In other words, the solvency of British imperialism depended on its colonial monopoly – a feature of its fundamental parasitism.

1.3 *Parasitism, the labour aristocracy and the working class*

Britain's colonial monopoly allowed it to continue by and large to maintain the conditions of the labour aristocracy through the last decades of the century. Although money wages remained fairly constant during this period, there was a significant fall in prices, especially of food, as a consequence of the vast improvement in transportation. Hence real wages continued to rise, especially for the more privileged strata of the working class: by 26 per cent in the decade of the 1870s, 21 per cent in the 1880s, slowing down to 11 per cent in the 1890s. Elie Halevy described the results:

12. *Marxist Study Course, Political Economy* vol 10a, Lawrence, circa 1932, p41.

Table 4[13] **(£000,000s)**

	Gross National Product	Merchandise Exports	Merchandise Imports	Overall Visible Balance
1870	947	246	279	–33
1880	1097	290	378	–88
1890	1389	334	387	–53
1900	1781	356	485	–129
1910	2050	536	632	–96
1913	2333	637	719	–82
	Net Export of Services	**Net Property Income From Abroad**	**Overall Invisible Balance**	**Overall Current Balance**
1870	55	35	+88	+55
1880	65	58	+121	+33
1890	67	94	+160	+107
1900	61	104	+163	+34
1910	104	170	+270	+174
1913	121	200	+317	+235

'[The fall in] ... current prices has enabled a very large body to come into existence among the British proletariat, able to keep up a standard of living almost identical with that of the middle class. The self-respecting workman in the North of England wanted to own his own cottage and garden, in Lancashire his piano. His life was insured. If he shared the common English failing and was a gambler, prone to bet too highly on horses...the rapid growth of savings banks proved that he was nevertheless learning the prudence of the middle class.'[14]

13. Drawn from B Mitchell and P Deane (eds), *Abstract of British Historical Statistics*, Cambridge, 1962, pp828-9 and 872-3. The slight discrepancy in the total balance of invisible trade arises from currency transactions.

14. E Halevy, *History of the English People,* Epilogue Book 2, Pelican 1939, p133.

The improvements were mainly confined to the labour aristocracy: in 1900, skilled workers could on average expect 40 shillings per week, unskilled workers 20-25 shillings, women workers and agricultural workers 15 shillings. But this only gives part of the picture, since on average unemployment was three times higher for the unskilled than for the skilled worker, and he or she was far more likely to be casually, seasonally or otherwise temporarily employed.

Poverty and destitution remained the norm therefore for masses of unskilled and semi-skilled workers: in 1911, for instance, it was estimated that 30 shillings per week was the minimum to sustain an adequate family existence, but five million out of eight million male manual workers earned less than this; the average for this five million workers was 22 shillings. Sir Leo Chiozza-Money in his 1905 study *Riches and Poverty*[15] estimated that 33 million out of a population of 43 million lived in poverty, and of these, 13 million lived in destitution. The benefits of Empire were very definitely confined to an upper layer of the working class

Not surprisingly trade unionism and political life remained the almost exclusive preserve of this layer. In 1892, out of 14 million people employed in industry and trade, only 1.5 million belonged to a trade union, and less than a million belonged to TUC-affiliates. With the very partial exception of the miners, these were still the old craft unions; the unskilled unions were at this time a negligible force. As a proportion of the workforce, trade union membership changed little until shortly before the war; only in 1906 did it exceed two million. Furthermore, the unions were still by and large benefit societies: the annual expenditure of 100 leading unions on strike pay or lock-out benefit only once exceeded 13 per cent of income between 1899 and 1909; during this period, expenditure on unemployment and friendly benefits averaged 60 to 70 per cent.

Suffrage was not quite so sharply restricted, but was still only available to a minority of the working class (and of course still excluded all women): the householding qualification of the 1867 Reform Act

15. Cited in I Cox, *Empire Today*, Lawrence and Wishart, 1960, p16.

had enfranchised an electorate of three million, half of them working class. This was raised only to five million by the 1884 Act when it extended the householder's franchise to the counties; such a property qualification meant that its beneficiaries were again drawn from the labour aristocracy. As the official Labour Party history described the situation in 1900: 'by far the greater part of the working men enfranchised thereby were approaching, or past, their middle years, and, not withstanding their memories, they were not the material out of which a Labour victory could be achieved.'[16]

This period, then, was one of political stagnation. British imperialism could still afford to make concessions to the labour aristocracy, in return for which it expected, and usually got, social peace. The exceptions were the free speech demonstrations in London of the late 1880s, and the explosion of unskilled unionism in 1889-90, particularly amongst the dockers and gasworkers. Both these events drove sections of the working class into an alliance with Marxists and revolutionaries; the fact that many of the dockers were Irish (and a large proportion of their strike committee as well) probably facilitated such a development. Not only would the craft unions with their Lib-Lab politics prove incapable of defending the mass of the working class, they were in fact utterly hostile to the revolutionary methods that the unions used, especially during the dockers' strike. George Shipton, Chairman of London Trades Council argued:

> 'When the people were unenfranchised, were without votes, the only power left to them was the demonstration of numbers. Now however, the workmen have votes.'[17]

Or, at least, the workmen who really counted for Shipton: it was precisely casual labourers such as dockers who were still excluded from the franchise, and therefore from bourgeois political life and

---

16. Lord Shepherd, in Herbert Tracey (ed), *The British Labour Party*, vol 2, Caxton, 1948, p192.
17. Quoted in T Cliff and D Gluckstein, *The Labour Party – a Marxist History*, Bookmarks, 1988, p9.

could only express their interests through revolutionary means. However, their alliance with the Marxists could not be sustained under the combined attack of the ruling class and its labour aristocrat allies, and within two to three years, the new unions had lost the majority of their members, falling from 300,000 members in 1890 (25 per cent of TUC membership) to 80,000 in 1896. By 1900, they constituted less than 10 per cent of the membership of the TUC. They began to ape the organisational and political methods of the old craft unions in order to preserve themselves, rejecting recruitment amongst the casual and unskilled labourers in favour of those in stable employment, for instance municipal gasworkers. In other words, the new unions themselves became corrupted by the prevailing trend of opportunism.

1.4 *The Independent Labour Party and the Fabians*

Since the passage of the 1867 Reform Act, politics for the privileged workers had been Liberal Party politics, and a few workers, mainly miners, had been elected to Parliament since 1874 on a Liberal ticket. But the competitive pressures on British industry at the start of the 1890s revealed that the Liberal capitalists who dominated the mining and cotton industries were every bit as ruthless as their Tory counterparts elsewhere. And it was the defeat of a strike in the cotton industry in 1892 that led to the first organisational break in the Lib-Lab alliance – the formation of the Independent Labour Party (ILP).

Keir Hardie, who was the prime mover behind the founding conference in 1893, was in favour of organisational independence from Liberalism, but not political independence. Hence the conference rejected the name 'Socialist Labour Party' in favour of 'Independent Labour Party' because 'they had to appeal to the vast mass of workers outside, and not only to Socialists' – in other words, to those skilled workers who possessed the vote but who were still quite happy with Liberalism. More than that, the name was a signal to the Liberals that there were no fundamental political disagreements between the two parties, at least none that might prevent them arriving at electoral agreements, open or otherwise. 'For its theories and its detailed facts', Francis Williams' official history notes, the ILP 'drew mainly upon the Fabian society';[18] hardly surprisingly, since most of its leaders were Fabians, Keir Hardie and Ramsay MacDonald amongst them.

The constituency of the ILP was identical to that of the contemporary trade union movement – the skilled working class. One commentary quotes a description of a Glasgow branch as typical:

> 'Except for an odd teacher and a few shop assistants, the members were all working men and their wives. For the most part the men belonged to the skilled trades as in England and were nearly always known as exceptionally good and steady working men. They were active trade unionists to a man. The ILP was not attracting as yet what are called the "unskilled workers" ...'[19]

In Sheffield, 'the unskilled, the irregularly employed and the slum dwellers remained almost completely impervious to the ILP appeal. Party organisers discovered that the "indigent have neither time nor opportunity to think out social problems for themselves".'[20]

While the bulk of the membership was drawn from the skilled working class, there was a substantial proportion drawn from the lower professional middle class: 'The formation of the ILP's internal structure, its political ideas, its leadership and organisers was, in fact, directly and substantially affected by the presence of middle class socialists ... Although small, this group forged the alliance between the ILP, the Radical Liberals and the TUC, and opened the way for the ILP's parliamentary breakthroughs of the early 1900s.'[21] Middle class socialists might be stretching it: Radical Liberalism was as potent an influence on the ILP as the Fabians. It was not just the case that middle class liberalism played a leading organisational and political

18. F Williams, *Fifty Years' March – The Rise of the Labour Party*, Odhams, circa 1950, p104.
19. S Pierson, *Marxism and the Origin of British Socialism,* Cornell, 1973, p209.
20. *ibid*, p210.
21. C Levy in ed C Levy, *Socialism and the Intelligentsia, 1880–1914*, Routledge and Kegan Paul, 1987, p136.

role within the ILP: they had the links with a variety of wealthy donors such as Cadbury whose financial donations were crucial to the survival of the Party at the turn of the century.

The Fabian Society, which was to prove so influential with both the ILP and the Labour Party, was an organisation of middle class socialists formed in 1884, although of significance only from the late 1880s. Never numbering more than a few hundreds, it saw its purpose as primarily educational. It consciously rejected the class struggle; indeed, it held the working class in complete contempt, as one of its leading figures, Beatrice Webb, argued in 1895: 'judging from our knowledge of the Labour movement we can expect no leader from the working class. Our only hope is in permeating the young middle class man.'[22] And: 'What can we hope from these myriads of deficient minds and deformed bodies that swarm our great cities – what can we hope but brutality, meanness and crime.'[23] In 1911, she was to condemn the Liberals' health insurance scheme for workers as 'wholly bad, and I cannot see how malingering can be staved off...What the government shirks is the extension of treatment and disciplinary supervision.'[24]

Initially opposed to independent labour representation, the Fabians accepted it in 1892 in the same period as they started to involve themselves in local government – 'gas and water' or municipal socialism. Their motivation was in part to create an alliance with middle class Radicalism – to 'permeate' it, but also for fear that unless something was done to improve municipal services, there might be terrible consequences, as Sidney Webb wrote in their programme for the 1892 London County Council elections:

> 'The largest city in the world, the capital of the Empire, cannot, in these democratic days, safely be abandoned to the insidious influence of its festering centres of social ulceration. We dare not

22. Quoted in J Callaghan, *Socialism in Britain*, Blackwell, 1990, p37.
23. Quoted in Cliff and Gluckstein, *op cit*, p18.
24. *ibid*.

neglect the sullen discontent now spreading among its toiling millions ... Metropolitan reform has become a national if not yet an imperial question.'[25]

By 1901, it had become an imperial question, when Webb noted that eight million destitute persons – a fifth of the population – constituted 'not merely a disgrace but a positive danger to our civilisation' and asked 'what is the use of an Empire if it does not breed and maintain in the truest and fullest sense of the word an Imperial race?'. He concluded that it was necessary to introduce a national minimum standard of life 'not merely or even mainly for the comfort of the workers but absolutely for the success of our industry in competition in the world.'[26] This imperialist and racist would, with complete justification, come to be described as 'the intellectual leader of the Labour Party'.[27]

Throughout the 1890s, Fabians, the ILP and radical Liberals were to establish a close alliance through the experience of municipal socialism. The ties were often very close: Ramsay MacDonald, for instance, was a leading figure within both the ILP and the Fabian Society at this time, and had a close political relationship of many years' standing with the Liberal anti-imperialist JA Hobson. This meant that middle class socialism was to play a vital role in formulating the political standpoint of the Labour Party.

1.5 *The Labour Representation Committee*

The initial response of the craft unions to the ILP was one of hostility. The 1895 TUC Congress approved a number of measures to isolate it. It adopted the block vote to determine policy – the ILP was stronger in the smaller unions – and ended trades council repre-

25 S Webb, *The London Programme*, 1891, Swan Sonnenschein, p6.

26. Quoted in Callaghan, *op cit*, p41.

27. Beatrice Webb in 1917, quoted by H Pelling, *A Short History of the Labour Party*, Macmillan, 1972, p42.

sentation, again because of the ILP influence in such local bodies. Lastly, it excluded delegates who were not at their trade; Keir Hardie was now working as a journalist, no longer a miner. However the pressure on British industry continued to grow throughout the 1890s onwards, forcing a series of confrontations, in which the unions suffered significant defeats: the Amalgamated Society of Engineers (ASE) in 1897 (after a lock-out organised by the Engineering Employers' Federation), and the South Wales miners the following year. The Lib-Lab alliance was no longer sufficient to defend the interests of the labour aristocracy; the 1899 TUC therefore voted to convene a conference to set up a Labour Representation Committee (LRC).

The Conference met in February 1900; delegates came from 65 unions with 568,000 members, and from political organisations such as the Social Democratic Federation (SDF), the ILP and the Fabians. The interests of the labour aristocracy dominated the proceedings: an SDF proposal that there be a 'party organisation separate from the capitalist parties based upon a recognition of the class war' was dismissed out of hand in favour of Hardie's formulation, moved by the general secretary of the ASE, that 'this Conference is in favour of working class opinion being represented in the House of Commons by men sympathetic with the aims and demands of the Labour movement', passed by 102 votes to 3. Such representatives were 'to form their own distinctive labour group and act in harmony with its decisions.' In other words, the Committee was to be first and foremost a parliamentary body.

The LRC was formed by a trade union movement which excluded 90 per cent of the working class: there were only about 100,000 organised unskilled workers out of a total of some 10 million. The electorate on which it could depend was again drawn from the upper ranks of the working class, since the majority were still without a vote. By its very nature, it was therefore an exclusive body, formed by the craft unions to represent their interests in Parliament more adequately than the Liberal alliance. It was not until 1906 that the LRC voted for universal male suffrage, and, separately, for women's suffrage on the same terms as men (and then only just, by 446,000 'votes' to 429,000). Parliamentary democracy was still a democracy for the privileged, and the labour aristocracy was in no hurry to change it: 'It is an inescapable fact that the early Labour Party took no more than a passing interest in electoral reform.'[28]

By the turn of the century, the competitiveness of British industry had declined to the extent that now even the labour aristocracy began to suffer deteriorating conditions. Between 1900 and 1910, real wages fell by 6 per cent,[29] whilst unemployment amongst trade unionists rose steadily from 2.5 per cent to nearly 8 per cent.[30] The response of the craft unions was, however, supine: the number and extent of strikes fell to a record low in 1904, a fact reflected in the parsimonious sums spent by the unions on strike pay. The Taff Vale judgment of 1901 removing trade union immunity for the consequence of strike action further reduced their strength, although reinforcing their need for parliamentary representation to offset the shortcomings of the Lib-Lab alliance.

Throughout this period, the Labour Party (as it was called from 1906) played second fiddle to the Liberals. Its main aim became the repeal of the Taff Vale judgment; for that it required a Liberal government. There was no attempt at political independence: Labour MPs were still elected courtesy of pacts with the Liberals, since the Party's electoral base was not adequate to guarantee election if candidates stood unaided. Ramsay MacDonald had assumed the leadership of the Party from Keir Hardie: as Cole and Postgate put it, 'He had a natural skill in parliamentary tactics ... his conviction that circumstances required an inflexible support of the Liberals reassured the trade unionists.'[31] The very meagre reward was the 1906 Trades Dispute Act which restored trade unions' immunity to damages arising from industrial action.

Two years later, the Osborne judgment which prevented unions

---

28. In H Tracey, *op cit*, vol 2, p193.
29. Aldcroft and Richardson, *op cit*, p105.
30. J Kuczynski, *Labour Conditions under Industrial Capitalism*, Muller, 1972, p109.
31. Cole and Postgate, *The Common People 1746-1938*, Methuen, 1938, p447.

from paying a political levy threatened the solvency of Labour. Not for five years until the 1913 Trades Dispute Act was the original legal position restored. In the meantime, the Parliamentary Labour Party, by this time consisting of some 40 MPs, acted as a support group indistinguishable from the Liberals, even though from 1910 it held the balance of power. At no point did it offer any opposition: its political dependence, epitomised by its secret electoral pact, was too great.

The last four years before the war has been seen as one of the high points of the British trade union movement. In contrast with the previous decade, resistance to the ruling class offensive was considerable. Strikes of seamen and dockers (1911), railwaymen and miners (1912) brought millions of workers into action. In Liverpool, there was a near insurrection against the army, with Tom Mann in the leadership: he was later gaoled for six months for supporting an appeal to troops not to fire on workers. During this period, the Labour Party and, to a large extent, the ILP leadership offered only condemnation, particularly of the syndicalist influence of leaders such as Mann. But as one delegate put it to the 1912 TUC: 'Syndicalism really is ... a protest against the inaction of the Labour Party'.[32] Four Labour MPs (including Arthur Henderson) meanwhile put forward a Bill which proposed making strikes illegal unless 30 days' notice had been given; those who struck illegally or incited others to strike illegally would be subjected to very heavy fines. Although the Bill was condemned by the TUC Parliamentary Committee, it demonstrated that even at this early stage of its history Labour would stand against the working class as a whole. As JR Clynes told the 1914 Labour Conference: 'too frequent strikes caused a sense of disgust, of being a nuisance to the community.'[33]

---

32. Quoted in Cliff and Gluckstein, *op cit,* p47. MacDonald agreed, 'Syndicalism is largely a revolt against Socialism [ie, the Labour Party – RC]. Socialism must be Parliamentary or it is nothing.' Quoted in *ibid*, p50.
33. Quoted in R Miliband, *Parliamentary Socialism*, Merlin, 1972, p38.

1.6 *The 1918 Constitution*

Until the 1918 Constitution, the Labour Party was a federation of trade unions, particularly the craft unions, and a small number of political organisations such as the ILP and the Fabians. There were no local parties; the Labour Party was represented locally by branches of the ILP in particular. That structure was sufficient for a Party which for all its organisational independence was content to act more or less as an appendage to the Liberal Party. It had to change:

> 'The war and the disruption of international socialism had landed the British Labour Party in a position it had not held before. Largely owing to the numerical strength – and the wealth – of the British trade unions, the Labour Party found itself willy-nilly the leading 'Allied' socialist party and the rock upon which European social democracy was already building its fortress against Bolshevism. Consequently, it appeared necessary to construct a political party appropriate to this industrial support.'[34]

It was not just the numerical and financial strength of the trade unions that would make Labour play this role: it was primarily the fact that Britain would emerge from the war still as the leading European imperialist power, and therefore the vanguard of the counter-revolution. However, growing internal unrest combined with the political impact of the Russian Revolution had a further consequence: it forced the ruling class to concede universal suffrage for men over 21 and women over 30. The Representation of the People Bill encompassing this proposal would more than double the electorate from 8.5 million in 1915 to over 22 million in 1922. Labour's social base amongst the more affluent sections of the working class, and in certain layers of the middle class, would in itself be a far too narrow electoral base to enable it to become a significant parliamentary force in the post-war world. To continue to defend their interests, it would have to broaden its electoral support, and the

34. R McKibbin, *The Evolution of the Labour Party 1910–24*, Oxford, 1973, p91.

only constituency it could appeal to was the newly enfranchised section of the working class. Labour had to establish proper local Party organisations which could serve to mobilise that vote; to prevent any challenge to the domination of the labour aristocracy it had to keep such organisations under tight central control.

Under the leadership of Arthur Henderson, a committee was established in September 1917 to draft the Constitution; it consisted of four craft union leaders, plus Ramsay MacDonald, Arthur Henderson, Sidney Webb and Egerton Wake, a Party organiser. The ILP were effectively excluded from playing any role, as most of the work of the committee devolved onto Henderson and Webb, the latter now acting effectively as Labour's ideological leader. Their draft proposed individual membership, allowed the unions to retain their block vote, and changed voting procedures for the National Executive Committee (NEC).

Henderson and Webb saw individual membership as a means of recruiting middle class support from both the Fabians and disaffected Liberals in organisations such as the Union of Democratic Control (UDC). In proposing that the conference voted for the NEC as a unit, the draft ended the practice whereby political organisations had an exclusive vote for their reserved seats: now the trade unions could cast their block votes for candidates for all seats. Hence the draft effectively gave the trade union leaders complete control over conference policy and the subsequently elected NEC.

A special conference in January 1918 considered and rejected the draft. The trade union leaders' only concern was to minimise the influence of the middle class socialists whom they felt were a major threat, mainly because they were associated with a pacifist position during the war. Sexton of the Dockers spoke of 'the cranks of the UDC and the Council of Civil Liberties avowedly opposing the policy of the Labour Party', and was echoed by Tom Shaw of the Textile Workers, a bastion of social imperialism. Henderson made a further concession: the trade unions would be given 13 out of 23 seats on the NEC rather than 11 out of 21. This was sufficient for a subsequent conference in June to accept it.

Clause 4 of the new Constitution, and its elaboration in a programme *Labour and the New Social Order*, were to be the basis for its electoral appeal to the working class. Sidney Webb wrote both, and restated in them the basic principles of Fabianism. Clause 4 itself was presented at the 1918 Special Conference, and aroused no interest let alone opposition amongst the trade union leaders:

> 'To secure for the producers by hand or brain the full fruits of their industry, and the most equitable distribution thereof that may be possible, upon the basis of the Common Ownership of the Means of Production, and the best obtainable system of popular administration and control of each industry or service.'

This differs only in form with the founding statement of the Fabian Society, for which Webb was also responsible some 30 years earlier:

> 'It [the Fabian Society] therefore aims at the reorganisation of Society by the emancipation of Land and Industrial Capital from individual and class ownership, and the vesting of them in the community for the general benefit ... The Society, further, works for the transfer to the community of the administration of such industrial capital as can conveniently be managed socially.'[35]

Nor was there anything new in *Labour and the New Social Order*: there was no attempt to hide the racist and imperialist prejudices of its author, since they would be shared by the social stratum the party represented. Thus it refers to the 'moral claims upon us of the non-adult races', and to the 'great Commonwealth', which was 'not an Empire in the old sense, but a Britannic Alliance'; whichever it was, 'the Labour Party stands for its maintenance and its progressive development', qualified by the vaguest of phrases, 'on the lines of

35. Quoted in E Hobsbawm, *Labour's Turning Point 1880–1900*, Lawrence and Wishart, 1948, pp55-56.

Local Autonomy and "Home Rule All Round"'.[36] And only an imperialist could declare 'As regards our relations to Foreign Countries, we disavow and disclaim any desire or intention to dispossess or to impoverish any other State or Nation. We seek no increase of territory',[37] since only an imperialist would feel the need to make such disavowals in the context of possessing the largest Empire the world had known. The programme's call for the introduction of a minimum wage together with an extended unemployment benefit system, the nationalisation of the mines, railways and power supply, and the establishment of a progressive taxation system with some kind of state welfare were the means to attract the working class vote.

However, there were also significant bribes for the professional middle class, whom Webb had always thought would be more interested in socialism than the working class. Thus the document is littered with statements that 'this is not a class proposal', whilst workers are always 'workers, by hand or by brain', as they are in Clause 4.

But the main purpose of Clause 4 and *Labour and the New Social Order* as far as Henderson was concerned was to provide a pole of

---

36. Sidney Webb *Labour and the New Social Order*, 1918, p22. The extreme racism of the Webbs had been voiced but five years earlier in an article in the *New Statesman* in 1913. Commenting on the falling white birth rate, they wrote, 'Into the scarcity thus created in particular districts, in particular sections of the labour market, or in particular social strata, there rush the offspring of the less thrifty, the less intellectual, the less foreseeing of races and classes – the unskilled casual labourers of our great cities, the races of Eastern or Southern Europe, the negroes, the Chinese – possibly resulting as already in parts of the USA, in such a heterogeneous and mongrel population that democratic self-government, or even the effective application of the policy of a national minimum of civilised life will become increasingly unattainable. If anything like this happens, it is difficult to avoid the melancholy conclusion that, in some cataclysm that it is impossible for us to foresee, that civilisation characteristic of the Western European races may go the way of half a dozen other civilisations that have within historic times preceded it; to be succeeded by a new social order developed by one or other of the coloured races, the negro, the kaffir or the Chinese.' Quoted in F Lee, *Fabianism and Colonialism – The Life and Thought of Lord Sydney Olivier*, Defiant, 1988, pp189-90.

37. *Labour and the New Social Order*, p22.

electoral attraction to the mass of the working class. Labour needed these votes if it were to become a significant parliamentary force, let alone form a government.

Some have seen in the 1918 Constitution and programme a break with the past, the culmination of a process whereby Labour could in some way represent the interests of the working class. Thus Miliband describes it as a 'considerable step forward';[38] Cliff and Gluckstein an 'extraordinary transformation', a 'commitment to socialism', a 'minimal anti-capitalist position' that now must be defended;[39] Coates that it marks a break with the past with its 'enormous' promise and its 'radical and uncompromising' rhetoric'.[40] But its racism and its imperialism? Some things, it appears, are best left alone.

In fact the rhetoric of *Labour and the New Social Order* is no different from that in any Fabian document, so that its 'uncompromising' character depends completely on the eye of the beholder. Its aims go no further than any put forward by the Fabians over the previous 30 years, so it takes a particular flight of imagination to characterise it as an 'extraordinary transformation'. In their apparent anxiety to show that Labour was now a progressive force, these historians have developed a complete blindness to imperialism and racism. However, sensing that all is not well, they cite a second reason for their claim that Labour was a working class organisation: its links with the unions. As we have seen, however, the unions which founded it as a matter of policy excluded 90 per cent of the working class, and represented only a privileged upper stratum. By the time the general unions had any influence, their structures also excluded the working class, and their leaders had become 'labour lieutenants of the capitalist class' par excellence. Neither in 1900 nor in 1918 did Labour represent the working class, either politically or socially. Quite the opposite: it was set up to exclude the working class from political life,

38. Miliband, *op cit*, p62.

39. Cliff and Gluckstein, *op cit*, p54 and p72.

40. D Coates, *The Labour Party and the Struggle for Socialism*, Cambridge, 1975, p14. For a discussion of Lenin's views on the Labour Party, see Appendix.

and ensure that a privileged stratum close to the middle class had a vehicle to defend its narrow, parasitic interests. That this necessarily involved defending Britain's imperial interests will be shown in the next section.

PART TWO

The Labour Party and British imperialism 1900–45

The Labour Party was established to defend the privileged interests of an upper stratum of the working class in alliance with a section of the middle class. These privileges depended on the relative strength of British imperialism; defending them therefore meant defending British imperialism. Throughout its history, Labour has proved itself equal to the task. In its politically corrupt world, 'democracy' became a particularly debased word: always used to denounce revolution, it was never applicable to the near 500 million people of the British Empire until it became politically convenient. Labour's hypocrisy and racism are founded in the material existence of the stratum which created and built it, since their political rights and privileges depended on the denial of those self-same rights to hundreds of millions of others. It therefore cannot be reduced to the inadequacies of individual leaders, or to weaknesses and deficiencies in the ideological foundations of Labourism. The terms 'trade union bureaucracy' or 'labour bureaucracy', which the left borrows from liberal sociology to analyse Labour, precisely obscure this political reality. In short, the Labour Party and British imperialism are inseparable: neither could survive without the other.

With very few exceptions, histories of the Labour Party refer very rarely to the existence of the British Empire or British imperialism. This may not be surprising for the more reactionary accounts such as those of Henry Pelling or Francis Williams (see Bibliography). However, there is no excuse for those who write from the left – Ralph

Miliband, James Hinton, David Coates or Cliff and Gluckstein from the Socialist Workers' Party (SWP); one can only say that they too have been caught up in Labour's web of corruption. To give an example, the index in Cliff and Gluckstein's book has no entries against either 'empire' or 'imperialism', but finds room for four under 'tokenism'. The reason for this is not hard to find: membership of the left is by and large drawn from better-off layers of public sector workers that British imperialism could afford to support in ever-increasing numbers in the post-1945 period. These 'respectable' people therefore find no relationship between the Labour Party on the one hand and the imperialist character of British capitalism on the other, because it they have no interest in looking for one.

It is as well to recall what constituted the British Empire, and the resources it contained. There was Ireland, of course, a source of cheap food and of cheap labour. India, with nearly ten times the population of Britain, and worth some £120 million net per year in the 1930s: it supplied over a million troops in each of the two world wars. Malaya with its rubber and tin. Swathes of West Africa with its cocoa and palm oil, and much of East Africa. The West Indies with its sugar. The settler Dominions – Canada, Australia and New Zealand; the mineral wealth of South Africa. Then there was the informal empire: most of Latin America prior to the First Imperialist War; Egypt and Palestine; Persia with its oil. After 1918, more ex-German colonies, and Iraq with even more oil. These were the victims on which the British imperialist parasite gorged itself: approximately 500 million people, the overwhelming majority of whom were kept in destitution if not starvation, who had no control over their destinies, and in whose name Labour was to govern on three occasions.

2.1 *From the Boer War to 1914*

The foundation of the Labour Representation Committee took place as British imperialism found itself bogged down in an increasingly brutal war against the Boer settlers of the Transvaal. The issue it posed was quite clear to the radical wing of the Liberal Party led by

JA Hobson: it was a struggle by British finance for control over the diamond and gold resources of southern Africa. In this struggle, the Radical Liberals took the side of the Boers. The ILP, under the influence of the Radicals, adopted a similar standpoint, arguing that the Government wanted 'to promote a war of conquest ... in the interest of unscrupulous exploiters'.[1] Keir Hardie was particularly forthright; the war was:

> '... a Capitalists' war, begotten by Capitalists' money, lied into being by a perjured mercenary Capitalist press, and fathered by unscrupulous politicians, themselves the merest tools of the Capitalists ... As Socialists, our sympathies are bound to be with the Boers.'[2]

However, the trade union aristocracy was split down the middle. Some stood completely with the ILP; others were more ambivalent, tinging their opposition with gross anti-semitism – John Burns, earlier a leader of the dockers' strike, preferring the Boer leader Kruger to 'the horde of Jews and greedy gentiles who ha[d] corralled the old fellow in'.[3] Still yet others, such as Havelock Wilson of the Seamen and Will Crooks of the Gasmen were strongly jingoistic. The 1900 TUC adopted an anti-war resolution, but as Poirier points out, 'patriotic sentiment and the fact that war production usually meant increased pay and more jobs could not be ignored, and the resolution passed by only a small minority.[4] Congress the following year refused to debate the issue further, a fact that was taken to indicate tacit support for the war. This kind of response was already leading Hobson to the conclusion that: 'in many towns, the most important trades are dependent upon government employment or contracts; the imperial-

1. ILP 1900 Annual Report, quoted in P Poirier, *The Advent of the Labour Party*, George Allen and Unwin, 1958, p101.
2. Quoted in B Porter, *Critics of Empire – British Radical Attitudes to Imperialism in Africa 1895–1914*, MacMillan, 1966, p128.
3. Quoted in Poirier, *op cit*, p102.
4. *ibid*, p103.

ism of the metal and shipbuilding centres is attributable in no small degree to this fact.'[5]

The Fabians were the one group which adopted an unequivocally pro-imperialist stance, and their overall position was set forth by GB Shaw in his pamphlet *Fabianism and Empire*. Shaw described the aim of the Fabians as the 'effective social organisation of the Empire', and argued that: 'the notion that a nation has a right to do what it pleases with its own territory, without reference to the interests of the rest of the world, is no more tenable from the international socialist point of view – that is, the point of view of the 20th century – than the notion that a landlord has a right to do what he likes with his estate without reference to the interests of his neighbours."[6]

Not that Hobson was an unconditional defender of the right of nations to self-determination either:

> 'Assuming that the arts of "progress", or some of them, are communicable, a fact which is hardly disputable, there can be no inherent natural right in a nation to refuse that measure of compulsory education which shall raise it from childhood to manhood in the order of nationalities.'[7]

It was a position shared by the ILP: Ramsay MacDonald, who had been a close colleague of Hobson since the early 1890s, drew heavily on his Liberal friend in a series of articles published in 1901. In them he proclaimed that: 'so far as the underlying spirit of Imperialism is a frank acceptance of national duty exercised beyond the nation's political frontier...[it] cannot be condemned.' Indeed, 'the compulsion to expand and to assume world responsibility is worthy at its origin.'[8] This allowed a completely pragmatic attitude to British imperialism in particular:

---

5. From JA Hobson, *Imperialism*, quoted in VI Lenin, *Imperialism, The Highest Stage of Capitalism*, CW, vol 22 p279.
6. Quoted in Porter, *op cit*, pp116-17.
7. From JA Hobson, *Imperialism*, quoted in Porter, *op cit*, p231.
8. Quoted in *ibid*, pp185-86.

'The question of Empire cannot be decided on first principles,so far as this country is concerned. We have a history, and it is an Imperial one.'[9]

It was not possible to: 'rewrite history, to undo evil ... we have gone so far in our imperialist history that we can hardly look back. We can be guided in our future work; we cannot re-cut and re-carve the past.' In the meantime, it was sufficient to 'rule our Empire wisely' and 'to take more interest in its welfare.'[10]

MacDonald would later intervene in a debate on 'socialist colonialism' at the 1907 Stuttgart Congress of the Second International, supporting the resolution that: 'Congress does not, in principle and for all times, reject all colonial policy, which, under a socialist regime may have a civilising effect' on the basis that 'we must have the courage to draw up a program of colonial policy ... Capitalists cannot do all they want to do in the sphere of colonial policy, for they are generally submitted to the control of Parliaments.'[11] In this he merely echoed the position of the German Social Democrat Bernstein, who had argued that: 'We must not assume a purely negative standpoint ... on the question of colonial policy, but instead must pursue a positive socialist colonial policy. We must get away from the utopian idea that aims at simply leaving the colonies ... The colonies are there. We must put up with this fact. A certain guardianship of cultured peoples over non-cultured peoples is a necessity, which should also be recognised by socialists.'[12]

MacDonald's colleague Philip Snowden, ILP member for Blackburn, put this view into practice when he was moved to applaud government support for the development of cotton plantations in East Africa in 1905:

9. *ibid*, p189.

10. *ibid*, p189.

11. Quoted in R Fox, *The Colonial Policy of British Imperialism*, Lawrence, 1933, p111.

12. Quoted in *Manifesto of the Revolutionary Communist Group*, Larkin Publications, 1984, p42. The German Socialist David was even more forthright, 'Europe needs colonies. She does not even have enough. Without colonies, from an economic point of view, we shall sink to the level of China.' Quoted in R Fox, *op cit*, p110.

'As a member for a Lancashire constituency which consumes more raw cotton than any other country in the world I cannot but look with approval on the proposal to grant a loan for the development of cotton growing in East Africa.'[13]

The influential cotton unions had always had an interest in Empire: in 1896, they campaigned against a decision by the colonial government in India to impose tariffs on cotton imports from Britain, and only gave up when an equivalent duty was placed on Indian imports into Britain. When this was lifted in 1915 as a sop to the Indian bourgeoisie, they unsuccessfully renewed their campaign, arguing: 'there is doubtless an existing body of opinion in favour of a measure of protection for native industries. But these classes ... are in no position to speak for the people of India at large, who are our wards, and towards whom we have great responsibilities.' Snowden was again prominent in their support.[14]

In 1921, as author of *Labour and the New World*, Snowden was to state that there were 'inexorable limits to the right of self-determination.' Using China as an example, he argued that it had no right to 'deprive the rest of the world of access to her material resources',[15] and, almost paraphrasing Shaw's *Fabianism and Empire*, he concluded:

'By no moral right may the ownership and control of the natural and material resources of a territory be regarded as the absolute monopoly of the people who happen to be settled there.'[16]

In practice, no section of the British labour movement considered the interests of the dispossessed black people of southern Africa. The Boer War was the only occasion on which a substantial section of the labour aristocracy was to adopt a position which was remotely opposed to British imperialism. The Radical Liberals created the

---

13. Quoted in Porter, *op cit*, p297.
14. Quoted in PS Gupta, *Imperialism and the British Labour Movement 1914–64*, Cambridge, 1975, p43.
15. P Snowden, *Labour and the New World*, Waverly, 1921, p289.
16. *ibid*.

space for this in their denunciation of the British financiers. It was however their swansong: the growth of banking capital and its merging with industrial capital was already undermining the Liberal Party as the representative of manufacturing industry. The future of the Radicals lay in an alliance with the labour aristocracy, but in conditions where British imperialism's colonial monopoly would be increasingly under challenge. In these circumstances, neither could afford themselves the luxury of such demonstrations of opposition: their existence was mortgaged to British imperialism. Their attitude to the 1913 Dublin Lock-Out showed this.

2.2 *The 1913 Dublin Lock-Out*[17]

Like the 1889 dockers' strike, the Dublin Lock-Out of 1913 involved an alliance between revolutionaries (Jim Larkin and James Connolly) and the mass of the disenfranchised working class. The response of the labour aristocracy was to be no less hostile. In 1907, Snowden had already defended the Government's 'employment of the military to quell disorder' when troops had been used in an attempt to defeat the unionisation of Belfast dockers under Larkin's leadership. At the TUC Congress on 1 September, six days after the Lock-Out started, James Sexton called for support for the Dublin workers 'black as James Larkin might be, and James Connolly too'. The day before, police had attacked strikers on a demonstration, killing two. 50,000 people attended the funeral of one of the victims on 3 September, the procession being guarded by Irish Transport & General Workers' Union (ITGWU) squads bearing make-shift arms. Throughout September, unofficial sympathy strikes took place on the British mainland, which leaders such as JH Thomas of the Railwaymen did their successful best to stop.

At the end of October, the TUC sent £2,000 for distribution amongst 'affiliated unions'; the ITGWU did not receive a penny

17. Much of this section is drawn from D Reed, *Ireland – the Key to the British Revolution*, Larkin Publications, 1984, pp30-39.

because it was not an affiliate of the British TUC. In mid-November, Larkin made a direct appeal to British workers in a series of meetings up and down the country. He had been released from a seven-month gaol sentence after serving just 17 days due to an active campaign. Calling for national strike action, he spoke to thousands of workers – 5,000 in Manchester's Free Trade Hall, with 20,000 outside. Under this pressure, the TUC convened a special Congress on 9 December. The day after this announcement, Larkin along with George Lansbury (editor of the *Daily Herald*) denounced the Labour Party and the TUC for their inaction: 10,000 came to the Albert Hall to hear him, again leaving thousands waiting outside.

The breaking point came when Larkin called on workers through the *Daily Herald* to tell their leaders to stand for trade unionism, and 'that they are not there as apologists for the shortcomings of the capitalist system'. The response was immediate. Havelock Wilson issued a manifesto denouncing Larkin and the methods of the ITGWU, whilst Snowden described strikes as 'demoralising'. Larkin told a mass meeting in London that 'I am not going to allow these serpents to raise their foul heads and spit out their poison any longer.'

At the TUC Conference, after Connolly presented the case for the Dublin workers, speaker after speaker, led by Ben Tillett, once one of the most radical leaders of the dockers, denounced the strike, condemning Larkin's unfair treatment of British trade union officials. Tillett went on to ask Congress to affirm its confidence in TUC officials to negotiate an honourable settlement, effectively over the heads of the ITGWU. Larkin responded against a growing uproar, denouncing the leaders for their betrayal. Tillett and the rest of the leadership had their way: isolated, the Dublin workers were eventually starved into submission. The opportunism of the privileged leadership of the British working class had triumphed.

2.3 *The First Imperialist War*

The advent of World War was to show how far Labour had travelled since the Boer War. Although Britain was in no immediate military danger, or indeed under threat of attack in those first four days of August 1914, there was no doubt that it needed to settle accounts with the German challenge to its colonial monopoly. Two days before the declaration of war on 4 August, massive demonstrations had heard Labour leaders denounce the impending threat and issue calls to resist it, in line with the policy of the Second International. But by 5 August, the trade union MPs – some 35 of them – had deserted to the ruling class, leaving but five ILP MPs, MacDonald, Hardie and Snowden amongst them, to wring their hands in dismay, supported by an equally small number of Liberals.

Within days, the Labour Party had called an industrial truce, to be followed shortly after by an electoral truce as well. It placed its national organisation at the disposal of the recruitment campaign. Union leaders such as Ben Tillett acted as recruiting sergeants, vilifying conscientious objectors. Havelock Wilson denounced ILP calls for a negotiated peace, saying: 'some of you would be content to meet these men! [the Germans] You would take the blood-stained hands of murderers in your own'.[18] A manifesto issued by the Labour leadership stated: 'The victory of Germany would mean the death of democracy in Europe ... Until the Power which has pillaged and outraged Belgium and the Belgians, and plunged nearly the whole of Europe into the awful misery, suffering and horror of war is beaten there can be no peace.'[19]

That the defence of democracy required an alliance with Tsarist reaction did not trouble such leaders at all. In February 1915, Labour convened a meeting of Allied Socialists which adopted a resolution declaring: 'The invasion of Belgium and France by the German armies threatens the very existence of independent nationalities, and strikes a blow at all faith in treaties. In these circumstances a victory for German imperialism would be the defeat and the destruction of democracy and liberty in Europe.'[20] Given Britain's colonial mono-

18. Quoted in Cliff and Gluckstein, *op cit*, p59.
19. Quoted in Tracey, *op cit*, vol 1 p105.
20. *ibid*.

poly, the reference to 'independent nationalities' was typical of Labour's corrupt defence of privilege. Pamphlets issued by Radicals such as ED Morel and Norman Angell showed the predatory nature of these treaties and the imperialist interests they expressed. But such opposition was isolated as the official labour movement sanctioned the most appalling slaughter the international working class had ever known to defend British imperialism.

In May 1915, Arthur Henderson, who had replaced MacDonald as leader of the Parliamentary Labour Party (PLP), joined a Coalition government which included Edward Carson as Attorney General and eight other Ulster Unionists. Truly by their friends shall ye know them! It was less than two years since Carson had openly prepared for military struggle against the Liberal's Home Rule Bill for Ireland. Now Labour was in alliance with those it had once denounced as the antithesis of 'democracy'. Imperialism needed Labour's involvement in order to mobilise the working class for war, to ensure a plentiful supply of recruits eager to defend 'democracy', and to impose discipline on the workforce left behind.

Although there were some within the ILP who were to maintain a courageous opposition, their leaders were not amongst them – not once did they oppose war credits. MacDonald himself called for the prosecution of the war to the end: 'Victory must therefore be ours. England is not played out, her mission is not accomplished ...We must go straight through...the young men of the country must, for the moment, settle the immediate issue of victory. Let them do it in the spirit of the brave men who have crowned our country with honour in the times that are gone.'[21] An ILP Manifesto published in late 1914 urged members to: 'carry on a general propaganda of socialism "though not dealing specifically with the war"'.[22] The change since 1900 was spelled out by Keir Hardie:

'A nation at war must be united, especially when its existence is at

21. Quoted in Cliff and Gluckstein, *op cit*, p21.
22. Quoted in R Fox, *The Class Struggle in Britain*, Lawrence, 1932, vol 2, p22.

stake. In such filibustering expeditions as our own Boer War ... where no national danger of any kind was involved, there were many occasions for diversity of opinion ...With the boom of enemy guns within earshot, the lads who have gone forth to fight their country's battles must not be disheartened by any discordant notes at home.'[23]

Meanwhile, the Irish people had chosen a different side. The ITGWU immediately denounced the war as imperialist, and organised protests against it. The fruits of Connolly's agitation came with the proclamation of the Irish republic on Easter 1916. The reaction from the British movement was unequivocal. On behalf of the ILP, *Socialist Review* pontificated 'We do not approve armed rebellion at all, any more than any other militarism or war ... Nor do we complain against the Government for having opposed and suppressed armed rebellion by armed force.'[24] Another ILP publication, *Labour Leader,* declared that Connolly was 'criminally mistaken', whilst George Lansbury described the uprising as a crime against the Irish people. After the suppression of the revolt, the War Cabinet authorised the execution of its leader; when news reached Parliament of Connolly's death, Arthur Henderson led other Labour MPs in a spontaneous round of applause.

When Labour dealt with the possible post-war fate of the Empire, it was quite clear that there was to be no change, especially in Africa. A December 1917 Memorandum on War Aims explained 'it is impracticable here (ie in Africa) to leave the various peoples concerned to settle their own destinies', describing them as 'non-adult races'.[25] In a more specific reply to Bolshevik peace proposals in January 1918, the Party stated: 'Nobody contends that the black races can govern themselves. They can only make it known that the particular government under which they have been living is bad in some or all

23. Quoted in Miliband, *op cit*, p44.

24. Quoted in D Reed, *op cit,* p59.

25. Quoted in Gupta, *op cit*, p53. The Memorandum was itself drafted by the ubiquitous Sidney Webb.

respects, and indicate the specific evils from which they desire liberation.'[26]

ED Morel, an ex-Radical Liberal who was on the advisory committee which formulated Labour Party colonial policy at the time, had written in 1911: 'in no period of time which can be forecast, will the condition of West African society permit of the supreme governing power being shared by both races.'[27] In other word, tutelage was to be indefinite. Racism was the very stuff of such politics; in April 1920, Morel wrote an article for Lansbury's *Daily Herald*, following the French Army's deployment of Moroccan troops during their occupation of Germany, in which he referred to France 'thrusting her black savages into the heart of Germany'. He went on to talk of the 'barely restrainable bestiality of the black troops', which had led to rapes and consequent injury and death for 'well-known physiological reasons'. The *Daily Herald* commended the article; a follow-up pamphlet was distributed at the 1920 TUC under the auspices of the Standing Order Committee, whilst Morel was able to involve well-known leaders like JR Clynes, Robert Smillie, Robert Williams and Ben Turner in his campaign.[28]

The end of the war led to an explosion within the working class, stimulated by the success of the Russian Revolution. Mutinies in the Army, massive strikes in industry, and a meteoric rise of trade union membership to eight million served notice to the ruling class that it would have great difficulty in enforcing its will. Yet Labour, in co-operation with the trade union leadership, ensured that such challenges were kept to a minimum. In September 1918, its executive had despatched Henderson to an Inter-Allied Conference of Allied Labour and Socialist parties with instructions not to 'approve or condemn Allied intervention' which British imperialism was leading in Russia, but to accept it 'as an accomplished fact'. In the absence of any organised opposition, they were able to get away with a tacit

26. *ibid*.
27. *ibid*.
28. For example, Callaghan, *op cit*, p93.

acceptance of British intervention. Later, in April 1920, dockers, led by Harry Pollitt amongst others, boycotted the *Jolly George* when they learned that it was to be loaded with arms to be used against the Red Army. In August, a specially convened conference of the Labour Party and TUC issued blood-curdling threats as to their response if British imperialism carried out its evident intention to send troops to support Polish aggression against the Soviet Union. The Polish victory shortly afterwards avoided the need to put this to the test.

2.4 *The Labour Party and the Second International*

The Second International[29] had collapsed at the outbreak of the war, as its leading parties rushed to the defence of their respective imperialist ruling classes. The major exception was the Bolshevik Party, who stood by the decisions made by the International in various conferences before 1914 calling for mass working class action against war if it should break out. The defection of the leaders of Social Democracy caused Rosa Luxembourg to describe the International as a 'mouldering corpse', and Lenin to fight for a new, Third International. In March 1918, a conference of Allied socialist parties – the open chauvinists – set up a committee to resurrect the Second International. Its first Conference took place in Berne in February 1919.

From the outset, the Labour Party, which had been an insignificant force in the pre-war International, played a leading role. Henderson was its first Chairman, and Ramsay MacDonald its Secretary. The Conference declared that: 'in full agreement with all previous

---

29. The Second International was formed in 1889 as the successor to the First International of Marx's day which had dissolved in 1876. The Second International was a loose amalgam of a variety of socialist parties and trade unions, which included open opportunists as well as revolutionary currents. Several Congresses, including the last one held at Basle in 1912, had declared the intention of the International to oppose any imperialist war by international action; August 1914 showed the extent of imperialist corruption when all the leading parties bar the Bolsheviks supported 'their' ruling class in the slaughter of the First Imperialist War.

Congresses of the International, the Berne Conference firmly adheres to the principles of democracy'. Hence, it proclaimed itself to be fully in favour of self-determination, but what this meant in practice was left 'to a future conference'. Its next Conference at Geneva in early 1920 defined the 'Political System of Socialism' in a resolution that drew heavily on *Labour and the New Social Order*, and so made no reference to the existence of the class struggle. In between the conferences, it had set up a Permanent Commission of seven members, three of whom were British. 'The headquarters [of the International] were placed in London, and in effect the British Labour Party took charge of its affairs.'[30]

The founding Congress of the Third International had taken place in March 1919; at its second, in August 1920, it established stringent conditions of admission to exclude not just the open chauvinists, but also the social-pacifists who wanted to reconstruct a united International. These last (including the ILP at a time when MacDonald was Secretary to the Berne International) set up the Vienna Union, or Two-and-a-Half International, in February 1921. From the outset, both the Second and the Two-and-a-Half Internationals were determined to isolate the Russian Revolution: led by the Labour Party, the former counterposed its empty concept of 'democracy' – which naturally excluded all the colonies – to that of 'Bolshevik dictatorship'. Its main attack on the new-born Soviet Union was over Georgia.

The October 1917 Revolution had no immediate echo in Georgia, where a Menshevik government had been set up. Following the Brest-Litovsk peace treaty of April 1918, German troops moved into Georgia. Despite the fact that the Georgian Mensheviks had wanted to continue the war against Germany, they loyally co-operated with the occupying army, the Menshevik President Zhordania declaring in September to the German commander: 'It is not in our interests to lower the prestige of Germany in the Caucasus.'[31] Within two

30. GDH Cole, *A History of Socialist Thought* vol 4 Part 1, Macmillan, 1958, pp329-30.
31. Quoted in Trotsky, *Social Democracy and the Wars of Intervention*, New Park, 1975, p24

months, he had to swallow these words, as the British moved in from Persia in the wake of the German defeat, occupied the main Trans-Caucasian towns and 'left the Georgian Menshevik government in office under their supervision.'[32] By January the following year, Zhordania could say of the British commander 'General Walker ... proved to be the first person that understood the state of affairs in our country.'[33] At the same time, another leading Menshevik was saying 'I assume that our republic will co-operate with the Allied countries in their fight against the Bolsheviks, with all the means at its disposal'.[34] The Georgian Mensheviks were as good as their word: throughout 1918 and 1919, they supported the counter-revolutionary armies of Kolchak and Denikin, and, in 1920, allowed the defeated Denikin forces to regroup under Wrangel. Zhordania himself made it quite clear: 'I know that our enemies will say that we are on the side of the imperialists. Therefore I must say most emphatically: that I prefer the imperialists of the West to the fanatics of the East.'[35] Domestically, the Mensheviks suppressed the Georgian Communist Party, put down numerous peasant uprisings particularly amongst the national minorities, and even engaged in a little war with Armenia over some disputed territory. In February 1921, the Red Army put an end to this bastion of counter-revolution.

However, Georgia was to become a *cause celebre* for the chauvinists. Self-determination may not apply to the colonies, to India or Ireland, but it was the absolute right of Georgia. Kautsky, MacDonald, and Ethel Snowden made visits to Georgia on behalf of the Second International to view the achievements of Georgian Mensheviks, using it to denounce the Russian Revolution. In May 1922, at a meeting of representatives of all three internationals chaired by the imperialist Tom Shaw, those from the Second and Two-and-a-Half

32. GDH Cole, *op cit*, vol 4 Part 1 p206.
33. Quoted in Trotsky, *op cit*, p45.
34. Quoted *ibid*, p25.
35. Quoted *ibid*, p54.

International denounced the Bolshevik 'occupation' of Georgia, and demanded the restoration of the Mensheviks, at the same time rejecting any joint campaign against the imperialist Versailles Treaty.

In May 1923, the depleted forces of the Two-and-a-Half International merged with the Second to form the Labour and Socialist International (LSI) with Tom Shaw as one of the two joint secretaries and Henderson remaining as chair. The headquarters remained in London 'where Arthur Henderson and the British Labour Party could keep a vigilant eye on its doings';[36] apart from the Austrian Adler, 'the Administrative Committee that took charge of the International's day-to-day affairs was made up entirely of British members'.[37] The British grip on the International ensured that it took no position on the issue of colonialism, least of all British colonialism, whilst constantly demanding a Menshevik restoration in Georgia. As one Communist wittily characterised the LSI position: 'There is another country to which the parties affiliated to the LSI must give special attention, ie, to Georgia ... The liberation of this country from the Bolshevik yoke constitutes one of the chief aims of the LSI. Every true social-democrat has two countries: his own, and Georgia.'[38] On the other hand, 'The LSI, whose activity is based on the idea of international solidarity and which opposes every nationalism except that which defends itself, is pledged to combat with special energy the Asiatic and African nationalism of the colonial and semi-colonial people.'[39] The LSI was a pawn in the hands of the Labour Party, defending the Versailles imperialist order and British colonialism in particular against the growing unity between the Russian Revolution and the anti-colonial struggle.

---

36. Cole, *op cit*, vol 4 Part 2, p684.
37. *ibid*.
38. G Valetzki in *Labour Monthly*, October 1925, p596.
39. *ibid*, p599.

2.5 *Labour and Ireland 1920–21*[40]

Labour viewed the renewed struggle for Irish independence as it always had done: from the standpoint of protecting Britain's imperial interests. *Labour and The New Social Order* recognised 'the claim of the people of Ireland to Home Rule, and to self-determination in all exclusively Irish affairs', and demanded that a 'wide and generous measure of Home Rule should be immediately made law and put in operation.[41] This meant rejecting any settlement leading to an independent republic. In June 1920, the Labour conference modified this standpoint, demanding 'free and absolute self-determination' for the Irish people, even if by a narrow majority.[42]

The situation was that the Irish people already had their own assembly – the Daíl Eireann, a constitution – the 1916 Proclamation and the 1919 Daíl Democratic programme for which they were fighting the terror of the Black and Tans. The issue was therefore not one of rights, but of acknowledging the *de facto* existence of the Republic. This Labour refused to do because the Daíl Eireann was in practice laying claim to the whole of Ireland, which Britain was not prepared to concede. In the meantime, Labour opposed the terror on the grounds that 'under such conditions it is practically impossible to bring the Irish Republican Army to bay ... Executions and torture are not deterrents; they have indeed, the opposite effect.'[43] This was to become a familiar Labour refrain: if it ever made a show of disagreeing with British imperialism it would not be over aims, but on the brutality of its means, and then not out of concern for its victims, but out of fear that it might be counter-productive.

Labour's position was made clearer in a 1920 report from a Commission chaired by Arthur Henderson, which declared that 'It is impossible to treat Ireland as a separate country from Great Britain for military purposes. An invasion of Ireland would be an invasion of

40. Again, this section draws on D Reed, *op cit*, pp64–72.
41. *op cit*, p22.
42. Quoted in D Reed, *op cit*, p70.
43. Quoted *ibid*, p69.

Britain ... the two islands should form a single unit for all war-like purposes.'[44] In December 1920, it arrived at its definitive position, which was for the withdrawal of troops and for the election of a constituent assembly which would work out 'without limitations or fetters, whatever constitution for Ireland the Irish people desire, subject only to two conditions – that it affords protection to minorities and that the Constitution should prevent Ireland from becoming a military or naval menace to Great Britain.'[45] In practice, this conceded both the need for partition and for a continuing military occupation.

The 1920 TUC met in September, as Terence MacSweeny, Mayor of Cork, neared death on hunger strike in Brixton prison. The TUC approved the sending of two telegrams to the Government, but JH Thomas as president of Congress refused to allow MacSweeney's sister to address it, evidently because she might call for some meaningful action. Sitting in the public gallery when he announced the decision, she shouted 'traitors' to the Congress and walked out.[46] 'Traitors' indeed: next year, when Partition was agreed, and the Treaty came before Parliament, it took a Communist MP, Shapur Saklatvala, to force a division and record any opposition to it. Henderson's party had indeed proved a 'bulwark against revolution', and the Irish people could well ponder Snowden's comments on the 'inexorable limits to the right to self-determination': Ireland was not Georgia.

2.6 *Labour and India 1919–23*

By the end of the war, India was in as much turmoil as Ireland. Britain had plundered it of manpower, finance and food resources. The first three years of the war had cost it £270 million: part of this was used to fund the one million strong army it provided to British imperialism, and which was crucial in preventing the German Army

44. Quoted in R Fox, *The Colonial Policy of British Imperialism*, p109.
45. Quoted in D Reed, *op cit*, p70.
46. From the Trades Union Congress 52nd Annual Report, 1920, p355.

from occupying the Channel ports in its 1914–15 campaign. But it also included a forced loan of £100 million, which George Lansbury was later to describe as a 'gift'.[47] And, at a time when two-thirds of the population was starving, Indian exports of wheat and cereals amounted to 2.5 million tons in 1917, and even more in 1918.

The mutinous state of the Indian Army, and the impact of the Russian Revolution, meant that some political concessions to the nascent Indian bourgeoisie were needed to stabilise imperialist rule. The Secretary of State for India, Edwin Montagu, touring India in 1918, described the 'seething, boiling, political flood raging across the country.'[48] He proclaimed the Government's aim as 'the gradual development of self-governing institutions with a view to the progressive realisation of Responsible Government in India as an integral part of the British Empire.' Together with the Indian Viceroy, Lord Chelmsford, he prepared a report on the necessary constitutional changes to buy off at least one section of the Indian bourgeoisie.

The Montagu-Chelmsford reforms were based on a plan devised by an Empire Federationist, Lionel Curtis. Responsibility for three departments, those of education, health and local government, would be transferred to elected ministers, but only at a provincial level: national structures would remain unchanged. Even then, the vital department of finance would remain under the control of the Indian Civil Service. There would be a franchise: three million out of 350 million people would be allowed the vote. The progress of these reforms would then be reviewed after a period of ten years. At the request of the Labour Party, Curtis produced a pamphlet explaining his proposals for use by Labour candidates in the 1918 general election. 'At present', he wrote, 'the number of people who could understand the vote is small. To grant full responsible government

47. G Lansbury, *Labour's Way with the Commonwealth*, Methuen, 1935, p51. It is difficult to conceive of what £100 million meant in 1915; certainly it is at least £20 billion in today's terms, and probably over £40 billion if it is assessed as a proportion of GDP.
48. *ibid*, p54.

outright ... would place government in the hands of a very few.'[49] At the Berne Congress of the Second International in 1919, Labour was to state its support for Home Rule, and claim that these reforms indicated that 'British policy has been tending in this direction for some time.'[50]

However, such reforms were irrelevant to the mass of the Indian people. Famine stalked the land: estimates as to the number who died from a combination of flu and starvation in 1918–19 range from 12 to 30 million. The countryside was a tinder-box, and, starting in the heartland of the cotton industry, Bombay, a massive strike wave spread throughout the major industrial centre. The only response was repression: a Bill enacting new measures to combat 'sedition' and 'terrorism' proposed by the Rowlatt Committee took effect in March 1919. On 13 April, a meeting against the Rowlatt Act took place in Amritsar in the Punjab. Under the command of General Dwyer, a column of troops opened fire on the peaceful crowd. 379 people were murdered, 1,200 injured.

Under Gandhi's reluctant leadership, the campaign spread throughout early 1921: spontaneous non-payment of taxes started in some areas; more ominously for the Indian landlord class, peasants started to go on rent strike. In January, Gandhi sent a letter to Chelmsford, stating that unless all prisoners were released and the Rowlatt Act repealed, he would authorise a campaign of mass civil disobedience ... in the District of Bardoli, home to a mere 87,000 people. Shortly after, irate peasants stormed the police station in the village of Chauri Chaura and burned 22 policemen to death. On 12 February, Gandhi unconditionally called off the campaign complaining that: 'the country is not non-violent enough', advising 'the cultivators to pay land revenue and other taxes due to the government, and to suspend every other activity of an offensive nature', and ordering the peasants that witholding of rent payment to the landlords was 'injurious to the

49. Quoted in Gupta, *op cit*, p42.
50. Quoted in R Fox, *The Class Struggle in Britain, op cit*, Part 2, p68.

best interests of the country.'[51]

During all of this Labour was guided by the notion that India, like Ireland, was above politics; it would differ from the Government, but only in detail, and not in substance. JH Thomas, to become Labour's first Colonial Secretary within three years, was of the opinion that: 'It is a fact that, at the moment, there would be very few people in India among the natives who would understand the significance of the power to vote. This means that responsible government, as in Canada, could not be arranged just now.'[52] In January 1922, at the height of the struggle, the TUC and the Labour Party joined together to issue a statement saying nothing about self-government, but stating: 'While realising the necessity of preserving order in India, the Council deplores the political arrests ... but deplores no less the action of the non-co-operators in boycotting the parliamentary institutions recently conferred upon India by which grievances should be ventilated and wrongs redressed.'[53]

2.7 *The 1924 Labour Government*

The December 1923 election returned 192 Labour MPs, who, with 157 Liberals, held a majority over the 258 Conservatives. With the failure of Tory diplomacy in Europe, the Middle East and India, British imperialism needed to adopt a less militaristic and more conciliatory guise: a Labour Government would suit it admirably. If matters got out of hand, it could be speedily brought down; in the meantime, it could learn how to administer the imperial machine. The Liberals agreed to support a minority Labour Government – consummating the alliance between the labour aristocracy and the middle class. JH Thomas was put in charge of the Colonial Office,

---

51. Quoted in R Palme Dutt, *India Today*, Left Book Club, 1940, pp316-17. Much of the material on the Indian struggle is drawn from this, undoubtedly the best book on the history of the Indian struggle.
52. JH Thomas, *When Labour Rules*, Collins, 1920, p139.
53. Quoted by Clemens Dutt in *Labour Monthly,* September 1926, p545.

announcing that he was there to ensure there was no mucking about with the Empire. As if to underline the point, Lord Chelmsford, now retired from India, was given the Admiralty, Sidney Olivier, a Fabian and former colonial governor, was given the India Office, Lord Haldane, a Liberal Imperialist who had supported the Taff Vale judgment, became Lord Chancellor, and the Tory Lord Thompson was put in charge of the RAF.

Labour had consistently denounced the Versailles Treaty even if it had prevented any action against it; as late as 1923, MacDonald had declared that: 'there will never be peace so long as the Versailles Treaty is in existence', arguing that 'pursuing the will-o'-the-wisp of reparations is the great curse of every country.'[54] Within 48 hours of coming into office, as he was later to boast, MacDonald had accepted the Dawes report in its entirety, and had made the chief object of his European policy its imposition on the German working class. The Dawes report, prepared on behalf of US bankers, accepted the premise of Versailles: that Germany should pay war reparations – it merely rescheduled them over a longer period. And what if Germany wouldn't accept? 'She must accept. We shall make her accept. We must have some settlement,' MacDonald declared at a meeting of the PLP.[55] At the 1924 London Conference, despite French misgivings, Germany did accept: Labour had committed itself to the Treaty it had denounced for the previous four years.

Given the make-up of the Cabinet, it is not surprising that there was indeed no mucking about with the Empire. Far from it. JH Thomas was all for exploiting the 'incalculable riches of our splendid possessions.' MacDonald as both Prime Minister and Foreign Secretary stated, in case there was any doubt, that:

> 'I can see no hope in India if it becomes the arena of a struggle between constitutionalism and revolution. No party in Great Britain will be cowed by threats of force or by policies designed

54. Quoted by 'UDC' in *Labour Monthly*, February 1925, p104.
55. *ibid*, p109.

to bring Government to a standstill; and if any section in India are under the delusion that is not so, events will sadly disappoint them.'[56]

On 6 February 1924, Olivier made his policy on the 1919 India reforms absolutely clear: to change it for the establishment of full responsible government:

> '...would be worse than perilous, it would be big with disaster to the people of India ... The programme of constitutional democracy ... was not native to India ... It was impossible for the Indian people or Indian politicians to leap at once into the saddle and administer an ideal constitution ... The right of British statesmen, public servants, merchants and industrialists to be in India today was the fact that they had made the India of today, and that no Home Rule or national movement could have been possible in India had it not been for their work.'[57]

No wonder *The Times* found these views 'reassuring' and 'deserving of full recognition'. And as if to underline its position, the Government sanctioned the passage of yet more repressive legislation, the Bengal Ordinance, which allowed for detention without charge let alone trial.

In the Middle East, the Labour Government consolidated British imperialism's grip on some of the prizes won from Versailles. It rubber-stamped a treaty with Iraq which gave Britain total control over Iraqi fiscal, foreign and military policy, and allowed it to garrison the country and set up air bases. It sanctioned the use of the RAF to

---

56. Quoted by MN Roy in *Labour Monthly*, April 1924, p207.
57. Quoted *ibid*, p209. Olivier had been Governor of Jamaica between 1907 and 1913 at a salary of £5,000 per annum – at 50 times average wage, over £1 million in today's terms – and had been a leading Fabian since the late 1880s, resigning over their support for British imperialism in the Boer War. However, he held no shrift for the rights of the colonial people, arguing: 'I have said that the West Indian negro is not fit for complete democratic citizenship in a Constitution of modern Parliamentary form, and I should certainly hold the same opinion with respect to any African native community.' Quoted in F Lee, *op cit*, p117.

support the campaign of the British puppet government against the Kurds, explaining that because the RAF dropped warning leaflets ahead of bombs and gas, no significant injuries took place. Lord Thompson was rather more frank about this than the Under-Minister for Air in the House of Commons when he remarked in November that the effects of air attacks in Iraq were 'appalling', and that panic-stricken tribesmen 'fled into the desert where hundreds more must have perished from thirst ...The British Air Force in Iraq was the cement which kept the bricks together.'[58]

Finally, the Government refused to accede to Egyptian claims on either the Suez Canal or the Sudan, the latter to the great relief of the cotton unions. For all its pious support for the League of Nations, it declined the proposal of the Egyptian leader Zaghlul Pasha to submit the issue of the British military occupation and control of the Suez Canal to arbitration by the League. MacDonald himself made clear that he adhered to the view that: 'absolute certainty that the Suez Canal [would] remain open in peace as in war for the free passage of British ships [was] the foundation on which the entire defence strategy of the British Empire rests.'[59] For the next 30 years, British control of the Suez Canal was to remain a *sine qua non* for the Labour leadership. Zaghlul Pasha, who only accepted office in the belief that a British Labour Government would support Egyptian independence remarked that MacDonald's position was not new but:

> 'What was new to Egypt was that the policy was approved by a Labour Government which had always been opposed to imperialist principles.'[60]

The first Labour Government lasted nine months; its work on Dawes and the Middle East complete, it was summarily despatched. It had demonstrated a fitness for office which was to be remembered five years later; on no issue of imperial defence had it been found

58. Quoted in Clemens Dutt, *Labour and the Empire*, CPGB, 1929, p12.
59. Quoted in Gupta, *op cit*, p98.
60. Quoted in *Labour Monthly*, October 1929, p620.

wanting. The issue was not whether it was constrained by its minority position: it had determinedly pursued the interests it had been placed in government to advance.

2.8 *Empire Socialism*

Whilst Britain had retained its position as the dominant European imperialist power, its underlying industrial strength was even less assured than it had been in 1914. Although it had made substantial gains from the carve-up at Versailles, especially in the extension of its informal empire in the Middle East, it did not address the fundamental problem of antiquated manufacturing plant and the resultant low level of productivity. In 1923, British exports of manufactured goods were in real terms 73 per cent of their 1913 level, whilst French and US manufactured exports stood at 117 per cent and 148 per cent.[61] In real terms, production in the years 1921-26 averaged 80 to 88 per cent its pre-war level.[62] Noting that 'A larger number of workers is employed today than before the war, but for a less total production,' Dutt concluded:

> '*What the decline in production reveals is that the productive workers are being thrown on the scrap-heap, while an ever increasing proportion of the working force of the nation is being consumed in unproductive parasitic occupations.*'[63]

Net property income from abroad throughout this period averaged £200 to £250 million per annum; although in real terms this was less than half the immediate pre-war rate, it still amounted to 50 per cent of the level of the gross trading profits of private companies. And capital continued to flood abroad: Dutt cites an *Economist* report which analysed new capital issues between 1921 and 1926 under a variety of headings, and showed that of £1,904 million new capital,

61 R Palme Dutt, *Socialism and the Living Wage*, CPGB, 1927, p39.

62. *ibid*, p40.

63. *ibid*, p41; emphasis in original.

only £431 million was invested in home industry; the bulk of the remainder went abroad. 'Parasitism was becoming a deadly growth on the productive forces of the metropolis'.[64]

Labour expressed particular concern at British imperialism's overall fragility, and the left in particular began to express support for Imperial Preference: that the Empire be consciously used as a protected market for the export of British goods. Thus John Wheatley MP declared 'Within the British Empire we have a nucleus of unity; therefore I am opposed to any policy of wrecking it.' He went on to argue that 'Whatever we think of [it], our duty as members of the Labour Movement is to see how we can utilise it to serve our purposes.'[65] Lansbury agreed with him during a parliamentary debate on the issue, during which David Kirkwood declared:

> 'I am all out for cementing the British Empire ... We are all out for universal peace. There is nothing that can accomplish that better than cementing the British Empire.'[66]

Such 'cement' was something which the Iraqi people had now experienced first-hand. This trend of Empire Socialism had other exponents: Tom Johnston, who voted with Lansbury, Kirkwood and about 20 other left MPs for Imperial Preference, argued that 'In some socialist circles – but these are smaller and fewer than they were a dozen years ago – there is a fixed belief that this Empire is an engine of grab and oppression and that it is and can be nothing more.'[67] The 1925 Labour Party conference adopted Empire Socialism, whilst the following year, the Hobsonian radicals on the Empire Policy Committee of the ILP 'welcom[ed] the possibility of closer economic relationships between the British nation and the various parts of the

---

64. R Fox, *The Colonial Policy of British Imperialism*, p36.
65. Quoted in S MacIntyre, *Imperialism and the British Labour Movement in the 1920s*, CPGB, 1975, p17.
66. Quoted in Clemens Dutt, *Labour and the Empire*, *op cit*, p13.
67. Quoted in JR Campbell, 'Must the Empire be Broken Up?' in *Communist Review*, 1924, p218.

Commonwealth.[68] This new twist to socialist colonialism was later to achieve full expression with the 1945-51 Labour Government.

2.9 *Labour and China 1927*

Labour's bipartisan approach to imperial diplomacy continued through the years between the first two Labour Governments, as its attitude towards China demonstrates. From the mid-1920s, Britain's dominant position in China was threatened on the one hand by US imperialist interests (against which Britain attempted to ally with the nascent Japanese imperialism), and on the other by rising Chinese Nationalist and Communist movements. The period was marked by the constant despatch of British warships and troops to safeguard British extra-territorial concessions and naval bases, many won following the Opium Wars of the 1830s, with Labour either directing operations, as it did in 1924, or giving eager support.

One such incident took place in August 1926, when after a shipping scuffle outside the Yangtze town of Wanhsien, a British gunboat bombarded the town, killing about 500 people. Sir Austen Chamberlain publicly thanked MacDonald for the support he gave to the Government during the episode. In June 1925, a joint Labour Party/TUC resolution argued that the 'point' had not yet 'been reached' where Chinese independence be recognised and British troops withdrawn; this followed an incident the previous month where British marines had fired on and killed a number of demonstrators at Shameen, near Canton (Guangzhou).

In 1926, an article in the ILP journal *New Leader* under the title 'Ah Sin at War with himself' referred to the struggle of the Chinese people as like 'our weary old Wars of the Roses', and expressed puzzlement at why 'should any human should among the indistinguishable millions of China care to risk life and all'[69] in the course of it. The article, with its references to 'Chinks', fully expressed what

68. Quoted in Macintyre, *op cit*, p18.
69. Quoted in *Labour Monthly,* March 1927, p141.

Palme Dutt described as 'the utter boorish self-centred indifference to every living human struggle, that is the heart and soul of the imperialist psychology in the labour aristocracy and the petty bourgeoisie...looking on with contemptuous indifference to the curious incomprehensible inferior races.'[70]

Early in 1927, a massive strike movement in Shanghai led to a number of incidents when Chinese workers attempted to reclaim the British concession, only to be fired on by British troops. Similar incidents took place in Hankou and Canton, where over 50 people were killed. 20,000 troops were despatched to deal with the threat from the Shanghai uprising. MacDonald argued that: 'the Chinese masses must not be mealy-mouthed as to the consequences of massing on the streets', and added: 'We have to turn to Mr Chen [the Chinese bourgeois nationalist leader] and say "your nationalist demands have our complete support, but we must warn you that if you cannot control mobs no effort of ours will be able to prevent trouble or keep those nationalist demands to the foreground".'[71] Ever the imperialist, JH Thomas was of the opinion that it was better to send a big army than a small one, and went on: 'For some unknown reason, the negotiations have broken down ... It is not statesmanlike or patriotic to hamper the Government in a question involving war and peace, or to attempt to make party capital out of the question'. He 'urged' Mr Chen to accept the agreement Britain was forcing on the Chinese people.[72] Meanwhile, George Lansbury in his *Lansbury's Labour Weekly*, also referred to the 'Chinese mobs', and stated: 'we owe a vote of congratulations to our comrades in the navy' for their role in the Hankou incident.[73]

The Shanghai strike movement developed into an insurrection, which was brutally put down by the bourgeois nationalist Kuomintang, aided and abetted by British and Japanese troops. For the left,

70. *ibid.*
71. Quoted *ibid*, p138.
72. Quoted in *League Against Imperialism, China's Appeal to British Workers*, 1927, p3.
73. Quoted in *Labour Monthly*, March 1927, p139.

George Lansbury asked whether there was not some power 'or any way to persuade the Japanese to use some other part of China to attack the Chinese?', for, as he explained, 'white people have lost faith in armaments and force and now want to depend on justice, truth and righteousness.'[74] Hundreds of thousands of Chinese workers died in the 1927 Shanghai massacres, leaving the various imperialist powers in possession of their concessions, and Britain the most powerful amongst them. No wonder that Tom Mann, returning from a visit to China in 1927, wrote of the Chinese people:

> 'They have no illusions about the Chinese capitalists, but the greatest curse, they declare, is the foreign imperialist, and in this they are undoubtedly right; and of all the imperialist forces in China beyond any question Great Britain is the worst.'[75]

2.10 *Labour and India 1927–31*

In late 1927, the Tory Secretary of State for India, Lord Birkenhead, decided to bring forward the statutory review of the progress of the Montagu-Chelmsford reforms in order to guarantee Tory control of the Commission that would carry it out. With the complete eclipse of the Liberals at the 1924 election, Labour had become the Loyal Opposition; this meant it would be entitled to seats on the Commission. In negotiations with MacDonald on its composition, Birkenhead's aim was to exclude any Indian representation, whilst MacDonald's was to ensure the presence of at least two Labour members. Both achieved what they wanted, and MacDonald overruled NEC objections on the absence of any Indians. The two Labour nominees were Clement Attlee and Steven Walsh, the latter a notorious imperialist.

The enabling act setting up the Commission under the Chairmanship of Sir John Simon was rushed through Parliament by Christmas

74. Quoted in H Rathbone, *China*, CPGB, 1930, p13.
75. Tom Mann in *Labour Monthly*, August 1927, p488.

1927. All sections of the Indian nationalist movement were outraged. The Indian TUC passed a motion demanding that Labour 'withdraw its members from the Simon Commission', and resolved that it itself would boycott it. Its President, Chaman Lal, protesting against what he described as MacDonald's 'imperialist proclivities' went on to say 'All classes are aghast at the betrayal by the Labour Party. The Simon Commission will register the middle class imperialist verdict.'[76] Pandhit Nehru, on behalf of Congress told the NEC: 'I am authorised to state that the action of the Labour Party, in not withdrawing its members from the Commission, and trying to effect some kind of compromise, is not supported by any responsible party in India.'[77]

The Simon Commission including Attlee arrived in India in February 1928, to be greeted by a general strike; three demonstrators were killed in a demonstration in Madras (Chennai). As it proceeded around the country it was greeted with mass demonstrations, strikes and riots. The Indian working class played a leading role: a colossal strike movement in 1928, with over 30 million days lost, was accompanied by a 70 per cent growth in union membership, and the massive growth of the revolutionary Bombay (Mumbai) Girni Kardar or Red Flag Union, with 65,000 members. Meanwhile the 1928 Labour Conference debated a motion opposing the Commission. Fortified by a TUC report which attacked the middle class leadership of the Indian trade union movement, the conference trounced opposition by three million votes to 150,000. No wonder Shapurji Saklatvala reported for the *Daily Worker*:

> 'It has been well-known for some time that the Commission would have a hostile reception from the Indian workers, who view it as the latest weapon of British imperialism ...When the Bombay workers burned the effigy of MacDonald in the streets along with that of Lord Birkenhead and others, they showed that

76. Quoted in Sehri Saklatvala, *The Fifth Commandment*, Manchester Free Press, 1991, p387.
77. *ibid*, p388.

> they viewed the Labour Party as nothing more or less than the willing hirelings of British imperialism.'[78]

British imperialism was given breathing space by a split in the Indian National Congress at the end of 1928: while the left wanted an immediate campaign for independence, Gandhi and the bourgeois wing made any campaign conditional on a British refusal to accept self-government by 31 December 1929. Imperialism had a year in which to prepare. In March 1929, all the most prominent leaders of the Indian working class, including the entire leadership of the Red Flag Union, were arrested and taken to Meerut, detained on a charge of 'attempting to deprive the King-Emperor of the sovereignty of India'. At a crucial stage in the liberation struggle, the working class movement had been decapitated.

At the 1929 Labour Conference, a resolution was put calling for the release of the Meerut detainees; Drummond Shiels, Labour's Under Secretary of State for India, replied that, 'the [Labour] Government accepted full responsibility for their present position'; and whereas the Government 'were in favour of the utmost freedom of speech in India consistent with the preservation of public order ... they took that attitude on the broad principles applicable to every civilised community, but they also took it in the interests of the uninformed humble people of India.'[79] The motion was defeated by a majority of ten to one.

The election of the Labour Government in May 1929 made not the slightest difference to British policy, either as far the Meerut prisoners were concerned, or in terms of any offer of self-government. Far from it: Labour was called into office, again with Liberal support, to continue the same policy but to serve it up in a dressing of socialist and democratic phrases. As to its imperialist credentials, there was no longer any doubt; as a demonstration of its *bona fides*, Snowden's statement just before the election that Labour would continue to insist on the German payment of war reparations was worth 'hundreds of thousands of votes to us' according to Mrs Snowden.

---

78. *ibid*, pp391-92.

79. Quoted in *Labour Monthly*, November 1929, p682.

The end of December 1929 came and went without any response from Gandhi, although there were vast demonstrations on Independence Day, 30 January 1930. In the meantime, Labour took the precaution of detaining the leading left-wing nationalist Subhas Bose. Then Gandhi announced a march on Dandi by a select band of followers to make salt in defiance of the Government monopoly, to be followed by a campaign of non-co-operation. On 6 April, Gandhi made his salt and the movement exploded once more, as peasants interpreted non-co-operation to mean non-payment of rent as well as taxes. The town of Peshawar fell into the hands of the people following hundreds of deaths and casualties at the hands of loyal troops. But one incident stood out:

> 'Two platoons of the Second Battalion of the 18th Royal Garwhali Rifles, Hindu troops in the midst of a Moslem crowd, refused the order to fire, broke ranks, fraternised with the crowd, and a number handed over their arms. Immediately after this, the military and police were withdrawn from Peshawar; from 25 April to 4 May the city was in the hands of the people.'[80]

At Sholapur in Bombay, the workers took over the administration for a week. Under Labour's direction, the response of the Government was brutal. Ordinance followed ordinance, creating a situation akin to martial law. Congress was banned in June, and Gandhi arrested. In the 10 months up to April 1931, between 60,000 and 90,000 people were arrested. Physical terror was the norm: 'The records of indiscriminate lathi charges, beating up, firing on unarmed crowds, killing of men and women, and punitive expeditions made an ugly picture.'[81] Between 1 April and 14 July 1930 alone, 24 incidents of firing had left 103 dead and 420 wounded; by the end of June, the RAF had dropped over 500 tons of bombs in quelling the disturbances.

The Simon Commission reported in June 1930 offering no significant concession, merely fuelling the anger. In an effort to break the

---

80. R Palme Dutt, *India Today*, *op cit*, p332.
81. *ibid*, p334.

impasse, Labour convened a 'Round Table Conference', inviting representatives from the three British parliamentary parties, some Indian merchants, industrialists and landowners and various feudal puppets from the Indian princely states. Opening it in January 1931, MacDonald declared that: 'I pray that by our labours, India will possess ... the pride and the honour of Responsible Self-Government'[82] – an offer which was to serve as a bait to Gandhi, but which committed the Government to nothing.

It was however enough for Gandhi; in March he persuaded Congress to call off the mass campaign for a few petty concessions, and to participate in the Conference it had sworn to boycott. There were no commitments on self-government or home rule. Ordinances were to be withdrawn, and prisoners released – except those guilty of 'violence' or 'incitement to violence', or soldiers guilty of disobeying orders. This formula allowed Labour and Gandhi to exclude the Meerut detainees from the amnesty, together with a group of Sikh revolutionaries who were forthwith hanged, and 17 soldiers from the Garwhali Rifles, who were given severe sentences. With that, Gandhi was released to attend the Round Table Conference, a charade that continued for a year without resolution. As a contemporary Communist wrote:

> 'Hanging, flogging, slaying, shooting and bombing attest the efforts of parasitic imperialism to cling to the body of its victim. The Round Table Conference beside these efforts is like the ceremonial mumblings of the priest that walks behind the hangman.'[83]

There were sound reasons for Labour's intransigence. As *The Manchester Guardian* pointed out in 1930, 'There are two chief reasons why a self-regarding England may hesitate to relax her control over India. The first is that her influence in the past depends partly upon her power to summon troops and to draw resources from India in

82. *ibid*, p336.
83. R Page Arnot, *Labour Monthly*, September 1930, p534.

time of need ... The second is that Great Britain finds in India her best market, and she has £1,000 million pounds of capital invested there.'[84] The annual tribute from India in the form of Home Charges, private remittances, and sterling indebtedness was currently of the order of £120-£150 million per annum. India absorbed 40 per cent of British cotton exports, which meant that the various Congress cotton boycotts had hit hard. That 'time of need' to which *The Guardian* referred was to occur once more with the financial crisis of 1931, when $180 million worth of gold was plundered from India between October 1931 and March 1932 to bolster the coffers of British imperialism. Well did *The Times* comment on 15 April 1930 that:

> 'Every farsighted view of our imperial interests, and of the hope of removing them altogether from party controversy, goes to show how important it is that a Labour government, and no other, should have the handling of the great external problems which are crowding upon us this year – the Naval Conference, the Imperial Conference, Egypt; above all, India.'[85]

A Naesmith, Secretary of the Weaver's Amalgamation, the largest textile union, echoed this view from the standpoint of the interests of the labour aristocracy when he told a mass meeting: 'they desired to see India and her people take their rightful place in the comity of nations, but not at the expense of the industrial and economic life of Lancashire and those dependent on it.'[86]

It had needed a Labour Government to re-establish British control over India. There is no more savage indictment of Labour than in its crushing of the Indian struggle of 1928–31, not even the crisis of 1931. Under a fog of democratic phrases, it acted savagely. It destroyed any chance of the Indian working class playing a significant role in the Indian liberation movement, which from thenceforward became

84. Quoted in R Palme Dutt, *ibid*, p497.
85. Quoted in R Page Arnot, *ibid*, p530.
86. Quoted in Gupta, *op cit*, p219.

the plaything of different bourgeois interests. In a debate in 1930, an ILP MP, WJ Brown, made a prophetic point when he told Parliament: 'I venture to suggest that we should regard it as a cardinal feature of British policy to carry Gandhi with us, for if we do not, we have to face the alternative to Gandhi, and that is organised violence and revolutionary effort.'[87] Partition, the reactionary solution of 1947, has its origins in this crucial phase of the struggle, when imperialism recognised that it would have to look to this bourgeois politician to safeguard its interests in any future independent India.

2.11 *The Middle East 1929–31*

Labour policy in the Middle East picked up where it had left off five years earlier. With Egypt, continuity of policy with the previous Tory government was to be a hallmark; as Arthur Henderson, now Foreign Secretary explained, it had been 'a conspicuous part of the policy of each Government, including the Labour Government of 1924, to raise the relationship between Egypt and this country above party.'[88] This included incidents in both 1926 and 1927, when battleships had to be sent to Alexandria to remind the Egyptian government of the substance of this 'relationship', which had drawn no complaint from Labour. Henderson was again adamant about the need for British troops to remain in Suez – 'located there for the purpose of ensuring the defence of that vital artery of British Imperial communications';[89] his attempt to force through a treaty legalising the de-facto British occupation failed as it had in 1924, without making the slightest difference to the substance of British policy.

Labour also needed to modify relations with Iraq in the face of nationalist rumblings; the 1924 Treaty was therefore re-negotiated with minor concessions: Britain was still left in control of foreign and military policy, was still to maintain its air bases, and could still occupy

87. Quoted by Clemens Dutt in *Labour Monthly*, June 1930, p333.
88. Quoted in D Carlton, *MacDonald versus Henderson – The Foreign Policy of the Second Labour Government*, Macmillan, 1970, p164.
89. *ibid.*

the country in the event of war – a power it was to use in 1941. Sidney Webb, now elevated to Lord Passfield, and Secretary of State for the Dominions and Colonies at the time explained:

> 'It may be asked, why do we want an alliance with Iraq at all? ... The answer to that question is, I think, that an alliance is vitally necessary in order to secure Imperial interests ... There is no other means of securing that unfettered use in all circumstances of our strategic air route, of adequately safeguarding our position at the head of the Persian Gulf.'[90]

In Palestine, a general strike during August 1929 by Palestinian workers and a revolt by the Arab peasantry against increasing Zionist expropriations was ruthlessly suppressed. 200 people were killed, mainly by British troops. On the direct orders of the Labour Government, nine Arab peasants were hanged, and several hundred more sentenced to long terms of imprisonment. Draconian legislation was passed which amongst other things made anti-imperialist agitation punishable by life imprisonment. A dispute between Lord Passfield and MacDonald over Jewish immigration, held to be at the root of the Palestinian uprising, was resolved in MacDonald's and the Zionists' favour to the extent that the apostle of Zionism, Chaim Weizmann, was to argue later that MacDonald's letter to him 'enabled us to make the magnificent gains of the ensuing years. It was under Macdonald's letter that Jewish immigration into Palestine was permitted to reach figures ... undreamed of in 1930.'[91]

2.12 *Labour after 1931*

The second Labour Government fell in August 1931 following MacDonald's defection as a result of the crisis over public expenditure. In the autumn general election, the Parliamentary Labour Party was reduced to an ineffectual rump of 52 MPs. The 1935 election brought

---

90. Quoted in Gupta, *op cit*, p165.
91. Quoted in S Palmer, 'The Labour Party and Zionism' in *Fight Racism! Fight Imperialism!* No 29, May 1983.

a partial recovery (see below); politically, in imperial affairs, there was no wish to do other than maintain the bipartisan approach. One instance reflects this unchanging attitude: the response to the Palestinian rebellion in 1936, during the suppression of which over 1,000 people were killed. The British TUC, whose leaders, in particular Sir Walter Citrine and Ernest Bevin, dominated the Labour Party in this period, declared 'the Congress hopes that the British Government ... will take all the necessary measures to bring the present disorders to an end.'[92] The Government certainly did: a further 5,000 Palestinians were killed before the uprising was finally crushed three months later.

On foreign policy, there were occasional disagreements, but these were verbal in nature. For instance, Labour condemned the National Government when it refused to sanction action by the League of Nations against Italy after the latter's invasion of Abyssinia in 1935. Yet such opposition was confined to gestures: any working class move to boycott Italian goods was also roundly condemned. It was the same after the renewal of Japanese action against China in August 1937. Labour called for League of Nations action, in the full knowledge that the Government would not accept such a course of action; when dockers at Middlesborough and Southampton refused to handle Japanese goods, they were censured.

The craven nature of Labour was most evident in its response to the fascist insurrection in Spain in July 1936. British imperial policy was one of 'non-intervention', which by treating the Republican government and the fascist rebels as equals, gave tacit support for the latter. On 10 September, Citrine told the TUC Congress that non-intervention 'while on paper preventing the Fascist Powers from supplying munitions, was in fact being held up in such a way as to give those governments all the opportunities they needed for supplying arms ... all the evidence proved you could not trust the word of Mussolini or Hitler'.[93] However, he then went on to argue

92. Quoted *ibid*.

93. Quoted in Miliband, *op cit*, p237.

the case for non-intervention 'unpopular though it may be with large masses of our own people who do not understand perhaps the niceties of the question, because we believe that policy is right, however distasteful, and the policy which your wisdom will commend.'[94] A few days later at the Labour Party Conference, Arthur Greenwood, opening the debate on the subject, could only say that 'it was felt by all those who have considered this matter, sad though they were about it, that in the circumstances of the time, there was no alternative but this very, very second best of non-intervention.'[95] The policy was endorsed by a majority of over three to one.

Labour was to formally reverse this policy a year later; but by this time, it did not matter: the outcome had already been decided even if the war was to drag on another two years. Many were the international meetings of socialists, many were the pleas to governments to send arms to Republican Spain. Ruled out were any calls for action, Citrine making it plain that in his view, industrial action would be illegal, and any joint action with the Communist Party completely unacceptable. All that remained was the ignominious acceptance that the Government would ignore their views anyway.

Labour expressed much concern about democracy when it saw its own interests imperilled, as in Spain; it would routinely denounce the 'dictatorial' nature of the Communist Party. However, democracy could never extend to the Empire, since that would also threaten its privileged position. Perhaps one of the perceptive writers on Labour imperialism at this time was George Orwell. In an essay deliberately and provocatively entitled *Not Counting Niggers*, he argued that 'above all in an imperialist country, left wing politics are always partly humbug', and criticised contemporary 'anti-fascism' because in proclaiming its defence of democracy it ignored a 'far greater injustice' – the British Empire. He went on:

> 'What we always forget is that the overwhelming bulk of the British proletariat does not live in Britain but in Asia and Africa.

94. Quoted *ibid*, p238.
95. Quoted *ibid*, p239.

> It is not in Hitler's power, for instance, to make a penny an hour the normal industrial wage; it is perfectly normal in India, and we are at great pains to keep it so.'[96]

To which might be added that the number of Indians who perished as a result of the famines that were a legacy of the British Raj were of the same order as those who died in the Nazi holocaust. Orwell was condemning those who were able to champion the superiority of British 'democracy' by conveniently forgetting to count the hundreds of millions of colonial slaves whose abject conditions made such a 'democracy' possible.

The outbreak of war in 1939 gave the Labour Party a new importance. The militarisation of labour would need the co-operation of the trade unions and the Labour Party; they were therefore drawn into the Churchill coalition of 1940. Labour's support for the coalition was to prove unconditional, despite the manner in which it prosecuted the war: securing British imperial interests first (the Middle East and the Mediterranean), before committing the resources necessary to defeat German fascism in mainland Europe. It also required very firm control of India, as it was to commit two million troops to Britain's war effort: it was also the last bastion against the westward drive of Japanese imperialism, and was critical to attempts to hold the Persian Gulf. Indian Congress support for the war was essential, and the Cabinet sent Stafford Cripps in March 1942 to negotiate with Gandhi. But Congress refused to accept any vague promise of self-government after the war, and initiated another campaign of civil disobedience. Once more, Congress and its associate organisations were banned and their leaders arrested, an act which occasioned protest only from Aneurin Bevan. On no issue involving colonial or foreign policy were there to be differences in substance between the two main partners of the coalition.

---

96. In S Orwell and I Angus (eds), *The Collected Essays, Journalism and Letters of George Orwell*, vol 1, Penguin 1970, p437.

PART THREE

Labour and the reconstruction of the imperialist order 1945–51

3.1 *Britain's post-war crisis*

At the end of the Second World War imperialism faced a serious political crisis. The Allied powers had prosecuted the war under the slogans of democracy and national freedom, enshrining them in the Atlantic Charter. However, the enormous growth of national liberation movements in the colonial and semi-colonial countries showed that people throughout the world were not only taking such commitments seriously, but were organising to ensure they were put into effect. Many of these movements such as those in China, Malaya, Greece, Yugoslavia and Vietnam were led by Communist Parties. In addition, a whole swathe of Eastern Europe was about to fall out of imperialist control, thereby greatly strengthening the position of the Soviet Union. Meanwhile, much of Western Europe lay in ruins, its industry destroyed and its economies bankrupt.

If the overall position of imperialism was weak, that of British imperialism was precarious in the extreme. If it lost its colonial empire, post-war reconstruction would have to be undertaken at the direct expense of the British working class, with all the attendant risks of social upheaval. But it could not carry on in the old way: it had to offer the semblance of democratic concession to colonial and semi-colonial peoples, if only to buy time. Of this the Tories were incapable: Churchill's war-time declarations against Indian independence, his openly-declared refusal to preside over the dissolution of the Empire, would unleash the international forces that British imperialism most feared. Hence it turned to Labour, with its ability to dress up the defence of imperial interests in the language of democracy, socialism and the Atlantic Charter.

The problems presented to the incoming Labour Government were formidable. British imperialism was practically bankrupt in 1945. It had run up a huge external debt of £3.65 billion, some 40 per cent of GNP. To finance its arms purchases from the US, it had disposed of £1 billion overseas investments; the consequent fall in invisible income meant that it could no longer cover its huge visible trade deficit. Its dependency on US imperialism, the undisputed master of the imperialist world, became evident in December 1945 when the latter unilaterally terminated the lend-lease scheme under which Britain had obtained favourable credit arrangements. Labour had to despatch a delegation to Washington to negotiate new credit, but at a market rate. The result was a loan of $3.75 billion, which was obtained at the expense of a commitment to allow sterling holders to freely convert their pounds into dollars – a direct threat to British financial control of the Empire.

The fundamental problem was the trade imbalance between the two imperialist powers: over the next two years, British imports from the US totalled £1 billion whilst its exports in return were a paltry £180 million. The economic weakness of British imperialism therefore expressed itself in the form of dollar-indebtedness. To resolve it, and thereby escape economic dependency on the US, Labour turned to the Empire; and despite the pressure to open it up to the US:

> '... the government exploited the colonies to the full. It required them to sell it their main export commodities at prices frequently well below world market levels. The government also accorded the colonies low priority for UK exports, preventing them from spending all their foreign exchange earnings. So the sterling balances grew in the late forties. Such high dollar earners as the Gold Coast [Ghana] and Malaysia were particularly ruthlessly exploited, being forced to add their dollars to the Sterling Areas

common pool, much of which was used to buy UK imports.'[1]

From 1948 in particular, the Empire was to be milked of all the dollars and superprofits it could earn. Resistance to this was be ruthlessly and murderously put down. Three areas were to be critical: the Middle East, Malaya and West Africa. Such plunder was to cushion the British working class from the worst effects of the crisis, and help prevent a repetition of the revolutionary struggles that occurred after the First Imperialist War.

3.2 *Greece*[2]

The immediate issues at the end of the war for the Labour Government were the need to forestall revolution in South East Asia, safeguard the position within the Middle East, and prevent the spread of revolution within Europe itself. This last possibility was very real: partisan forces in Yugoslavia, Albania and Greece had effectively driven the German occupation forces out of their countries. Greece was of particular strategic importance because of its dominant position in the Eastern Mediterranean. The democratic movement had to be crushed if the approaches to the Middle East were to be safeguarded.

The intent was already clear when British troops landed in Greece in October 1944 and their commander, General Scobie, demanded that the Greek liberation force, EAM, and its armed wing, ELAS, both of which had overwhelming popular support, give up their arms. British imperialism's aim was to install a puppet government, supported by reactionary monarchist and quisling forces to guarantee its position. After a series of fascist attacks on ELAS supporters, the EAM called a general strike in Athens on 4 December. Scobie promptly placed Athens under martial law and insisted that ELAS withdraw. Fighting broke out the following day; Churchill instructed Scobie to

---

1. P Armstrong, A Glyn and J Harrison, *Capitalism since 1945*, Blackwell, 1991, pp61-62.
2. The material in this section, including all quotations, is drawn from R Clough, 'The Labour Party and Greece' in *Fight Racism! Fight Imperialism!* No 36, February 1984.

'act as if you are in a conquered city where a local rebellion is in progress' and, later, 'the clear objective is the defeat of EAM. The ending of the fighting is subsidiary to this.'

Despite this blood-curdling threat, British forces were soon reduced to holding a few enclaves in Athens. Help was at hand from Labour, which was by happy chance holding its Conference at the same time. Bevin, who as a member of the coalition Cabinet had been party to all its decisions, stated: 'The British Empire cannot abandon its position in the Mediterranean.' A motion condemning the British attack and calling for the withdrawal of British troops was overwhelmingly defeated, to be replaced by one calling on the Government 'to take all the necessary steps to facilitate an armistice without delay.' But the Government was doing just that, rushing in the reinforcements it needed to defeat ELAS. It took a force of 40,000 troops as well as RAF air support before it finally drove ELAS forces out of Athens in early February.

The following month saw fascist terror unleashed against EAM/ELAS under the direction of a British military occupation. By December 1945, 50,000 people had been prosecuted for EAM/ELAS activity, 18,000 were in gaol, and hundreds murdered, including Aris Velouchiotis, ELAS Supreme Commander. As Foreign Secretary in the new Labour Government, Ernest Bevin made clear nothing was to change: 'His Majesty's Government adheres to the policy which they publicly supported when Greece was liberated.' Sir Walter Citrine, still TUC General Secretary, was sent to Greece in January 1945; thoughtfully provided with an interpreter whose royalist father had been shot by ELAS for collaboration with the Nazis, he dutifully compiled a report informing the British labour movement of ELAS 'atrocities', referring to the Royalists' 'isolated acts of reprisals'.

As the terror continued, Labour ordered elections to be held in March 1946. Their own puppet 'liberal' prime minister complained about the fascist terror, an opinion dismissed by Bevin:

> 'I am much surprised by your statement that armed "X" [former collaborationist security forces] organisations will be reinforced

> by almost the whole of the police and gendarmeries. Such a statement is not borne out by the reports which I have received. In any case, I cannot see how "X" organisations can compel the electors in the countryside to vote in a manner contrary to their convictions, provided a secret ballot is secured.'

And this an election where women were not allowed to vote (although they had in EAM-liberated areas) and a quarter of the electoral register did not exist! No wonder a Greek opportunist socialist, who, unlike EAM, decided to participate in the elections, declared 'We socialists in Greece are compromised by his [Bevin's] policy, as the people say to us: "If you are of Bevin's party, we cannot join you," and they turn more to the left.'

As the terror continued, ELAS re-grouped and started armed resistance from late 1946. The Royalist army, with British military backing, was unable to make any headway; by the beginning of 1947, the cost to Britain would approach £20 million per month. In February, Prime Minister Attlee told US President Truman that Britain could no longer afford the commitment, and would have to withdraw. British imperialism had forestalled the Greek revolution, but it could no longer be the lone policeman of the imperialist world. It would be left to US imperialism to fund the final destruction of ELAS in 1949.

3.3 *South East Asia: Vietnam*[3]

Whilst US imperialism took responsibility for forestalling revolution in North East Asia – in particular, China and Korea – Britain took responsibility for the South East – Vietnam, Indonesia and Malaya. Following the defeat of Japan, insurrection swept Vietnam under the leadership of the Viet Minh; revolutionary forces took over Hanoi on 19 August, Hue on 23 August, and Saigon two days later. On 2

3. Drawn from S Palmer, 'The Labour Party and Vietnam' in *Fight Racism! Fight Imperialism!* No 31, August 1983.

September, a million people crowded into Hanoi's Ba Dinh Square to hear Ho Chi Minh read a declaration of independence, and proclaim the Democratic Republic of Vietnam (DRV).

On 11 September, an advance guard of over 20,000 British (in fact, overwhelmingly Indian) troops arrived in Saigon under the command of Major General Gracey. Under direction from the Labour Government, he refused to recognise the DRV and gave the job of maintaining law and order to re-armed Japanese troops. A general strike on 17 September was met by a proclamation threatening summary execution for anybody taking part in a demonstration or public meeting or breaking the curfew. Next day, Gracey issued arms to French quisling colonial troops, who promptly organised a coup d'etat with his blessing.

With 40,000 Japanese troops at his disposal, Gracey started to clear the Viet Minh out of the major cities of the south, while French reinforcements were shipped in. In response to protests from Fenner Brockway, Prime Minister Attlee wrote 'the government is carrying out the principles for which it has always stood', a fact that is uncontestable. Four days later, Bevin as Foreign Secretary had a meeting with the French Ambassador, and signed a secret agreement which guaranteed a British handover of Indochina in exchange for French withdrawal from Syria and Lebanon. In Parliament on 24 October, Bevin dishonestly claimed that the DRV was a Japanese creation, and confirmed that:

> 'every effort is being made to expedite the movement of French troops to Saigon in sufficient numbers to enable them to take over from the British forces.'

The British intervention was critical. The French were in no position to play a significant role in quelling the Viet Minh until early 1946. But for Labour, there would have been a revolutionary government in a united Vietnam in 1945, not in 1975. The cost of Labour's restoration of the French can be measured in terms of 30 years' continuous war, millions of Vietnamese lives, and a ruined country.

3.4 *Indonesia*

A similar tale unfolded in Indonesia: of British intervention to restore a colonial power, and of secret agreements to support such intervention.

It started on 15 August 1945, when the Japanese surrendered to the Indonesian National Liberation forces, which then established a provisional government with Soekarno as president. On 15 September, the first British troops landed in Java under General Christison, who announced 'We are not going to put the Dutch back in power.' But with him came instructions that the Japanese army was to help restore the status quo and repress any disturbances, together with further orders banning all popular assemblies, the raising of the new national flag, and the carrying of arms. During September, Australian troops under overall British command were able to occupy Borneo and Sulavesi with little resistance, since the liberation forces were relatively weak on these two islands, and thus start the process of restoring the Dutch colonial administration.

At the same time, British reinforcements landed on Java, whilst Japanese forces took control of the major towns of Badang and Samarang in Sumatra in anticipation of a British invasion. On 25 October, British troops landed at Surabaya, preceded by a small Dutch party, which was promptly detained by the Indonesian republic. Two weeks later, in an effort to buy time, the Dutch made an 'offer' to the provisional Indonesian government: provided it disarmed, ended the republic and recognised Dutch rule, there would be a 'reconstruction' of the colonial government at some time in the future involving directly elected representatives, on a suffrage subject to further discussion. Noel-Baker, Labour Minister of State at the Foreign Office, described the suggested surrender terms as 'generous and far-reaching'; not surprisingly, the Indonesians themselves rejected them out of hand. Two weeks later, Bevin declared in the House of Commons:

> 'It is clear that HM Government have a definite agreement with [the Dutch] to provide for the Dutch East Indies Government to

> resume as rapidly as practicable full responsibility for the administration of the Netherlands Indian Territories.'[4]

This was the first indication that there had been a secret agreement with the Dutch to restore colonial rule in Indonesia, an agreement which had in fact been concluded as early as 24 August. Its full import became apparent at Surabaya, a stronghold of the liberation movement. In an attempt to force the republic to give up its Dutch captives, the RAF dropped leaflets on 9 November demanding the unconditional surrender of its leaders together with its arms. The following day, the city was shelled by 25-pound field guns, by a cruiser and four destroyers, and bombed by the RAF. Using tanks and armoured cars against youths armed with rifles, bows and arrows and machetes, the British took four weeks to capture the city, with the assistance of re-armed Japanese soldiers, an achievement which was then repeated at Bandung. By the time British troops withdrew in November 1946 they had inflicted 40,000 casualties, and left Dutch imperialism to impose a favourable neo-colonial solution.

3.5 *The Middle East*

Control of the Middle East was a crucial plank in Labour's foreign policy. Its aim was to restore as much of the status quo before the war as possible – in other words, retain control of the Suez Canal and sustain the string of puppet regimes through which British imperialism had controlled the oil reserves of the region since 1918.

After the unsuccessful efforts of Labour in 1924 and 1929, British imperialism had finally imposed a treaty on Egypt in 1936: its terms formalised British control of Egyptian foreign and military policy, and allowed 10,000 British troops to be stationed in Suez for the next 20 years, that is until 1956. But by March 1946, mass demonstrations were demanding its abrogation. Labour was not to be moved: it would not withdraw troops unless the Egyptian government were to

4. Quoted in A Clegg, *Hands Off Indonesia*, CPGB, 1946, p12.

sign a 'mutual defence' pact which would allow Britain unfettered use of the Canal, and it would not concede Egyptian demands for federation with Sudan. In January 1947, Labour broke off negotiations, retaining 80,000 troops in the Suez bases for the remainder of its term of office.

No long-term solution was possible in Iraq either: the awakening of nationalist opinion required re-negotiation of the 1930 Treaty. Labour was determined to ensure that even if it had to relinquish direct control of the Iraqi government, it should retain its RAF bases to assure control of Iranian as well as Iraqi oil. The Treaty was signed in Portsmouth in 1948; the immediate response was a near-insurrection in Baghdad, which forced the puppet regime to reject it. Once again, stalemate resulted: in practice, the Treaty operated even if it were not accepted; however, Britain's position had been fatally weakened, and it was to be expelled within ten years.

The most serious debacle was in Palestine. The 1944 Labour Conference, as well as supporting intervention in Greece, took a rabidly pro-Zionist standpoint: 'Let the Arabs be encouraged to move out as the Jews move in. Let them be compensated handsomely for their land and let their settlement elsewhere be carefully organised and generously financed ... Indeed, we should re-examine the possibility of extending the present Palestinian boundaries, by agreement with Egypt, Syria or Jordan.' The Zionist leader Chaim Weizmann was alarmed that Labour 'in their pro-Zionist enthusiasm, went far beyond our intentions.'[5]

However, in power, Labour was more concerned about its alliances with the puppet Arab regimes than with Zionist demands for the partition of Palestine. Bevin was opposed by the Labour left, led by Bevan and Michael Foot (whose support for Zionism was expressed in racist contempt for the Arab people) who argued that a Zionist state would anyway be a far better bulwark against the Soviet Union. The Zionists retaliated with a terror campaign directed against Palestinians and British troops alike. They were comforted in the

5. Quoted in S Palmer, *op cit.*

knowledge that they were backed by US imperialism, which saw in the conflict the lever with which it could evict British imperialism from its predominant role in the region. Labour announced it would withdraw troops from Palestine in May 1948; by carefully reinforcing the TransJordanian army, it hoped that in a war with its Arab neighbours, the Zionist forces would be humiliated. Labour's calculations proved erroneous, and the legacy is the ethnic cleansing of the Palestinian people today.

3.6 *India*

The 1945 Labour Election Manifesto *Let Us Face the Future* had said nothing about the colonies except that in relationship to India it was prepared to offer self-government. However, Congress leaders, who had spent most of the war in gaol, were in no position to accept this: there were widespread mutinies amongst Indian troops, and a full-scale revolt in the Navy in February 1946. The Indian people had few enough illusions in Labour: Cripps, who was still outside the Party in 1942 having been expelled in the 1930s, was now back in, and many remembered that he had endorsed suppression of Congress after the failure of his mission in 1942.

Imperialist policy had been to encourage the formation of a bourgeois Muslim movement as a counter-weight to the mainly Hindu, but equally bourgeois, Congress. There were real material differences between the two bourgeoisies, but the suppression of Congress during the war had given space to the Muslim League to mobilise the bulk of the Muslim population behind a plan for a state separate from India. The consequences of the Meerut trial were now evident: only the working class movement in the vanguard of the oppressed could have prevented the disintegration of the liberation struggle into a factional struggle between competing bourgeois interests. Despite these divisions, there was no chance for British imperialism to reassert its pre-war position, and in March 1947, Labour appointed Lord Mountbatten as Viceroy of India, with a commitment to bring about a British withdrawal by June 1948.

Even this timetable proved optimistic: within three months, the date for withdrawal had to be advanced to August 1947, as India proved completely ungovernable. Attlee himself was to concede 'No doubt we could have held India for two or three years longer. But we could have done so only at the cost of a great expenditure of men and money.'[6] Such men – in fact, Indian troops – would have been at best unreliable, and, given the precarious financial state of British imperialism, the money was not there to finance them anyway. Lord Ismay, Mountbatten's Chief of Staff,was more blunt in his assessment: 'India in March 1947 was a ship on fire in mid-ocean with ammunition in the hold. By then it was a question of putting out the fire before it reached the ammunition. There was, in fact, no option before us but to do what we did.'[7] Labour conceded independence, not because it had wanted to, but because there was no other way. Hundreds of thousands were to die in a series of communal massacres as the Muslim and Hindu ruling classes staked their territorial claims. India and Pakistan had been saved for imperialism.

3.7 *Oil and Iran*

British oil interests in the Middle East after the war were still enormous: the Anglo Iranian Oil Company (AIOC) controlled all Iranian oil output, and owned the biggest oil refinery in the world at Abadan, a capital asset of £350 million. It owned 25 per cent of the Iraqi Petroleum Company (with Shell owning a further 25 per cent), and 50 per cent of the Kuwaiti Oil Company (with Shell again effectively having a 25 per cent holding through an agreement with Gulf), and overall still directly controlled 58 per cent of Middle East oil reserves against the US's 35 per cent. The average cost of producing Middle East oil at this time was around $0.10 per barrel, compared with $0.50 per barrel in Venezuela, at that time the world's largest oil exporter, and $1.10 in the US. But through their monopoly control of

6. Quoted in B Moore, *Labour-Communist Relations 1920–51*, Part 3, Our History Pamphlet 84/85, CPGB, 1991 p15.
7. Quoted in Palme Dutt, *op cit*, p191.

Table 5 Iranian oil revenues 1946–50[8]

Year	Iranian Oil Production (Million tons)	AIOC Net Profits (£000s)	AIOC British Tax Payments (£000s)	AIOC Royalty Payments (£000s)
1946	**19.2**	**9,625**	**10,279**	**7,132**
1947	**20.2**	**18,565**	**15,266**	**7,104**
1948	**24.9**	**24,065**	**28,310**	**9,172**
1949	**26.8**	**18,390**	**22,480**	**13,489**
1950	**31.8**	**33,103**	**50,707**	**16,032**

the world's oil resources, the seven US and British oil giants set the price of oil to ensure the profitability of domestic US production. Fabulous profits could be made in the Middle East. As post-war production of oil boomed to meet increasing demand, so did the profits of AIOC (Table 5).

Total declared remittances to Britain came to some £54 million in 1946–7, and climbed to £177 million over the next three years, when royalty payments to Iran came to less than £40 million. Even this is an underestimate: gross profits in 1950 were £147 million. The Iranian government received little more than 10 per cent of this total. Not for nothing had Bevin declared of the Middle East:

> 'His Majesty's Government must maintain a continuing interest in that area if only because our economic and financial interests in the Middle East are of vast importance to us ... If these interests were lost to us, the effect on the life of this country would be a considerable reduction in the standard of living ... British interests in the Middle East contribute substantially not only to the interests of the people there, but to the wage packets of the

8. From Z Mikdashi, *A Financial Analysis of Middle East Oil Concessions 1901–65*, Praeger, 1966, p110.

9. Quoted in R Palme Dutt, *The Crisis of Britain and the British Empire*, Lawrence and Wishart, 1954, pp336-37.

workpeople of this country.'[9]

Incensed by the nakedness of this plunder, the Iranian people forced the Mossadeq government to nationalise AIOC in 1951. The response of Labour was immediate: it despatched a cruiser and destroyers to Abadan and imposed a world-wide oil embargo on Iran; only its weakened military status prevented it going to war. It was left to the incoming Tory government to conclude the matter by organising a coup with the CIA which destroyed Mossadeq and brought Iran and its oil back under imperialist control – with Britain retaining only a minority stake.

British control of Iranian oil was not only vastly profitable in the years to 1951, it also avoided expenditure of dollars. However, if AIOC was brazen about its profitability, its larger cousin by a factor of four, Royal Dutch Shell, was far more secretive. Shell's holdings lay traditionally in Dutch East Indies and Latin America, but its increasing Middle East interests also boosted profitability to a level which dwarfed AIOC: gross profits were £190 million in 1950 and no less than £249 million in 1951, which at about 2 per cent of contemporary British GNP would be equivalent to about £30 billion today.

Bevin understood very well the nature of parasitism.

3.8 *Malaya: rubber and tin*

Through its occupation of Malaya, Britain controlled the source of 45 per cent of the world's natural rubber, and 30 per cent of the world's output of tin. It monopolised a natural resource which was vital to US imperialism, since most of the remainder of the world's rubber and tin reserves lay in Indonesia. 'Plunder' does not even begin to describe how this was used to bolster Britain's financial position.

From 1946 to 1951, total British exports to the US amounted to £515 million. Over the same period, total Malayan exports to the US came to £460 million. In 1950, when British exports to the US came to £127.3 million, Malayan exports came to £122 million; in 1951, the respective figures were £154.7 million and £166 million. A US

Mission despatched to Malaya in 1950 noted the high rate of return on British investment in Malaya and stated:

> '[Malayan] exports to the US were valued at $215,426,831 in 1948 and $182,809,000 in 1949. The area is the largest net dollar earner in the whole sterling area. Malaya's exports, especially of rubber and tin, to dollar markets are of critical importance in the effort to achieve a balance of payments between the sterling and dollar area. Without these dollar earnings, the UK would ... face a noticeable reduction in its already austere standard of living.'[10]

The Malayan workers bore the full brunt of Labour's need for dollars, and in particular the Indian and Chinese labourers who had been imported to work the plantations and mines. Between 1939 and 1949, their real wages fell by nearly 80 per cent, while the plantation owners announced record dividends. While the Labour government attempted to forge a racist constitution which would guarantee a privileged position to the feudal sultans on the one hand, and the indigenous middle class Malayans on the other, the national liberation forces succeeded in building a trade union movement, the Pan Malayan Federation of Trade Unions (PMFTU) which united all workers.

Labour's hostility was undisguised: 'The parliamentary Under-Secretary of State for Colonies, Ivor Thomas, became concerned. after a visit to Malaya in February 1947, to ensure the unimpeded production of rubber, "a dollar earning commodity". He also shared the anti-Chinese and pro-Malay bias of Gent [Governor of Malaya], blamed the estate workers for strikes and frequent wage demands and recommended flogging and banishment as punishment for breaches of law and order.'[11]

Working class resistance was met with brutality; workers were regularly gunned down by police; in April and May 1948, eight workers were killed; on 1 June, seven plantation workers were beaten

10. Quoted in M Caldwell, in M Amin and M Caldwell (eds), *Malaya – The Making of a Neo-Colony,* p248.
11. PS Gupta, in J Winter (ed), *The Working Class in Modern British History*, Cambridge, 1983, p114.

to death for refusing to end an estate occupation. 12 days later, the government banned the PMFTU, and arrested hundred of its leaders. In May 1949, its former President, SA Ganapathy, was hanged for alleged possession of a gun, to be followed the next day by the former Vice-President, Veerasenam.

The destruction of the trade union movement left the Malayan Communist Party (MCP) no option but to resort to armed struggle, a struggle that was to last in all for 12 years before it was finally defeated. The Labour Government rushed huge forces to Malaya to deal with what it referred to with racist contempt as the 'bandits'. It set up concentration camps, put prices on the heads of known MCP leaders, used assassination squads, and even unleashed Dyak head-hunters to terrorise the nationalist population. After all, as the then Labour left Tribunite Woodrow Wyatt asked: 'What would happen to our balance of payments if we had to take our troops out of Malaya?'[12]

3.9 *West Africa: cocoa and vegetable oil*

The two major West African colonies – Nigeria and the Gold Coast – were sources of cocoa, and palm nut and ground nut oil. During the War, British imperialism had set up a system of Marketing Boards in these colonies to act as monopoly purchasers of the cash crops grown by African farmers. The Boards would buy the complete annual crop, ship it to Britain, and then re-sell it on the world – or, rather, the US market. In 1947, therefore, the Gold Coast Cocoa Marketing Board bought the entire cocoa crop at £67 per ton in sterling, and re-sold it all in London in dollars to the US chocolate manufacturers at £177 per ton. This netted the British government £16 million in 1947, and together with the Nigerian cocoa crop, £38 million in 1948. By simultaneously holding down imports into these colonies, British imperialism was able to build up a huge surplus on their trade (Table

12. Quoted in R Palme Dutt, *ibid*, p104.

Table 6 Trade surplus of Gold Coast (Ghana) and Nigeria 1946–51[13] **(£000s)**

Year	Nigeria			Gold Coast		
	Imports	Exports	Balance	Imports	Exports	Balance
1946	19,824	24,626	+4,802	13,220	20,303	+7,083
1948	41,947	62,741	+20,524	31,378	56,115	+24,737
1949	58,231	81,067	+22,836	45,416	49,927	+4,511
1950	61,866	90,168	+28,302	48,129	77,407	+29,278
1951	84,554	120,064	+35,510	63,793	91,900	+28,197

6), and convert them into forced loans in the form of sterling balances.

The net surplus from 1948–51 from these two colonies came to over £190 million. The plunder was naked: in 1946–7, the West Africa Produce Board bought palm oil from farmers at £16 15 shillings per ton and resold it in London at £95 per ton; in the same year, ground nuts were bought at £15 per ton, while their oil was realising £110 per ton. The power that British imperialism had given itself as a monopoly purchaser in 1939 served it well in the post-war years: '... a system of bulk buying, which began life as a wartime device, was prolonged after 1945 as part of Labour's system of tapping colonial resources.'[14]

No wonder Stafford Cripps, the Chancellor of the Exchequer, had argued during the acute crisis of November 1947 that: 'the whole future of the sterling group and its ability to survive depends, in my view, upon a quick and extensive development of our African resources.' He went on to argue at a conference of African governors:

13. Drawn from R Ekundare, *An Economic History of Nigeria 1860–1960*, Methuen, 1973, p412; also, GB Kay (ed), *The Political Economy of Colonialism in Ghana*, Cambridge, 1972, p326.

14. DK Fieldhouse in R Ovendale, *The Foreign Policy of the British Labour Governments 1945–51*, Leicester, 1984, p97.

> 'You will, I understand, be considering the question of the development of manufactories and industries in the colonies. Though I take the view that such development is highly desirable so long as it is not pushed too far or too quickly, yet it must be obvious that with the present world shortage of capital goods, it is not possible to contemplate much in the way of industrial development of the colonies.'[15]

His conclusion?

> 'Our desperate need in the next few years is, first, to find ways of increasing our capital resources available for investment, and, secondly, to invest that capital in the most profitable way so as to bring in quick results. The colonies can make their contribution to the first need by reducing demands for unnecessary current consumption and devoting some of their own earnings to capital purposes.'[16]

This view was echoed by the former 'extreme' leftist John Strachey, by now a far more 'realistic' Minister of Food:

> 'By hook or by crook the development of primary production of all sorts in the colonial territories and dependent areas in the Commonwealth and throughout the world is a life and death matter for the economy of this country.'[17]

The infamous Tanganyika groundnuts scheme was precisely the sort of project Labour had in mind. Initiated by the Chairman of the United Africa Company (UAC), a Unilever subsidiary, it proposed the development of vast groundnut plantations in Tanganyika, to supplement those in West Africa, where UAC already held a monopoly. So enthusiastic was the Government as to its prospects – it estimated an annual dollar saving of £10 million – that it increased the size of the

15. Quoted in R Palme Dutt, *ibid*, p248.
16. Quoted in G Padmore, *Africa – Britain's Third Empire*, Dobson, 1948, p190.
17. Quoted R Palme Dutt, *op cit*, p249.

initial project by 50 per cent, bringing the total acreage to 3.25 million, or some 5,000 square miles. At the end of 1946, the Treasury advanced £25 million to the UAC to commence clearing operations. However, Tanganyika was not a British colony, but an ex-German territory which Britain held now as a UN Mandate. Under the terms of the mandate, Britain was obliged to consult the UN before undertaking such a development. Labour was in too much of a hurry for such niceties, so, 'without consulting the Trusteeship Council of the UN, on whose behalf the Labour Government is supposed to hold the territory in trust until the Africans are able to take over the administration, Mr Creech Jones agreed to alienate some 3,250,000 acres of native land and hand it over to the Ministry of Food at an annual rental of five cents an acre.'[18] In March 1949, John Strachey was already revelling in the possibilities:

> 'If the British Empire does not flourish, the sovereignty over those areas which is at present held by this House will be lost to the House because the one thing that will not happen is that these areas will be left barren and undeveloped. If we do not do the job, some other Power or persons will, because the world cannot tolerate that this vast land should be left in the state in which it has too long lingered ... I have the perfect confidence that in a very few years the groundnut scheme will be one of the acknowledged glories of the British Commonwealth.'[19]

Too soon, however, for later that year, after the expenditure of £23 million, only 26,000 acres had been brought under cultivation owing to the difficulties of clearing the land; even worse, the yield was less than the seed used. The scheme was reduced in scope first to 600,000 acres, and then to 200,000. Defending it just before it was abandoned

18. Quoted in Padmore, *op cit*, p176. Creech Jones' position contrasts with what he had argued in *Tribune* in 1944 in an article on the Cameroons. His view then was that 'Trusteeship is cant and humbug unless it is implemented in constructive terms of development and social targets, and unless that development is for and in the interests of the African people.' (Quoted *ibid*, p187).
19. Quoted in Amanke Okafor, *Nigeria – Why We Fight For Independence*, 1950, p26.

as a complete fiasco with a loss of £36 million, Strachey said:

> 'The scheme is a thoroughly hard-headed and not philanthropic proposition ... painful readjustments for the African population ... this is not a philanthropic scheme started purely and solely for the African's benefit.'[20]

In 1948, the then Governor of Tanganyika had explained clearly what he thought was of benefit to the African population when he defended the practice of flogging as 'a suitable punishment' before the UN Trusteeship Council on the grounds that 'imprisonment was not understood, since in prison the Africans would be better off than at home.'[21]

3.10 *Sterling balances and overseas investment*

The massive trade surplus of the colonies did not just mean super-profits for the companies involved, let alone dollars for the British Empire. Labour was able to use Britain's financial control of its colonies to retain part of the payments for the colonies' exports as a loan whose rate of interest and date of repayment were determined by British imperialism. These credits were originally a method of pooling the hard currency earnings of the colonies to pay for US goods during the war; Britain bought such hard currency at the rate of exchange it chose to establish, and in return credited the colonies with an appropriate sterling balance. These balances had increased enormously during the war, those credited to India alone rising by £1.3 billion between 1939 and 1946, even though it was nominally a Dominion. Things did not change with the end of the war; in fact, the sterling balances of the colonies continued to rise as those to the Dominions fell. As Palme Dutt observed,

> 'This post-war increase in the colonial sterling balances represents

20. Quoted R Palme Dutt, *op cit*, p250.
21. Quoted in A Medora and J Woddis, *Social Security in the Colonies*, World Federation of Trade Unions, circa 1952, p47.

Table 7 Sterling balances 1945-51[23] (£000,000s)

	1945	1948	1951	Increase	
UK Sterling Debts to:				Total	%
Sterling Area:					
Colonies	446	556	964	+518	+116
Other Sterling Areas	2007	1809	1825	–182	–9
Non-Sterling Area	3663	3701	3807	–192	–16

a further volume of goods drawn from the colonial countries, and used in practice to meet Britain's dollar deficit, without any current payment to the colonial peoples other than a depreciating and irredeemable paper credit in London...The increase in the colonial balances is a measure of the increase in the special intensified exploitation of the colonial peoples during these years, additional to the "normal" flow of colonial tribute.'[22]

A condition of the 1945 US loan was that these sterling balances become freely convertible into dollars a year from the date the loan was finally approved. When that date, July 1946, arrived, a huge run on the pound started; by mid-September most of the loan had been used trying to defend the sterling area. Convertibility had to be suspended, since British imperialism had proved too weak to survive without the enforced financial support of the Empire. When in 1949 Labour finally devalued the pound, its control of colonial currency allowed it to maintain a fixed exchange rate with the metropolitan currency, with the result that:

'the British, while having to devalue the pound against the dollar ... kept the pound strong against all colonial currencies (in most cases at par) by devaluing them at the same time and to the same extent. In short, the sterling area was used after 1945 as a device

22. Quoted in R Palme Dutt, *op cit*, pp266-67
23. *ibid*.

for supporting the pound sterling against the dollar long after it had lost its legitimate function of pooling Empire and Commonwealth resources for the fight against fascism. At the same time the pound was kept strong against the colonial currencies to avoid an increase in the real burden of blocked sterling balances. In both ways, the colonies were compelled to subsidise Britain's post-war standard of living.'[24]

The increase in these forced loans co-incided with a huge increase in overseas investment by British imperialism – a total of £659 million between 1948 and the first half of 1951 alone. Hugh Dalton, Chancellor of Exchequer before Cripps, described the relationship between Britain and the colonies in the form of a fictional conversation with an Indian:

'For years you have been in debt to us, and you have paid up: our political control of you ensured that. Now the wheel of fortune has turned full circle: we are indebted to you. It is true that you are poor and we are rich, and that you need our funds for your economic development. But I am afraid we are not going to pay up.'[25]

Fieldhouse has argued that the period of post-war shortages and the Korean commodity boom represented the best conditions for the impoverished colonies to begin to create an infrastructure which would allow for a substantial economic development. However, 'these opportunities were lost because the Labour Government used the colonies to protect the British consumer from the high social price which continental countries were then paying for their post-war reconstruction. Consciously or not, this was to adopt "social imperialism" in an extreme form.'[26] Oliver Lyttleton, shortly to become Tory Colonial Secretary, put it more succinctly when he commented

24. DK Fieldhouse in R Ovendale, *op cit*, p96.
25. Quoted in DN Pritt, *The Labour Government 1945–51*, Lawrence and Wishart 1963, p136.
26. In R Ovendale, *op cit*, p99.

during the October 1951 election campaign that: 'The Government claims that the dependent territories were exploited in the past, but are not being exploited now. But in fact, the Socialist Government seems to be the first government which has discovered how to exploit the colonies.'[27]

3.11 *The African empire*

Since its 1917 response to the Bolshevik peace proposals, Labour had not changed its stance on the African colonies. Creech Jones wrote in 1944, two years before he was to become Colonial Secretary: 'Socialists ... cannot stop their ears to the claims of the colonial people and renounce responsibility towards British territories because of some sentimental inclination to "liberation" or internal administration. To throw off the colonial empire in this way, would be to betray the peoples and our trust.'[28] In line with this reasoning, not one African colony received independence from the Labour Government, as it took literally its 1943 policy document that 'the inhabitants of the African territories are "backward" and "not yet able to stand by themselves",' and opposed any reference to the Atlantic Charter because it mentioned self-government.[29]

The 'responsibility' with which Creech Jones was so concerned became evident during the Seretse Khama affair. Seretse Khama was heir to the chiefdom of Bechuanaland, a British protectorate bordering on South Africa. When he was formally elected chief by a huge majority, the apartheid regime protested because he had had the temerity to marry a white woman, and demanded his removal. In March 1950, Labour banished him from his homeland to maintain favour with South Africa, which had become an important ally, both economically and strategically. Already in early 1948, Harold Wilson as President of the Board of Trade, had singled it out 'as one market of

27. Quoted in R Palme Dutt, *ibid,* p270.
28. Quoted *ibid*, p335.
29. Quoted in Gupta, *op cit*, p276.

particular importance in view of its position as an important gold producer. Exports to this market may indeed not only save dollars but earn us gold',[30] whilst Dalton as the Chancellor of Exchequer had found South Africa 'particularly helpful' during the sterling crisis of 1947. From 1946 to 1955, British investments there were to total some £500 million. Nor was it just the economic significance: there was the Simonstown naval base, and perhaps most importantly of all, uranium – in fact the only uranium source outside US or Soviet control. With Labour now secretly committed to the development of a British A-bomb, there was not the slightest chance it would jeopardise its relationship with the apartheid regime with a dispute over the chieftanship of an 'insignificant' colony.

The Seretse Khama affair was one in a series of episodes which displayed an underlying sympathy with minority settler regimes. Already, in 1946, Labour had conceded the mandate over the former German colony South West Africa (now Namibia) to South Africa, and later supported the apartheid regime in its resistance to giving up control to the United Nations, arguing that South Africa had a perfect right to retain the ex-colony. A White Paper in March 1947 granted an unofficial majority to white settlers in Kenya in the legislature, based on communal representation. When in the following year the Kenyan African Union (KAU) adopted a democratic programme, Creech Jones commented that: 'democratic government in the hands of ignorant and politically inexperienced people can easily become unworkable'.[31] Two years later, the Communist-led East African TUC called a boycott of a visit by the Queen: the boycott itself was declared illegal, and when its leaders were detained, the response was an 18-day general strike. Labour rushed in troops, arrested hundreds of workers and banned the union. In December 1950, the new Colonial Secretary, James Griffiths, conceded the possibility of future self-government for Kenya, but by failing to

30. Quoted in P Foot, *The Politics of Harold Wilson*, Penguin, 1968, p270.
31. Quoted in E Abrahams, 'The Labour Party and Kenya' in *Fight Racism! Fight Imperialism!* No 32, September 1983.

suggest that it would be based on one person one vote, in fact accepted settler demands for parity with other races.

The other demonstration of pro-settler sympathy came with the proposal for a Central African Federation, which would include both Southern Rhodesia (now Zimbabwe), Northern Rhodesia (Zambia) and Nyasaland (Malawi). Again, nuclear technology was a prime consideration for British imperialism: Southern Rhodesia was a crucial sterling area source of chromium. The federation would of course be dominated by the tiny settler populations; for Labour, this was not an obstacle, neither were the unanimous objections of the African population led by the likes of Hastings Banda. By the time Labour left office, it had sanctioned Federation, with Griffiths an enthusiastic supporter.

Such sympathy was not to be dispensed when Africans insisted that they were more than capable of self-determination. When the influential Fabian Colonial Bureau (Creech Jones was its effective spokesman) organised a conference in January 1946, inviting various colonial representatives, Rita Hinden, its secretary, clashed with Kwame Nkrumah:

> 'When Mr Nkrumah said "we want absolute independence" it left me absolutely cool. Why? ... British socialists are not so concerned with ideals like independence and self-government, but with the idea of social justice. When British socialists look at the Eastern Europe of today they ask themselves whether independence is itself a worthwhile aim.'[32]

From its tiny population of three million, the Gold Coast had provided 70,000 servicemen for the imperialist war effort. The response was a 1947 constitution where the appointed Governor had an absolute veto over a legislative council, two fifths of which was made up of appointees. On 28 February 1948, police fired on a demonstration of demobilised servicemen protesting against the rising cost

32. Quoted in Gupta, *Imperialism and the British Labour Movement*, *op cit*, p326.

of living. Two were killed; there was a massive uprising in response. A split appeared in the existing bourgeois freedom movement, the United Gold Coast Convention, one wing under Joseph Danquah attempting to restrain the struggle and compromise, the other, under Nkrumah's leadership, adopting a programme of social reform and immediate self-government. Creech Jones attempted to exclude Nkrumah from the political scene by making concessions to Danquah: 'The Gold Coast is on the edge of revolution. We are in danger of losing it', he told the Governor of the colony.[33] Faced with such manoeuvering, the mass of the people forced an open split, and at a 60,000 strong meeting in June 1949, Nkrumah split along with the mass of the UGCC membership to form the Convention People's Party.

In October 1949, a revised constitution was presented, making no significant concessions other than to the lawyer-merchant class led by Danquah; its terms of reference had specifically excluded any consideration of self-government. On 20 November, a representative constituent assembly of 500 organisations including the trade unions demanded immediate dominion status, and proposed amendments to the constitution to frame this. The demand was immediately rejected by the Colonial Secretary, and a civil disobedience campaign started. The Gold Coast TUC called a general strike on 8 January 1950; in response the Governor declared a state of siege. Nkrumah along with other CPP and Gold Coast TUC leaders were arrested. However, as a tactical move, the CPP decided to contest elections to be held under the new constitution, and obtained a landslide victory. Labour had to backtrack and release Nkrumah lest events moved completely out of control. The Gold Coast thus became the only African colony to make significant progress towards independence, and the biggest obstacle it faced was the Labour Government's determination to maintain direct control of its dollar-earning capacity.

33. Quoted in B Lapping, *End of Empire*, Guild Publishing, 1985, p373.

3.12 *NATO and the Soviet Union*

Labour could not rebuild the world imperialist order on its own. There might be some with delusions that Britain was still a great power on a par with the US, but the latter's economic might was overwhelming, and could be expressed in a myriad of ways – from the termination of Lend-Lease to its refusal to share atomic secrets with Britain. But the initial confrontations with the Soviet Union were led by Britain as it tried to reclaim its empire. Indeed, there were a number of sharp disagreements in the aftermath of the war where the US, anxious to break up the old European empires, seemed to some to be too close to the Soviet Union: US observers in Vietnam were opposed to the British actions; there were also disagreements over the British role in Greece and Indonesia, not to mention over Zionist claims to Palestine.

The first serious disagreements between Britain and the Soviet Union took place within a couple of months of the end of the war: they concerned British plans for the former Italian colonies in Africa (Somalia and Cyrenaica, the latter now part of Libya), its designs on Persia (now Iran), and the British role in South East Asia, and shortly afterwards the division of Germany. In Persia, Soviet backing for an Azeri republic in the north of the country was faced down by Britain, and Soviet troops withdrew in May 1946: 'Iran settled down again into its traditional client role of indirect tutelage, an intrinsic element in Britain's economic and strategic "lifeline" as proclaimed by Bevin.'[34]

It was in fact early 1946 when US policy seemed to swing definitively behind Labour's in isolating the Soviet Union. It supported Britain in Persia and started to play a more active role in the rebuilding of capitalist Europe. It was also getting increasingly involved in the civil war in China; in the four years from 1945 it spent over $3 billion in economic and military aid in bolstering the reactionary Chiang Kai Shek against the Communist-led liberation struggle. The point at which it definitely took over the leadership of the imperialist

34. KO Morgan, *Labour in Power 1945–51*, Oxford, 1985, p251.

alliance from Britain was in March 1947, when Labour announced that it could not defeat the Greek revolutionary movement and would have to withdraw its forces. US President Truman declared 'that it must be the policy of the United States to support free peoples who are resisting attempted subjugation by armed minorities or by outside pressure.' Truman's announcement was followed by the immediate despatch of economic and military aid to both Greece and Turkey. In short order there followed the eviction of the Communist Parties from both the Italian and French Governments, and the establishment of the Marshall Plan to promote European reconstruction.

The military corollary of this process was the establishment of NATO in 1949, in which Bevin played the leading role. NATO was needed to contain the Soviet Union, not because it might march through Western Europe, but rather to isolate it from the growing anti-colonial movement which was now in the vanguard of the revolutionary struggle. In other words, NATO was a thinly-veiled warning to the Soviet Union to either drop or severely curtail any support for national liberation struggles. The Labour left was an enthusiastic supporter of such intimidation: *Tribune* was writing regularly about the dangers of appeasement, and had applauded the 1948 re-election of Truman to the White House. Thus there was never any question of Labour's commitment to NATO from the outset: even when it adopted a policy of unilateral disarmament in the early 1980s, it never dropped its allegiance to the imperialist alliance.

3.13 *The Korean War*

The final shame of the Labour Government was its support for the neo-fascist Syngman Rhee regime in South Korea. In August 1945, Korea had been partitioned along the 38th Parallel. In the North, the regime, made up of veterans of the war against the Japanese occupation of both Korea and Manchuria, had instituted a widespread land reform, and purged the state apparatus of those who had collaborated with the Japanese colonialists. In the South, under the direction of the

US, quite the opposite had happened: there was no land reform, and the regime was controlled by former stooges of the Japanese occupation.

The political stability of the regime in the North allowed the Soviet Union to withdraw its forces in 1948: it was a different story in the South. Peasant-based guerilla warfare started in 1946 as the popular land reform committees set up after the defeat of Japan were brutally repressed. Between 1946 and the outbreak of war in June 1950, an estimated 100,000 people in South Korea had been killed in what was to all intents and purposes a war of national liberation. The US could not withdraw since without its military and economic support, the Rhee regime would collapse overnight, with an incalculable political impact on Japan and the rest of South East Asia; a view shared by the Labour left:

> 'If she [the US] allowed South Korea to be occupied without coming to her help then the prestige of the West in Asia would have suffered severely. The repercussions would been felt in Malaya, Indo-China, Burma and indeed throughout South East Asia.'[35]

The issue then in June 1950 was not who started the war, but the substance of it: and that was the ending of partition imposed by imperialism. As the North Koreans swept south, forcing the numerically superior and far better-armed US and South Korean troops to flee for their lives, the popular committees took over the state administration, purging it of the former collaborationists and instituting widespread land reform. South Korean forces fell back to a small enclave in the South, butchering tens of thousands in widely-reported atrocities. To this were added even more when, backed by huge US firepower, they moved back and over the 38th Parallel towards the border with China.

As it was to do in 1990 over the Iraqi occupation of Kuwait, the US turned to the UN to provide a smokescreen for its intervention. the

35. *Tribune*, 7 July 1950.

Labour Government supported it completely, committing 12,000 troops, the largest foreign contingent after the US. In this action, the Government was enthusiastically supported by the Labour left; as a *Tribune* editorial put it on 30 June 1950 just after the start of hostilities:

> 'In the face of such action [the alleged North Korean invasion], the US government has in our view taken the correct and inevitable course. First, it has taken every step with the approval of the necessary majority in the UN Security Council. Second, it has made it clear that even if it fails to preserve the South Korean government, it will resist to the utmost Communist expansion anywhere else in the east.'

and added that the US had:

> 'demonstrated that there is no possibility of Communist aggression succeeding by reason of Western appeasement. The West has shown that it has preferred to fight, if need be, and that is a lesson that will not be lost on the Russians.'

The following week, in an editorial 'Some thoughts about Appeasement', *Tribune* opined:

> 'Of course the prospect of war by atom bomb or hydrogen bomb opens up a vista of infinite horrors. But they are not the only horrors. For example in the last war, how many more people, Jews and others, were killed by the Nazis in their extermination camps than were directly killed by the use of atom bomb. The answer is 100 times more. It is worth pondering these figures in considering whether there is any short cut to peace, or whether appeasement pays.'[36]

This was of course little more than an incitement to use the bomb, presumably to help the 'prestige' of the West in Asia. In view of the evident character of the Rhee regime and the real nature of the war, bravely reported by journalists like Rene Cutforth, James Cameron,

---

36. *ibid.*

Alan Winnington and Wilfred Burchett, the revolting corruption of the Labour left seems almost staggering. Indeed, even more so when the use of nuclear weapons was actively considered on numerous occasions by the US.

Labour re-introduced national service – again with the support of *Tribune* – initially for a period of 18 months, later extending it to two years. Rene Cutforth and James Cameron were subjected to abuse and vilification for reporting the absolute barbarity of the Rhee regime, and the collusion of the US. The Cabinet discussed the possibility of prosecuting Alan Winnington, a Communist, for treason after he wrote a pamphlet *I saw the truth* about these brutalities; they were only dissuaded because the mandatory sentence for the offence was death.

In November 1950, as US forces aimed for the Chinese border with the clear indication that they would cross it if necessary, the People's Republic of China intervened. The combined Korean and Chinese forces drove the US and South Korean forces back down to the 38th parallel, where a bloody stalemate ensued. The retreating Rhee regime carried out more reprisals, including a mass execution witnessed by British troops. The British ambassador made representations to the US to 'dissuade the Korean authorities from running unnecessary risks' – the risk being 'an incident' if British troops were again subjected to 'the spectacle of mass executions.'[37] A Foreign Office official wrote 'The continuing reports of "atrocities" and "political shootings" are, as you know, giving us a lot of trouble.'[38] The response was a much tighter military and political censorship. Hence it was not reported until later that Labour had indicated it would be prepared to consider supporting direct military action against China on two occasions – in May and September 1951. And if it boasted it had opposed the US's use of nuclear weapons when Truman suggested it publicly at the end of November 1950, this

37. Quoted in J Halliday and B Cummings, *Korea – The Unknown War*, Viking, 1988, p137. This excellent book is also the source of later material on dummy nuclear bombing runs.

38. *ibid.*

meant little because it had no control. The US never ruled out the use of nuclear weapons; in April 1951, bombs were despatched to Okinawa and Truman approved a request that they be available if there were further significant Chinese reinforcements. In September 1951, lone B-29 bombers made dummy runs over North Korea simulating a nuclear attack by following the attack lines they had taken over Hiroshima and Nagasaki. The nature of these runs would have been obvious to North Korean radar operators – whether or not they were simulation of course they could only guess.

When the war finally ground to a halt in 1953, some three million Koreans had been killed. But already by 1951, the US airforce had been grounded because there were no more targets for it to attack – everything north of the 38th Parallel had been utterly destroyed. Labour had even in this its last days of government shown an unquestioning determination to defend the world-wide interests of imperialism; the left's virulent support had destroyed any opposition. Only the CPGB took a remotely principled line, and many of its meetings were anyway violently broken up; but years of adaptation to the Labour Party had reduced its political impact. On the other hand, the non-Communist left echoed *Tribune*; the founders of the Socialist Workers' Party, for instance, keen to protect the Labour Party and their alliance with its left wing, declared their opposition to North Korea, describing it as a Russian stooge. Political expediency came before the interests of the Korean people.

3.14 *Summary*

It is safe to say that without the Labour Government, the reconstruction of the world imperialist order would have been a far more hazardous proposition. For two crucial years, 1945–47, it provided the political and military lead in confronting liberation movements throughout the world. At that point, it handed the baton over to US imperialism, and concentrated on building up the British economy at the expense of the Empire. A Tory government could not have achieved this: Churchill's leadership would have provided too naked an expression of British imperialist interests.

By basing British recovery firmly and squarely on the exploitation of the Empire, Labour's record turned into a consummation of the theory of 'socialist colonialism' discussed at Stuttgart in 1907, and enthusiastically approved by Ramsay MacDonald. Labour felt no compunction at exploiting the Empire in this way; racism was endemic within its leadership. When Hugh Dalton was offered the chance of becoming Colonial Secretary after the 1950 election, he turned it down, noting in his diary: 'I had a horrid vision of pullulating, poverty-stricken, diseased nigger communities, for whom one can do nothing in the short run, and who, the more one tries to help them, are querulous and ungrateful.'[39]

Labour's foreign and colonial policy during these six years can now be seen as of far greater historical significance than anything it achieved domestically. Full employment and nationalisation have long since gone; state welfare is also disappearing. Yet on the foreign stage, Labour constructed the imperialist alliances which were eventually to destroy the Soviet Union; it kept Greece, Indonesia, and Malaya in the imperialist camp; it was responsible for wars in Vietnam which were to claim the lives of millions. Labour never had to kill one British worker at home to rebuild British imperialism. But it had to kill untold thousands in the rest of the world, often with the enthusiastic support of its left wing. Hence those who seek to show that Labour played a progressive role between 1949 and 1951 can only do so on the racist assumption that the lives of the colonial people are of far less importance than those of British workers.

39. Quoted in Gupta, *op cit*, p336.

PART FOUR

Labour and British imperialism since 1951

4.1 *Labour in opposition 1951–64*

The defeat of the Labour Government in 1951 was a prelude to the long imperialist boom of the 1950s and 1960s. The Conservative Government, free from the most pressing and immediate effects of the post-war crisis, set about establishing a neo-colonial solution to the problem of empire. This involved building up the bourgeois component in the national liberation movements, whilst suppressing ruthlessly any influence from the working class or peasantry; it was a process completely supported by Labour, as in Guyana and Kenya.

The first elections ever in British Guyana, under a Labour-inspired constitution, were held in April 1953, and resulted in a landslide victory for the mildly-reforming, non-racial Peoples' Progressive Party (PPP) under the leadership of Cheddi Jagan. The PPP extended trade union rights, reformed education, ended corrupt expenditure of money on colonial officials, and introduced basic social legislation. On 4 October, the Tories suspended the constitution, and sent in troops, alleging that the PPP was organising a communist takeover. At issue were the bauxite resources of the colony. The British TUC weighed in with its support, accusing the PPP of waging a communist policy, of supporting the World Federation of Trade Unions as opposed to the CIA International Congress of Free Trade Unions, and of endeavouring to destroy the ManPower Citizens Association, a company union. The Labour Party NEC then banned affiliates from inviting PPP speakers to present their case, so effectively isolating them.

The Kenyan people had already served notice during the life-time of the Labour Government that they wanted their freedom. In 1952, following the suppression of the East African TUC, the KAU was also banned, and trade unionists and political leaders were gaoled. With the normal channels of bourgeois protest exhausted, the struggle of the Kenyan Land and Freedom Army – the Mau Mau – started. From the outset, Labour's support for British imperialism was assured: James Griffiths declared:

> 'from the beginning we have given the Government our fullest support in any steps that are required to suppress Mau Mau.'[1]

Labour might distance itself from what it regarded as Tory 'excesses' but only because such excesses 'will have the effect of creating in Kenya a whole people who will be resentfully against us in the future.' Griffiths himself was concerned at 'the danger of driving all the Kikuyu people into the hands of the Mau Mau', and thought it of 'the utmost importance' that there be 'a responsible political organisation to which the Africans can look for leadership' – that is, a bourgeois leadership willing to accept a neo-colonial settlement. Fenner Brockway for the left concurred; he found the Mau Mau 'an ugly and brutal form of extreme nationalism', and urged the government to 'accept the offers of African leaders to take their part' in the campaign against the Mau Mau. The suppression of the Mau Mau allowed British imperialism and Jomo Kenyatta to find this neo-colonial solution, one which leaves the Kenyan people dependent on imperialism today.

Labour played the same refrain during Suez, cautioning the Tories against playing into 'communist' and 'extremist' hands. Nasser's coup in 1952 had given the Tories no option but to move troops out of Suez – no longer was there a puppet government which might protest but do nothing. When in 1956 Nasser nationalised the Suez

1. Quoted in E Abrahams, *Fight Racism! Fight Imperialism!* No 32, *op cit.*

Canal to help pay for the Aswan Dam project, Gaitskell denounced the action as 'high-handed and totally unjustifiable', comparing Nasser to Hitler and Mussolini, and urging the supply of more arms to the Zionists. However, as the crisis developed, and it became apparent that there was not to be any US support for military action, Labour ruled it out, and moved to criticise the Tories' tactics, arguing that if the Government used force, 'they will leave behind in the Middle East such a legacy of distrust and bitterness towards the West that the whole area will be thrust almost forcibly under Communist control. This is the greatest danger of all.'[2]

Hence, when the invasion came in October 1956, Labour condemned it, not because of the violation of Egyptian sovereignty, or because of the slaughter of Egyptian civilians, but because the Government had lost an opportunity to attack the Soviet Union when the latter moved troops into Hungary.

4.2 *Back in office 1964–70*

By 1964, when Labour returned to office with a slender majority, Britain's dominant position in relation to its European competitors had disappeared. Rates of industrial growth, investment and increases in productivity lagged as capital was preferentially exported to where a quicker profit could be found. Labour's answer was the rejuvenation of the economy through the 'white heat' of a 'technological revolution', while continuing to act as a very junior partner of the US in defending world imperialist interests.

In Aden, Labour policy followed a now very familiar pattern: repression of the progressive wing of the national freedom struggle, cultivation of the reactionary side.[3] The National Liberation Front had been formed in 1962 to fight British-backed counter-revolution against the revolutionary republic established in North Yemen. The

2. Quoted in *Fight Racism! Fight Imperialism!* No 64, November 1986.
3. Material and quotations drawn from B Hughes, 'The Labour Party and South Yemen', in *Fight Racism! Fight Imperialism!* No 43, October 1984.

NLF represented the peasantry and Adeni working class, and launched armed struggle in 1963. However, Labour was quite clear it needed to retain Aden as a military base when it came into office, and one of its first acts was, in Harold Wilson's words, 'preparing for inevitable martial take-over, suspension of the constitution and a declaration of a state of emergency.' Sir Richard Turnbull, who had supervised the defeat of the Mau Mau, was appointed High Commissioner. The NLF was outlawed, and soon after so was trial by jury. Widespread torture was practised; when it was exposed by Amnesty International, George Brown as Foreign Secretary declared the policy 'had operated with considerable success, having provided information leading to the discovery of numerous arms caches and to the arrest of a large number of terrorists.'

Labour's attempts to cultivate relations with the feudal sultans and the Adeni bourgeoisie via the Front for the Liberation of South Yemen (FLOSY) were doomed as the expense of supporting 17,000 troops came to more than British imperialism could bear in the midst of serious balance of payment problems. On 30 November 1967, the British were finally driven from South Yemen.

Meanwhile, the Government was backing the US war against Vietnam to the hilt,[4] not least because at critical moments it was dependent on the US to provide it with loans to fend off frequent attacks on sterling. There was direct support: the training of thousands of South Vietnamese in jungle warfare at a school in Malaya, paid for by the Foreign Office; supplying arms, radar, and hovercraft for use in the Mekong Delta. Then there was the political support, complete and unconditional. The 1965 Party Conference voted to support the US, a position put in the 1966 Election Manifesto. In June 1965, the US commenced bombing Hanoi and Haiphong, with Wilson's sympathy and understanding expressed in a cablegram to Johnson:

> 'I wholly understand the deep concern you must feel at the need to do anything possible to reduce the losses of young Americans

4. Material and quotations drawn from S Palmer, *op cit*.

> in and over Vietnam ... our reservations about this operation will not affect our continuing support for your policy over Vietnam.'

The sympathy also extended to that year's Labour Party conference, as it obligingly voted down a resolution dissociating Labour from the US. Two years later, Wilson was to express 'the sense of outrage' he felt at the news of the Tet offensive which so nearly came to victory. Even later on in 1974, Labour would continue to back the South Vietnamese puppet regime, eventually welcoming Nguyen Van Thieu, the puppet ruler, after his defeat in September 1975 and settling him in Wimbledon.

Throughout this, the Labour left acted spinelessly, concerned as they were with not being seen to split the Party, something of far greater concern to them and their careers than the slaughter in Vietnam. The most honest statement from a Labour member was made by Bertrand Russell in a speech on 14 October 1965:

> 'When I compare the horrors of the Vietnam war with the election manifesto of the Labour Government, I find myself confronted with the most shameful betrayal of modern times in this country. Hitler, at least, seldom professed humanity, but these men who now pollute the chairs of office professed, before election, the most noble and lofty ideals of human brotherhood ... I can no longer remain a member of this so-called "Labour Party", and I am resigning after 51 years.'

At the end of his speech, he tore up his membership card and called for a new party to be built.

Following Labour's defeat in 1951, the Tories had continued with the Central African Federation project; established in 1953, it collapsed ten years later because it could not control either what was to become Zambia or Malawi. It left the Southern Rhodesian settlers on their own, faced with a movement led by the newly-formed Zimbabwe African National Union (ZANU) and Zimbabwe African People's Union (ZAPU). A Labour mission was sent out in February 1965 to negotiate with the settlers, bur made no progress. The only thing Labour made clear was that it would not use force to impose majority rule. This was a green light: Labour was using force in Aden at the time, and was backing the US in Vietnam. Wilson himself went to Salisbury (Harare) in October, to be boycotted by the settlers; when he returned to Britain he told ZANU and ZAPU leaders to take a more realistic stand and not hope that Britain would defend the Africans' rights by force. The settlers got the message, and declared independence on 11 November.

Wilson's response was to rule out any negotiations with the settlers, impose a series of sanctions, but at the same time to repeat the assurance that no force would be used. Within months, he had backed down, and 'talks about talks' started in early 1966. Then in December, he met the Southern Rhodesia prime minister Ian Smith on *HMS Tiger*. The document presented for discussion was an abject capitulation to the racists; it made clear, contrary to previous practice, that independence need not be accompanied by universal franchise: 'The British Government has repeatedly said that majority rule could not come about immediately but should be reached through merit and achievement.'[5] It therefore proposed to establish a Royal Commission, which it conceded would have to sit 'for several years' to work out ways to end racial discrimination. Knowing that sanctions would be circumvented through Portuguese Mozambique or South Africa, the settlers felt safe in rejecting Labour's pusillanimous proposals. The sanctions that Wilson promised would work 'in weeks rather than months' never worked at all: it took the armed struggle of ZANU and ZAPU to force the settlers to Lancaster House in 1980.

With South Africa itself, Wilson was keen to retain trading relationships, arguing in very familiar terms that sanctions 'would harm the people we are most concerned about, the Africans and those whites fighting to maintain some standard of decency.'[6] One of the first actions of the 1964 Government was to continue the supply of Buc-

---

5. Quoted in P Foot, *op cit*, p266.
6. Quoted in C Brown, 'The Labour Party and South Africa' in *Fight Racism! Fight Imperialism!* No 30, June 1983.

caneer bombers despite a commitment to stop them; the subsequent arms ban did not prevent the supply of Landrovers and other paramilitary equipment. By 1967, South Africa was Britain's second largest export market, and Crosland could write 'Our concern to see this valuable trade develop and to avoid any economic confrontation with South Africa has been repeatedly made clear in Parliament and the UN.'[7]

Indeed it was, as Britain vetoed any resolution calling for a mandatory trade embargo. This period saw a rapid growth in British investment in apartheid, as domestic profitability fell: from £30 million a year in 1964 such investment rose to £70 million in 1969. In 1968, Tony Benn signed a contract with Rio Tinto Zinc for the illegal extraction of 7,500 tons of uranium from the Rossing mine in Namibia, an episode which never seriously damaged his later image as a leader of the left.

With one exception, there was no significant organised opposition to the Government's support for apartheid, especially in comparison with the movement against its policy over Vietnam. This was because the character of the Anti-Apartheid Movement (AAM) was quite different to that of the Vietnam Solidarity Committee: the former was tied to the Labour Party, and anything it did was circumscribed by the need to protect the interests of Labour.[8] Hence, although several government ministers were members, the AAM refused to take action against them even though their own Government actively encouraged links with apartheid.

The only effective action against British links was in fact organised outside of the AAM, and in face of its opposition: the Stop the Seventy Tour Campaign against a visit from the Springboks rugby and cricket teams. It organised large and militant demonstrations against the rugby team between November 1969 and January 1970, drawing tens of thousands of people into active campaigning against apartheid

---

7. *ibid.*

8. Drawn from C Brickley, T O'Halloran and D Reed, *South Africa – Britain out of Apartheid, Apartheid out of Britain*, Larkin Publications, 1986, pp25-29.

for the first time, and forced Labour to 'persuade' the MCC to cancel the cricket tour organised for the summer of that year. After the campaign ended, the AAM subsided into inactivity, and distinguished itself only by its sectarian hostility to the most radical sections of the Southern African liberation movements. Hence, to the bitter end, it refused to give any support to ZANU in Zimbabwe whatsoever, and only under extreme pressure would it acknowledge the existence of the Pan African Congress of Azania or sections of the Black Consciousness Movement.

Its irrelevance continued into the next Labour administration. In 1975, Labour nationalised British Leyland; when workers in its South African plants sought support in a unionisation drive, the Government refused to support them, saying that the issue was left to the 'commercial judgement' of the local management. At the end of 1976, total British investment in South Africa stood at just short of £11 billion, 50 per cent of total foreign investment. In January the following year, through its representative on the IMF Board, it agreed a loan to the apartheid state. Just to put the record straight, the British Ambassador declared in a broadcast in March 1977 'In particular, I must remind you that the only four occasions on which my Government, Britain, has exercised the veto in the Security Council during the life of the present Government has been in favour of South Africa.'[9] What more could be said?

4.3 *Labour and Ireland from 1969*[10]

But if there is one thing for which the 1964 Labour Government should be remembered, it is the despatch of troops to the Six Counties of Ireland. The sectarian statelet had come under increasing challenge from the mid-1960s onward, as the Nationalist people organised to demand an end to gerrymandering and other forms of discrimination. The widely-televised spectacle of the RUC violently

9. Quoted in C Brown, *Fight Racism! Fight Imperialism!* No 30, *op cit.*

10. Material drawn from D Reed, *op cit*, pp113ff.

batoning a Civil Rights march on 5 October 1968 in Derry was one landmark in the developing mass movement, followed in March 1969 by the election to Parliament of Bernadette Devlin as a united anti-Unionist candidate. Throughout the early summer of 1969, there were repeated confrontations between the Nationalist people unwilling to accept the cosmetic reforms they had been offered, and a Unionist Government incapable of giving any more. When the Stormont Government refused to ban the Apprentice Boy's annual march round Derry on 12 August, the people of the Bogside served notice that they would defend their community. Barricades went up on the night before: for three days, the RUC attempted to break through using armoured cars against a hail of petrol bombs – 43,000 bottles went missing from the local dairy. On 14 August the exhausted RUC admitted defeat, and that afternoon British troops arrived to relieve them. The following day, the Army was deployed in Belfast's Falls Road, after a night of unbridled Loyalist terror supported by RUC armoured cars and B-Specials had failed to crush the resistance of the Nationalist people despite claiming six lives.

Labour had sent in the troops firstly to contain the insurrection in Derry, and only after that to Belfast to prevent the possible outbreak of civil war. Without the enormous resistance there would have been no talk of reforming the Northern Ireland statelet; time would tell that it could never amount to any more than talk. Once again, however, Labour had found sycophants to its left who were prepared to support its despatch of troops – the Tribune group, of course, the CPGB, Militant and the International Socialists (now the SWP). This would be a foretaste of the future, where the numerically significant forces on the left would show themselves at best indifferent to, and often in support of, British imperialist policy in the occupied Six Counties.

By the time Labour returned to government in 1974 after the 'Who Rules Britain?' election, a war of national liberation in Ireland was in full swing. The British Army had been as ineffective as the RUC in forcing the Republican minority to submit: the Tories had introduced internment on 9 August 1971, with the accompanying physical and psychological torture of the first detainees. A protest demonstration on 30 January 1972 in Derry turned into Bloody Sunday as 14 civilians were murdered by the Paratroop regiment. The resultant explosion forced Conservative Prime Minister Edward Heath to suspend Stormont on 20 March and later replace it with the Sunningdale power-sharing agreement. This was unacceptable to the Loyalists, who threatened to destroy it; in May 1974, the threat became a reality as the Ulster Workers' Council organised a general strike to bring it down. With the Army unwilling to intervene, Labour caved in and abandoned power-sharing, leaving it no option but to strengthen direct rule. Within short order, it presided over the framing of Judith Ward, the Guildford 4, the Maguire 7 and the Birmingham 6, and passed the Prevention of Terrorism Act in the wake of the Birmingham bombings at the end of the year.

Not until December 1975, however, was internment finally ended, following an agreement between the Republican movement and the Government earlier in the year. It was replaced by judicial internment, carried on through the juryless Diplock courts. Labour's strategy was one of complete repression: the widespread use of torture to extract confessions from detainees; the use of Diplock courts to almost guarantee a conviction, and the ending of Special Category status, so as to criminalise the prisoners. The aim was to establish sufficient political stability to allow the return of government to the Six Counties – 'Ulsterisation'.

Torture was officially sanctioned by the McGonigal judgment, which ruled that 'a certain roughness of treatment' of detainees was quite acceptable, and certainly different from 'torture'. Between 1975 and 1979, between 93 and 96 per cent of all cases appearing before Diplock courts resulted in conviction; of these, between 70 and 90 per cent depended either wholly or mainly on a confession. After Roy Mason became Secretary of State for Northern Ireland at the end of 1976, the use of torture became even more extensive. By autumn 1977, allegations about its use were so widespread that an ITV programme was broadcast on the subject. Mason, who had earlier described the consequent injuries to prisoners as 'self-inflicted', dismissed it as 'cheque-book television', but the following week, Amnesty International announced it would send a team to investigate. Its report, published in May 1978, concluded that there was widespread maltreatment of suspects, and recommended a public inquiry. This call was dismissed by Mason, who set up a private inquiry to ensure that there was as little publicity as possible over the affair. Torture of detainees continued.

Mason was also responsible for the use of SAS shoot-to-kill tactics which cost the lives of 11 people between late 1977 and 1978, including several unarmed civilians. But it was the criminalisation policy which was to galvanise Nationalist opposition once again. On 14 September 1976 Kieran Nugent became the first political prisoner to refuse to wear the prison clothing that became obligatory with the ending of Special Category Status. By March 1978, over 300 prisoners were on protest, all subjected to constant beating from the prison warders in an effort to make them submit. By this time, they had also been forced to start the 'no wash' protest because leaving their cells for a shower or to use the toilet had become without fail an occasion for a vicious beating. Outside, working class women had started to organise support for the prisoners 'on the blanket', forming themselves into local Relatives' Action Committees. By 1978, regular demonstrations of over 10,000 people were being held – the attempt to isolate the Republican movement had ended in failure.

Not that Labour was daunted. In an attempt to keep themselves in office over the winter of 1978, they offered a deal to the Loyalist MPs which would give them extra parliamentary seats in return for their support against the Tories. This vulgar horse-trading was to continue in March 1979, when they vainly sought the support of both Gerry Fitt of the SDLP and the Irish independent MP Frank Maguire to defeat a motion of no confidence. Labour had become the victim of the policy it had embraced so enthusiastically in the years beforehand.

4.4 *Labour imperialism during the Thatcher years*

Forced into the election of June 1979, Labour lost support from significant sections of the poorer working class – black people, low-paid public sector workers and, of course, Irish people. A campaign of disruption of rallies addressed by Labour leaders exposing the record of torture and criminalisation led by the Revolutionary Communist Group (RCG) obtained significant publicity; in contrast, the rest of the left called for a vote for Labour, once again showing its contempt for the struggles of the oppressed. The advent of the Tories signalled that British imperialism was in no mood for compromise, and neither were the prisoners. The first hunger strike ended with an agreement which the British Government almost immediately betrayed, setting the scene for the second, started by Bobby Sands on 1 March 1981.

By the time it was over, ten men had been murdered. Michael Foot, by now leader of the Labour Party, had made clear that he stood full-square with the Government, to the extent of sending Don Concannon, shadow spokesman on Northern Ireland, to tell Bobby Sands on his deathbed that Labour did not support the demands of the hunger strikers. This was at a time when Labour was supposed to be falling under the control of the left: not one Labour MP openly supported the five demands of the hunger strikers, and the only parliamentary protest came from an obscure right-winger, Patrick Duffy.

Whenever Ireland has become an issue since, Labour has proved it to be above party interest. In 1982, Michael Foot supported the banning of Gerry Adams and Danny Morrison after they were invited to London by Ken Livingstone. In 1983, Kevin McNamara, Labour spokesperson on Northern Ireland, opposing the renewal of the Prevention of Terrorism Act, said 'Ordinary decent coppers using ordinary decent police methods apprehended those responsible for the Birmingham outrage',[11] perhaps an unwitting confirmation that torture, forgery and perjury are 'ordinary decent police methods'. At the end of 1987, Labour leader Neil Kinnock cautioned Charles

11. Quoted *ibid*, p408.

Haughey against using the extradition issue to obtain reforms of the Diplock courts. In 1988, Labour congratulated the Tories on the murder of the Gibraltar 3. It abstained on the vote to renew the Prevention of Terrorism Act just after the European Court of Human Rights had ruled that the seven-day detention rule breached the Convention on Human Rights. In December that year, Labour's National Executive Committee stated 'the Party has never declared the Birmingham 6 or the Guildford 4 to be innocent. It does not believe the Party is in a position to declare them innocent' – not surprisingly, since they were convicted under a Labour Government.[12]

The stance that Labour adopted during both the Falklands and the first Gulf War was no surprise, no accident, no expression of a rightward drift within its leadership. Labour leader Michael Foot said of the Task Force in 1982 'our first concern in the Labour Party as in the country as a whole must be for their safety and success.'[13] Without his benediction, it is unlikely that the force could have been sent. The Labour left wanted neither to condemn British imperialist ambitions nor undermine its radical credentials; hence Tony Benn argued for more time for economic sanctions to work, but made clear he agreed on fundamentals: 'There is unanimity in the House on the question of opposing the aggression of the Junta. There is also unanimity on the right of self-defence against aggression.'[14]

This refrain was to be familiar during the lead-up to the first Gulf War. The Labour leadership was if anything more rabid than Thatcher. Gerald Kaufman as Shadow Foreign Secretary denounced the Tories as 'slack, lax and negligent' in their response to the invasion of Kuwait; this was a at a time when Thatcher was warning US President Bush not 'to go wobbly'. Kaufman boasted that Labour had insisted on Iraqi war reparations fully one month before the Tories

12. Decision of December 1988 NEC, quoted by Maxine Williams *Fight Racism! Fight Imperialism!* No 84, February 1989, p5.
13. Quoted in the Editorial, *Fight Racism! Fight Imperialism!*, No 20, June 1982.
14. Quoted *ibid*.

took it up. Benn meanwhile wanted more time for economic sanctions to work; these were eventually to kill hundreds of thousands of children. He made it clear that he opposed Iraqi 'aggression' against British interests. During both wars, Benn and his allies played that familiar role of the Labour left: accepting the substance of the leadership's position – protection of British imperialist interests – whilst choosing to distance themselves from the means with some pacific and even democratic phrases. The Labour left's role allowed others outside the Labour Party to offer praise, magnify their significance, pretend that they represented the true working class heart of the Party, and thus justify their own continuing alliance with it. Thus it was that during both wars, no significant section of the left was prepared to act independently of Benn, because their need for an alliance with Labour forced them to oppose the emergence of any separate movement.

4.5 *The Labour Party and British imperialism: conclusion*

Orwell may have had many political deficiencies, but he knew hypocrisy and political corruption when he saw them. He was always quite frank about the nature of the Labour Party; in *The Lion and the Unicorn*, he argued that Labour 'has never possessed a genuinely independent policy', and that 'This meant that all through the critical years it was directly interested in the prosperity of British capitalism. In particular it was interested in the maintenance of the British Empire, for the wealth of England was drawn largely from Asia and Africa. The standards of living of the trade union workers, whom the Labour Party represented, depended indirectly on the sweating of Indian coolies.'[15] Hence his earlier description of the humbug of left wing politics, which could casually describe Britain as a democracy, and ignore the slavish conditions of those whose exploitation provided the basis for that democracy – the colonial oppressed. Orwell saw the connection between imperialism and political corruption

15. G Orwell, *The Lion and the Unicorn,* Penguin, 1982, p96.

within the 'democratic' or 'socialist' movement. That this is a rare insight can be gathered from its exclusion from the vast majority of histories of the Labour Party.

Labour, in or out of office, whatever the decade, wherever the colony or dependency, took as its starting point the defence of Britain's imperialist interests. 'Old Labour' never adopted an anti-imperialist position on any issue. More than that: it never had a significant anti-imperialist current within it. From time to time, the left wing may have protested against the methods; it never disputed the aims. It never championed the struggle of the Irish people. It never stood up for the masses of India. It regarded French Senegalese troops in the Ruhr as 'black savages', had contempt for 'Chinks' in 1927, mused on the use of the atom bomb in Korea in 1950, vilified the Mau Mau a few years later. In other words, its political culture was always as corrupt as the leadership's, although the language it used might have sounded more radical.

Labour then was always first and foremost an imperialist party, with an imperialist and racist culture. That culture is the culture of privilege, of a section of the working class whose conditions of life are maintained through the parasitic relationship of British imperialism to the rest of the world. It was, and is, corrupt and corrupting; it extends beyond the Labour Party to affect those who then seek to protect it, who themselves reveal an 'utter boorish self-centred indifference to every living human struggle, that is the heart and soul of the imperialist psychology in the labour aristocracy and the petty bourgeoisie.' That privilege has been preserved against the interests of the oppressed through out the world; it has also been preserved against the interests of the mass of the British working class, as we shall now see.

PART FIVE

Labour and the working class 1918–45

5.1 *British imperialism between the wars*

The period between the wars was one of painful and, in the end, only partial reconstruction of British manufacturing and industry. The effect on large sections of the working class was however enormous; by 1939, its structure had changed significantly. In addition, it created a huge reserve army of labour, an oppressed section of the working class ignored and isolated by the Labour Party and the TUC and organised only by Communists. During the late 1930s, as the economy boomed in the South East and the Midlands, the structure of the working class in these areas started to take on the features that are developed to such a high degree today, and which are a product of the most parasitic side of British imperialism.

On the face of it, the British economy had suffered lightly during the First Imperialist War compared to its main competitors such as France and Germany, which had experienced enormous destruction. It was still a creditor nation – its debts of $4.7 billion to the US was more than balanced by credits of $8.6 billion if the Russian debts cancelled by the Bolsheviks are ignored. In addition, it had emerged as the supreme power in the Middle East, with a mandate over Palestine and with oil-rich Iraq firmly in its orbit.

But the underlying problems had not been resolved, and as European reconstruction started, so the uncompetitive nature of much of British industry became more and more apparent; its most significant feature, a major deterioration in export performance (see Table 8), brought considerable pressure on the balance of payments. No longer could these deficits be made up through overseas income, since a substantial proportion of overseas assets had been liquidated to help pay for the war effort. Although strenuous efforts were made to rebuild them, this required much borrowing on the open market: hence the phenomenon of 'lending long and borrowing short' – building up long-term assets through short-term borrowing. The nature of these assets was such that they could not be easily liquidated in the event of sudden financial shocks, so, with low levels of gold reserves, the financial structure of British imperialism was to be extremely shaky, as the events of 1931 were to prove.

Following the brief inflationary boom of 1920, output did not substantially exceed the 1913 level until the year following the defeat of the General Strike, 1927. However, while the level of imports

Table 8 The British economy 1913–37[1] (£000,000)

Year	National income at current prices	National income at 1900 prices	Exports & re-exports at 1913 prices	Imports at 1913 prices
1913	2265	2021	634.8	768.7
1921	4460	1804	368.3	493.4
1923	3844	1917	459.8	560.3
1925	3980	2070	540.7	770.0
1927	4145	2259	507.3	742.8
1929	4178	2319	521.1	758.2
1931	3666	2270	315.6	598.1
1933	3728	2422	304.3	492.7
1935	4109	2616	348.2	588.7
1937	4616	2728	395.0	680.6

1. Calculated from B Mitchell and P Deane (eds), *op cit*, 1962, pp828–29 and 872–73, and from J Kuczynski, *op cit*, p131.

matched that of 1913, the level of exports and re-exports was down 20 per cent, a deficit which had to be compensated by what was in real terms a smaller surplus on invisibles. Put another way: whilst exports covered more than 80 per cent of the value of imports in 1913, in the 1920s this had fallen to about 70 per cent. The parasitic features of the British imperialist economy thus became more and more dominant.

Although there was a steady increase in productivity, this was achieved more through speed-up and the intensification of labour, or through concentration and cartelisation than it was through new investment, which in real terms stagnated. The series of 'more loom' disputes in the textile industry were an example: productivity was intensified through the simple device of making workers operate more looms. This led to a series of disputes which accounted for two-thirds of all days lost in strikes between 1926 and 1934. Industrial stagnation was then the norm for the 1920s: as the then Chancellor of the Exchequer, Churchill, stated in his budget speech on the eve of the General Strike:

> 'The basic industries of the country, those which employ the largest number of workpeople, nearly all continue obstinately depressed under their heavy burdens.'[2]

It was those basic sectors on which the industrial wealth of British imperialism depended that suffered most: coal, iron and steel, textiles and shipbuilding; Palme Dutt cites evidence that overall, British industrial output averaged 80-88 per cent of its 1913 level between 1921 and 1926; national income as presented in the table above also includes the parasitic, luxury sectors which were already expanding. Hobsbawm also describes such stagnation:

> 'Between 1912 and 1938 the quantity of cotton cloth made in Britain fell from 8,000 million to barely 3,000 million square yards; the amount exported from 7,000 million to less than 1,500

2. Quoted in Palme Dutt, *Socialism and the Living Wage,* CPGB, 1927, p52.

> million yards. Never since 1851 had Lancashire exported so little. Between 1854 and 1913 the output of British coal had grown from 65 to 287 million tons. By 1938 it was down to 227 million and still falling. In 1913 12 million tons of British shipping had sailed the seas, in 1938 there was rather less than 11 million. British shipyards in 1870 built 343,000 tons of vessels for British owners, and in 1913, almost a million tons: in 1938 they built little more than half a million.'[3]

The effect on employment was dramatic: the labour force in the cotton industry fell by over half between 1912 and 1938 (from 621,000 to 288,000),[4] the number of miners from 1,200,000 in 1923 to 700,000 in 1938; more generally:

> 'At all times between 1921 and 1938 at least one out of every ten citizens of working age was out of a job. In seven out of those eighteen years at least three out of every twenty were unemployed, in the worst years one out of five. In absolute figures unemployment ranged from a minimum of rather over a million to a maximum (1932) of just under three million; at all events, according to official figures, which for various reasons understated it. In particular industries and regions the record was even blacker. At its peak (1931–2) 34.5 per cent of coalminers, 36.3 per cent of pottery workers, 43.2 per cent of cotton operatives, 43.8 per cent of pig-iron workers, 47.9 per cent of steelworkers, and 62 per cent – or almost two in three – of shipbuilders and ship-repairers were out of work.'[5]

Branson and Heinemann make the essential point, that Britain's privileged, imperialist position 'was also a source of weakness. The tendency of British investors to export capital to the colonies, rather than invest it in modernising production at home, had contributed to the technical backwardness of the older basic industries in Britain,

3. E Hobsbawm, *Industry and Empire*, Pelican, 1969, p207.
4. *ibid*, p209.
5. *ibid*, pp208–09.

which by their very age included a great deal of obsolete plant ... It was these industries which were hit hardest by the slump.'[6]

The overall impact of the slump on British imperialism was however less than in the US or Europe, partly because it could turn to the protected markets of the Empire, partly because there was still the cushion of imperial tribute from overseas investment, even if at a lower level, and partly because basic industries had been anyway generally depressed beforehand. In specific areas, it was of course quite devastating: in the coalfields of Scotland and South Wales, the steel and coal regions in Northumberland and Durham, the cotton areas of Lancashire, not to mention any shipbuilding area, unemployment in the 1930s would be 30, 40 per cent and more; the peak in Jarrow when Palmer's shipyard closed was 80 per cent. 20 to 25 per cent of the population lived in areas which remained severely depressed until the war.

Recovery when it came was therefore patchy and localised, and presented new parasitic features. Firstly, growth was concentrated overwhelmingly in London, the Home Counties and the Midlands. Between 1932 and 1937, the number of insured workers in Greater London rose 14 per cent; in the same years, of the net increase of 644 factories, 532 were in the Greater London area.[7] These new factories were mainly in the luxury good sector: vehicle manufacture, electrical trades, household goods. But the biggest increases in employment were in the distributive trades (up 807,000 from 1923 to 1937), public and private 'services' (up 560,000), building and construction of public works (up 485,000). As against this, there was an overall increase in manufacturing employment of only 219,000.[8] 'Napoleon is said to have called Great Britain "a nation of shopkeepers"; by 1938 it seemed to be turning into a nation of shop assistants, clerks, waiters and machine attendants.'[9]

The most visible signs of the boom of the 1930s was the growth of

---

6. N Branson and M Heinemann, *Britain in the 1930s*, Panther, 1971, p13.

7. *ibid*, p81.

8. Cole and Postgate, *op cit*, p605.

9. *ibid*, p609.

the middle class, for whose spending power much of the new industry catered. As in the 1980s, the extension of credit was to play a vital role in creating a new affluence for the middle class and small sections of the working class. This was particularly important for stimulating a housing boom which created the suburbia of Greater London, the Home Counties and the Midlands. This building formed a huge portion of Gross Domestic Capital Formation (GDCF): in 1913, 11.9 per cent of GDCF was made up of new dwellings; in the 1930s, it was never less than 34.9 per cent. In 1932, and from 1934 to 1936, it exceeded 40 per cent, while in 1933 it was over 50 per cent. Net of dwellings, it was not until 1937 that GDCF was to exceed the 1913 level as a proportion of National Income. From 1931 to 1939, private industry built just short of two million new houses, whilst local authorities built fewer than 600,000.[10] The peak was in 1935, when private enterprise built over 287,000, seven times the number built by local authorities.

Most of these houses were built for sale: the period saw the transformation of the building society into the 'foremost investment agency in Great Britain.'[11] In 1913, building societies lent £9 million; in 1935, £135 million. Mortgage loans doubled between 1929 and 1936 (from £268 million to £587 million),[12] whilst the incurred debts were being paid off at £80 million per year. Cole and Postgate point to this as:

> '... an immensely significant social phenomenon. In 1938, the "blackcoats" and the top layer of the manual working class, as well as the middle classes, largely bought their houses, instead of renting them.'[13]

The new municipal housing estates also benefited the more privileged sections of the working class: their quality made them more

10. Branson and Heinemann, *op cit*, p222.
11. Cole and Postgate, *op cit*, p615.
12. Aldcroft and Richardson, *op cit*, p244.
13. *op cit*, p615.

expensive than private rented accommodation; they were also mainly located in city outskirts, so with the additional cost of travel to work, they were beyond the reach of the mass of the working class. In the meantime, 20,000 people in Liverpool and 200,000 in Glasgow lived three to a room,[14] and there were still 5.7 million houses classed as slums.

The general effect of the crisis on real wages was far more serious for the worse-off sections of the working class, for a variety of reasons. First, there was a far greater pressure to cut money wages in the most backward industries such as coal mining and cotton manufacture. Second, such industries also had far more short-time working. Thirdly, the means test meant that many workers still employed in areas of high unemployment had to support relatives who were out of work. Hence, although prices fell throughout the period, and especially during the early 1930s, it was only those in steady employment, living in areas of low unemployment such as London, the Midlands and the South East, who benefited.[15] For vast sections of the working class, little had changed since before the war, while for some, for instance in the mining and cotton industries, conditions had become distinctly worse.

The slump of 1929–31 was in fact to greatly accentuate the parasitic features of British imperialism. From covering 70 per cent of the value of imports in the 1920s, exports covered about 60 per cent in the 1930s, whilst the balance of invisible exports (including income on overseas investment) rose from just over 50 per cent of visible export income to just over 60 per cent on average. Despite the fact that there were substantial defaults on overseas loans with some being written off altogether, accumulated overseas investment fell only slightly, from £3.738 billion in 1929 to £3.692 billion in 1938 – possibly a slight rise in real terms. Once again, British usury provided a cushion; monopoly control of Empire food and raw material prices enabled it to make maximum advantage of the general fall in world

14. Branson and Heinemann, *op cit*, p203.

15. See Branson and Heinemann, *op cit*, pp150-164 for a good discussion of this point.

prices for such commodities. Well might Hobson's description of the Home Counties in 1900 apply in 1938:

> 'Could the incomes expended in the Home Counties and other large districts of Southern Britain be traced to their sources, it would be found they were in large measure wrung from the enforced toil of a vast multitude of black, brown or yellow natives, by arts not differing essentially from those which supported in idleness and luxury Imperial Rome.'[16]

And equally, Palme Dutt denounced:

> '... the system of parasitism which has grown up to the most extreme point as the characteristic expression of British imperialism more than any other – the system of increasing dependence on world tribute alongside of actual productive decay. Imports unpaid by exports; declining role of industry and production; increasing role of the rentier and financial profits; declining exports and rising imports; decline of the basic industries (coal, iron, steel, engineering, shipbuilding, textiles) and the rise of the luxury "industries" (hotels, restaurants, shops, stores, artificial silk, motor cars, personal service, commerce, finance); mass unemployment and multi-millionaires; falling real wages and rising super-tax incomes – this has been every year more and more the picture of modern capitalist Britain, a picture of rotten capitalist decay ...'[17]

5.2 *Labour between the wars*

As we have seen, the Labour Party was originally the creation of the skilled unions. By the end of the war, however, the new general unions, organising mainly semi-skilled workers, had gained much greater influence. These were not the general unions of 1889, but

16. Quoted in Lenin, *Imperialism*, *op cit*, p280.
17. R Palme Dutt, *Crisis – Tariffs – War*, CPGB, 1932, p7.

ones whose traditions were based on those of the old skilled unions, with a substantial bureaucracy which had gained extensive experience in running the affairs of the imperialist state during the Great War. Their leaders, epitomised by Ernest Bevin, were the new 'labour lieutenants' of the capitalist class, and it was they who were to ensure that the incipient revolutionary challenge to British imperialism in 1919–21 was stifled and then destroyed.

For two brief years, the British working class was in turmoil: demobilising soldiers mutinied, then rioted when they found no jobs in the 'land fit for heroes'. Even the police went on strike, escalating ruling class' fears that events were moving beyond their control. In May 1920, dockers boycotted *The Jolly George* with its shipment of arms to Poland to help it in its war against the Bolsheviks. By summer, it was evident that the Government, having already sent troops to Archangel in the north and Baku in the south of the Soviet Union, was contemplating a far more extensive military commitment in support of Polish aggression. After the appalling slaughter of the war, there was no question of the working class tolerating a call to defend imperialist interests again, especially against the Soviet Union. On 13 August, a special joint Labour Party and TUC conference called for a general strike if such intervention took place, people like JH Thomas and Ramsay MacDonald taking the lead, for fear of losing all control altogether. The Government backed off.

The end of 1920 spelled the end of the brief, inflationary post-war boom. By March 1921, unemployment had leapt to over 11 per cent, compared to 2.4 per cent on average the previous year and 5.8 per cent in December. The Government announced it would terminate the subsidies which had enabled the coal mines to keep in operation from 31 March. The mine owners immediately announced new rates of pay, which would cut wages in some areas by up to 50 per cent. The miners refused to accept, and invoked the Triple Alliance of railway and transport workers to come to their aid. After two days of confusion, on Black Friday, 15 April, the union leaders called off a strike they had sanctioned on the Wednesday, and 'brought an epoch in the labour movement's history to an end.'[18] What would in effect have been a general strike was avoided. A million miners were left to fight alone, before being crushed three months later. Within months, they had been followed by the engineers.

Black Friday put the labour aristocracy back in control. By the time of Red Friday – 31 August 1925, when a threat of a general strike forced the Government to commit itself to nine months' subsidies for miners' wages – and the General Strike itself the following year, the Labour and trade union leadership were in a far more assured position. The defeat of the General Strike was a precondition for the re-establishment of some of the fortunes of British imperialism. Preparing the confrontation with meticulous care, the British ruling class was confident that it could rely on the official labour movement to deliver the final blow. The General Council of the TUC, mindful of its obligations to British imperialism and its constitution, duly obliged: the miners were to fight on for another six months, under constant attack from the leadership of the Labour Party. The organised working class was to play no further significant role between the wars.

5.3 *The struggle of the unemployed*

This did not mean the end of all resistance to the effects of the reconstruction of British imperialism, but it did mean that it had to be organised from outside the official movement. In practice, it fell to the Communist-led National Unemployed Workers' Committee Movement (NUWM) to mount any challenge. As in 1889 or 1913, the official movement was to stand against the interests of the poorer sections of the working class and seek to isolate them. And equally, it was to take revolutionaries to give expression to their demands and to organise them into any kind of force.

18. At greater length, Cole argued that Black Friday brought the 'period of post war industrial militancy to a decisive end', and that the impact of the defeat was compounded by the onset of the slump which saw unemployment soar from 5 per cent in 1920 to 17 per cent in 1921. (GDH Cole, *A History of Socialist Thought*, *op cit*, vol 4 Part 1 p430).

There had already been a number of riots and demonstrations at the end of the war over unemployment; in October 1920, a demonstration in support of London mayors lobbying the Ministry of Health for better treatment of the unemployed was viciously attacked by the police. A special joint conference of the Labour Party and TUC was held in January 1921 to discuss unemployment:

> 'The conference was to report back on the feelings of Labour Party and trade union members about taking "direct action" on unemployment. Yet the meeting place was kept secret, and a motion passed against hearing from the unemployed themselves. Strike action was rejected, and people simply advised to join the Labour Party. Jimmy Thomas, the right wing leader of the railwaymen, was in the chair and refused to allow any motion other than an officially prepared one to be put. The meeting ended in uproar caused by delegates incensed by Thomas's ruling, and was followed by a march by 10,000 workless from outside the congress hall (the venue had not been a very well-kept secret) to Hyde Park .'[19]

Right from the beginning, the official movement had made its position clear; not surprisingly, Wal Hannington described the conference 'not only an absolute farce but an abdication.'[20] On 15 April 1921, Black Friday, delegates from local unemployed committees met to discuss the formation of a national movement. 'Even as the unemployed movement was being established, then, the trade union leaders were demonstrating that they had no real support to offer fellow trade unionists in, let alone out of, work.'[21]

One of the first acts of the new movement was to organise a march from London to Brighton in the summer where the Labour Party Conference was meeting; a deputation which addressed the conference bitterly attacked both the Labour and trade union leaderships,

---

19. R Croucher, *We Refuse to Starve in Silence*, Lawrence and Wishart, 1987, p39.
20. *ibid*, p40.
21. *ibid*.

demanding some action: all they got was a collection from the delegates. Reflecting on this, one of the founders of the NUWM, Albert Hawkins appealed to the official movement to accept the NUWM as an affiliate body, arguing that 'Either the movement will take a recognised place in the ranks of the organised workers, or it will develop in the future upon independent and antagonistic lines. Whichever happens will depend on the attitude of the Labour Party.'[22]

Yet Labour was already showing its attitude in Poplar, east London. The Poplar Board of Guardians since the end of the war had paid outdoor relief (relief which did not require the recipient to enter the work-house) at a rate adequate to support the unemployed – much higher than the accepted norm. The growth in unemployment in 1920–21 meant that either it cut these rates, or defaulted on payments to certain London-wide Metropolitan funds. The Guardians, led by George Lansbury, chose the latter course, and were imprisoned for their pains. Throughout, they had massive local working class support, which forced the Government to introduce a scheme whereby funds were diverted from affluent middle class boroughs to the poorer ones. But this did not prevent the Labour leadership attacking their stand, and when Labour did less well than expected in the 1922 election, JH Thomas argued:

> 'Of course many of our political opponents will construe the election as a rebellion on the part of the people against the Labour policy ... I do not interpret the result as a determination on the part of the people not to trust Labour, but I do frankly admit that it is a revolt against the kind of Poplar method of administration, which certainly alarmed people.'[23]

In response, Lansbury argued that 'Sooner or later the Labour Party must face all the implications of administrative responsibility. The workers must be given tangible proof that Labour administration

22. A Hawkins in *Labour Monthly*, November 1922, p277.
23. Quoted in *Labour Monthly*, June 1922, p383.

means something different from Capitalist administration, and in a nutshell this means diverting wealth from wealthy ratepayers to the poor. Those who pretend that a sound Labour policy can be pursued either nationally or locally without making the rich poorer should find another party.'[24]

But in the conflict between Lansbury's hopes and sordid reality, reality triumphed as always. Poplar was isolated, no other councillors being prepared to court illegality, and when in 1925 the High Court ruled that Poplar would have to cut the rates it paid to its council workers, Lansbury succumbed. Forgetting his own advice of three years before, Lansbury pleaded successfully for the Poplar workers not to strike, the start of an odyssey which was to lead him to urge Labour councils to apply the means test – but humanely.

In late 1922, the NUWM organised the first national hunger march: throughout the winter marches from various localities arrived in London, to be greeted by large demonstrations. The constant pressure saw the TUC make a small concession by establishing a Joint Action Committee with the NUWM; the last thing it was intended do, or in fact did, was organise action, joint or otherwise.

Although unemployment had fallen somewhat by the time of the first Labour Government of 1924, it was still in excess of 10 per cent. The Government instituted some reforms to unemployment insurance: the period of benefit was extended from 26 to 41 weeks, and the weekly rates were improved. On the other hand, a clause in the relevant Bill allowed benefit to be refused if it was felt that the claimant was not genuinely seeking work; the 'not genuinely seeking work' clause would shortly be used to exclude hundreds of thousands from receiving benefit. Furthermore, the Government did not change the situation whereby out-door poor relief could be offered as a loan or in kind; nor did it abolish the Guardian's discretion in refusing out-door relief and offering the workhouse.

However, it was the Blanesburgh Unemployment Insurance Committee, set up in November 1925, and which reported at the

24. *ibid*, p388.

beginning of 1927, which was to herald a vicious attack on the unemployed. Benefits were to be reduced, savagely so for those in the 18-21 age range, and contributions were to be raised to help reduce the insurance fund debt. More seriously, the system of extended benefit, whereby claimants under certain conditions could get more than 26 weeks' benefit in any one year, was to be abolished; instead, claimants might be entitled to a new 'transitional' benefit provided they had made more than 30 contributions in the previous two years. This would eliminate seasonal workers and the long-term unemployed, since the entitlement to transitional benefit would be reviewed every 13 weeks to determine whether the 30-contribution rule still applied. Stringent conditions were attached to the receipt of normal benefit: in particular, the 'not genuinely seeking work' clause was stiffened by requiring claimants to give positive evidence of seeking work. Finally, it disallowed benefit for strikers completely.

Workers whose benefit had terminated would under normal circumstances have recourse to Poor Law relief; the Committee proposed that those who were struck off benefit as a result of their proposals should be denied it:

> 'We understand that the Poor Law Acts and regulations made thereunder prohibit, except in special cases, the unconditional outdoor relief of able-bodied persons, and although the Minister of Health has found it necessary, during the extreme post-war depression, to assent to a widespread use of the regulation permitting unconditional relief in special cases, we think ... that in so far as it deals with the able-bodied unemployed, Poor Law relief should retain the deterrent effect which now attaches to it, or may be applied thereto.'[25]

What made this so outrageous was that there were three Labour representatives on the Committee, all of whom signed the report: Frank Hodges, former secretary of the Miners' Federation, AE Holmes,

25. Quoted in W Hannington, *Unemployed Struggles*, EP Publishing, 1977, p171.

and Margaret Bondfield, a member of the TUC General Council who was to become Minister of Labour in the 1929–31 Labour Government. A special joint conference of the Labour Party and the TUC in April 1927, called under pressure to discuss the report, ruled a motion of censure on the three submitted by the Miners' Federation out of order, and in the end merely called on the Parliamentary Labour Party to try to amend the report.

At the same time, the Conservative Government sought to bring the local Boards of Guardians which administered Poor Law relief under more centralised control. Agitation by the NUWM had forced many Boards to use their discretionary powers over the distribution of relief in favour of the unemployed. Elected representatives to the Boards were replaced by appointed commissioners, who were to practice a ruthless economy.

The effect of these changes was dramatic. Between March 1927 and March 1928, 441,000 people were disqualified from receiving unemployed benefit; another 205,000 were disqualified in the next four months, most on the grounds of 'not genuinely seeking work', by which time one and a half million people were thrown on to Poor Law relief.[26] Yet this was a matter of indifference to the Labour and trade union leaders. The defeat of the General Strike had allowed them to move decisively in isolating the Communists, issuing a series of bans and proscriptions. In March 1927, just before the special conference on the Blanesburgh Report, the TUC unilaterally wound up the Joint Action Committee with the NUWM, General Secretary Citrine saying it would not serve any useful purpose. When, in November 1927, the NUWM organised the second national hunger march, made up of miners from South Wales – there were by this time 350,000 miners out of work – the TUC and Labour Party circulated affiliates instructing them not to support it.

In September 1927, the TUC opened discussions with some industrialists who represented the monopoly or cartelised sections of British industry, led by Sir Alfred Mond, founder of the new ICI. In a

26. *ibid*, p176.

letter to the TUC he wrote: 'We realise that industrial reconstruction can only be undertaken with the co-operation of those empowered to speak for organised labour ... We believe that the common interests which bind us are more powerful than the apparent divergent interests that separate.'[27] The General Council concurred with the Mond group that the tendency towards rationalisation and trustification in industry 'should be welcomed and encouraged'. Although no formal machinery arose from the discussions, the talks, whose direction was supported at the 1928 TUC Congress, gave a clear indication of where the TUC's priorities lay. This self-same TUC Congress in Swansea had to be protected from the unemployed by the police acting in co-operation with Henderson and Citrine.

The NUWM organised a further national hunger march, directed specifically against the 'not genuinely seeking work' clause, starting in January 1929. Once again, the TUC and Labour leadership instructed local affiliates not to render any assistance. The Ministry of Health, responsible for administering Poor Law relief, weighed in by instructing local authorities to treat hunger marchers as 'casuals' or tramps; this meant that a series of regulations were to be applied:

i) every man had to be searched on entering the workhouse, and he had to give his name and address;
ii) the regulation diet could not be exceeded (two slices of bread and margarine and a cup of tea for supper and breakfast).
iii) no man could leave the institution on the day of entering.
iv) a task had to be performed next morning before leaving.
v) no smoking, singing or meetings could be held in the institutions.

Contingents set off from Scotland, Durham, Yorkshire, Liverpool, Manchester, South Wales and Plymouth; all refused to accept the Ministry of Health regulations, and faced every evening a battle over accommodation which they generally won. They encountered police sabotage, especially in Birmingham; but the final demonstration in London on 24 February mobilised tens of thousands of workers

27. Quoted in A Bullock, *The Life and Times of Ernest Bevin*, MacMillan, Vol 1 p393.

despite the opposition of the official movement.

Six weeks later, the then Chancellor of the Exchequer, Winston Churchill, in his budget speech, extolled the virtues of Empire:

> 'The income which we derive each year from commissions and services rendered to foreign countries is over £65 million. In addition, we have a steady revenue from foreign investments of close on £300 million a year ... That is the explanation of the source from which we are able to defray social services at a level incomparably higher than that of any European country or any country.'[28]

Very little of it got to the unemployed.

5.4 *The unemployed and the 1929–31 Labour Government*

Within three weeks of the hunger march, the second Labour Government had come into office. Nothing of substance was to change. Between June and September 1928, 58,000 claimants had been disqualified for 'not genuinely seeking work'; the corresponding figure for the same four months of 1929 under Labour was nearly 80,000. Arthur Greenwood as Minister for Health proved equally vicious as his Ministry of Labour counterparts. He opposed an established scale of Poor Law relief, leaving it entirely to the discretion of the Boards of Guardians. He insisted on the continuation of 'test and task' work by able-bodied claimants – a form of forced labour which was a condition for obtaining relief. Lastly, he threatened to remove Boards of Guardians which discontinued the collection of relief debts incurred by miners. This was particularly odious. Miners who had been locked out in the great struggles of 1921 and 1926, or lost their jobs as a consequence, had often received poor relief in the form of a loan. Their wages savagely reduced when they were able to get work, they were frequently incapable of repaying such debts. Some Labour-dominated boards had stopped trying to deduct the repayments;

28. Quoted in R Palme Dutt, *The Crisis of Britain, op cit*, p80.

when they applied to the Labour Government for the cancellation of the debt, they were threatened with surcharge and suspension.

In February 1930, the NUWM organised a further march against the 'not genuinely seeking work' clause in the light of the Government's refusal to abolish it. Greenwood followed the example of his Tory predecessor in ruling that the marchers were to be treated as 'casuals', with as little success. Although smaller than its predecessors, it was during the march that the Government finally abolished the 'not genuinely seeking work' clause; the final demonstration on 1 May was estimated at some 50,000 strong.

Under Labour, unemployment soared as capitalist rationalisation was officially encouraged; by December 1930, it had reached 2.6 million, nearly 20 per cent of the workforce. The Government appointed the Gregory Commission to study the solvency of the unemployment insurance scheme; it reported in June 1931 with a whole series of proposals limiting benefits and eligibility to them, to bring annual savings of £42 million. On behalf of the Government, Margaret Bondfield said: 'The Government agree in principle with the recommendations of the Royal Commission and we propose to place before the House proposals to give legislative effect substantially to these recommendations.' This took the form of the Anomalies Act; passed into operation in October 1931, it resulted in the disallowance of benefit to 77,000 claimants within six weeks, and 134,000 by the end of the year.

However, it was the report of the May Committee that spelt the end of the Government: recommending a 20 per cent cut in unemployment benefit together with the application of a means test for the extension of that benefit, cuts in wages for teachers, civil servants and the armed forces and sundry other economies, it forced the Government to act to balance the budget. The final Cabinet vote, on a 10 per cent cut in benefit, gave a small majority in favour; but the condition of US bank loans to bail out the Government was unanimous support, and on that basis, MacDonald dissolved it.

5.5 *The unemployed and the National Government*

The provisional National Government took over on 8 September 1931; the day beforehand, Citrine had once more called in the police to protect the TUC Congress in Bristol as 20,000 workers protested outside. Huge demonstrations of the unemployed took place up and down the country, organised by the NUWM: 50,000 in Glasgow, fighting off police attacks, 30,000 in Manchester. *The Daily Herald*, whose editorial policy was now firmly controlled through Odham's Press by Citrine and Bevin, condemned them: 'The remedy is in [the unemployed's] hands. Not in rioting and futile demonstrations, not in pointless collisions with the police, who are also victims, but in a determined effort to win the election for Labour.'[29]

Throughout September and October, huge demonstrations of the unemployed continued, frequently attacked by the police. Naval ratings mutinied on 12 September in protest at a shilling a day wage cut, which amounted to a 20 per cent reduction; they were quickly deemed a 'special case', and the cut greatly reduced. Teachers and civil servants too demonstrated; their cuts were limited to 10 per cent. The Government also pressed ahead with a 10 per cent cut in unemployment benefit, reducing the allowance for an adult man from 17 shillings to 15 shillings 3d, that for his wife from nine shillings to eight shillings, although the children's allowance of two shillings was left untouched. But the main economy was in the application of the means test. Unemployment benefit was now automatically cut off after 26 weeks, to be replaced by a new 'transitional benefit'; this transitional benefit would only be granted after an exhaustive test of the means of the family by the Poor Law authority, and could not exceed unemployment benefit.

On the day after the benefit cuts took place, 8 October, 150,000 marched in Glasgow and 100,000 in London three days later. Fire-hoses and mounted police failed to disperse 80,000 in Manchester; there were baton charges in Port Glasgow on 15 October, and in

29. Quoted in Cliff and Gluckstein, *op cit*, p161.

London and Cardiff the next day. On 27 October, the general election returned the National Government with a landslide, and on 12 November the means test came into operation. More demonstrations, more police attacks: but it was the NUWM organising the protests, not the official movement. Between 12 November 1931 and 23 January 1932, 270,000 were excluded by the means test from claiming any benefit whatsoever; by 20 February 1932, this had risen to 377,000. Some 900,000 of the unemployed were on transitional benefit, so that less than half the unemployed were left drawing full unemployment benefit.

The Public Assistance Committees (PACs) had extensive discretion in deciding the scale of transitional relief for the unemployed: in Lancashire, fewer than 16 per cent received the maximum, and a third were excluded altogether from the means test. It was this discretion that led to rioting in Birkenhead and Belfast in 1932. In Birkenhead, a demonstration in September protested against the fact that the local PAC rates were three shillings below the maximum. It was viciously attacked by the police; four days of rioting and fighting with the police took place which forced the PAC to raise its scales. Where PACs had been appointed from Labour-controlled authorities they tended to pay maximum transitional benefit and either ignore the means test or interpret it liberally. However, the Ministry of Health cracked down, and replaced some of the PACs with appointed commissioners to administer the test properly:

> 'One by one the other recalcitrant PACs drew in their horns and appeared to be toeing the line. West Ham made a public statement: "We were threatened with supersession, and in face of that threat we prefer to keep the poor under our own care and do what we can for them rather than hand them over to an arbitrary Commissioner from whom they could expect little humanity".'[30]

However, it must not be thought that Labour control of the local PAC

30. Branson and Heinemann, *op cit*, p38.

necessarily meant greater sympathy for the plight of the unemployed, as the murder of Arthur Speight in Castleford, Yorkshire in the summer showed:

> 'During a demonstration to the PAC, the Labour representatives on the PAC voted against receiving a delegation from the unemployed and that evening the unemployed demonstrated to the Trades and Labour Council in protest at the attitude of the Labour representatives. When the Council broke up, shouting at the Labour men became hostile, and the police (mainly from outlying districts) made a fierce baton charge which left women, men and children badly beaten and an NUWM member, Arthur Speight, dead. Several local leaders of the movement were arrested, and the following day the Labour magistrate refused to grant any adjournment to the severely injured defendants and proceeded to sentence them immediately.'[31]

A further national march was organised for September and October: it coincided with the huge battle in Birkenhead, which was followed by one in Belfast, where for the first and only time ever, Nationalists and Loyalists together fought the army and police after a severe cut in Poor Law relief. The march itself was also attacked by the police when it reached London and, when NUWM leader Wal Hannington was arrested, rioting took place throughout central London in protest.

NUWM organisation against the cuts continued with a further national march in early 1934; when it reached London, MacDonald as Prime Minister refused to receive a delegation, citing as precedent the actions of both the TUC and the Labour Party. Nevertheless, following a huge demonstration on 16 April, the Government was forced to restore the cuts of 1931, despite a declaration just beforehand that it saw no need to.

New regulations, to be introduced in early 1935 when there were still nearly two million unemployed, proposed a more stringent means

31. Croucher, *op cit*, p132.

test, and the establishment of 'training' or labour camps for those who were on transitional benefit having exhausted their 26 week entitlement. Once more it fell to the NUWM to campaign against them; the official labour movement offered no response. The capacity of the NUWM to mobilise tens of thousands of people remained undiminished: 10,000 marched in North Shields, breaking a police ban, followed by 300,000 in various parts of South Wales on Sunday 3 February. Cuts in transitional benefit were withdrawn as a result of the rising level of opposition.

The NUWM mobilised the unemployed and sections of the organised working class throughout this period because there was no other force capable of representing their political interests. The Labour Party at each and every stage, along with the TUC, sought to isolate and destroy the NUWM, aided by the police and forces of the state. Many NUWM leaders served prison sentences as they stood with the unemployed.

In contrast, Labour Party representatives co-operated in the administration of the means test; George Lansbury arguing at the 1932 conference that 'whilst it was true that when you are in a minority you cannot do much, you can do a little to soften the business' (ie, administer the means test).[32] There was no practical challenge from the Labour left either: to take up the cause of the unemployed would have involved a break with the Party which was trying to crush their struggle.

The bitter hostility of the labour aristocracy towards the unemployed was all the more evident in their attitude to the 1936 Jarrow Crusade. This was the one march not organised by the NUWM: it was organised as a 'non-political' march which excluded known Communists, accepted every police rule, and in return was supported by the churches and local Tory and Labour parties. Yet still Labour and the TUC circularised their local affiliates instructing them not to support the march or to provide it with any assistance, to the extent that in at least one place, where the local Labour Party and Trades Council

32. Quoted in Miliband, *op cit*, p212.

refused to assist the march, it was the local Tory Party which organised food and accommodation.

Labour's response to the struggle of the unemployed has been often condemned but little understood. For instance, James Hinton has suggested that 'During the 1930s unemployed activism and local authority defiance of central government continued, but no effective way was found to direct this militancy into the national politics of the Labour Party',[33] while John Saville has described their opposition to Jarrow as the best example of Labour's 'stupid, reactionary and politically self-destructive' attitude in this period,[34] and Ralph Miliband argued that 'Given the fact that Britain was in 1931 one of the richest countries in the world ... it is surely amazing that there were actually found rational men to argue that the saving of a few million pounds a year on the miserable pittance allowed to unemployed men and women and their children was the essential condition of British solvency.'[35]

Yet what else could have been the case? Maintaining the pre-1931 levels of unemployment benefit would have undermined the solvency of the most depressed industries which now absolutely depended on speed-up and wage cuts. The stagnant condition of the British economy meant that adequate conditions could not be sustained for the mass of the working class, but only for a minority. Militancy did not find its way in to Labour politics because it was well and truly kept out, with the use of the police if necessary. Resistance by the poorer sections was a threat to the conditions of the better-off layers of the working class which Labour represented. Once again, none of these authors understand the political significance of a divided working class. Labour's attitude was certainly reactionary, but equally certainly not 'politically self-destructive' – after all, within ten years of the Jarrow march, it was to achieve a landslide parliamentary majority.

33. J Hinton, *Labour and Socialism – A History of the British Labour Movement 1867–1974*, Wheatsheaf, 1983, p135.

34. In A Briggs and J Saville (eds), *Essays in Labour History 1918–39*, Croom Helm, 1977, p240.

35. Miliband, *op cit*, p185.

PART SIX

Labour and the working class 1945–97

Introduction

Between the electoral landslides of 1945 and 1997 a process occurred whereby the Labour Party changed from one reactionary form – so-called 'Old' Labour – into an equally reactionary form – 'New' Labour. 'Old' Labour was a continuation of the alliance between the labour aristocracy – a small, privileged stratum of the working class organised in skilled trade unions – and a radical section of the petit bourgeoisie that founded the Labour Party to represent its interests. Until the late 1980s, the trade unions were the major force in the alliance, bankrolling the party and dominating conferences with the block vote. Under 'New' Labour the petit bourgeoisie became the predominant force: public sector managers and directors, accountants, management consultants, lawyers, journalists, the upper echelons of the media, NGOs and so on. The trade union leadership remained important only for its financial backing even though the unions continued to organise more affluent workers particularly in the public sector. Labour had broken all connection with the working class.

The seeds of this process were sown during the post-war boom as the structure of the working class started to change: manufacturing employment declined continuously whilst public sector white-collar employment rose. The process accelerated rapidly with the onset of the crisis in the mid to late 1970s, as the more parasitic features of British capitalism came to the fore and British imperialism utilised its dominance in the financial services market to shore up its domestic position. From 1979, the Tory Government progressively lifted regulations on the operations of the City of London and, along with a massive outflow of investments, employment in finance and business services expanded massively in the 1980s and 1990s, creating many highly-paid jobs. Despite Tory rhetoric, public sector employment also continued to rise. Labour had lost the 1979 election because a large section of the skilled and more affluent layers of the working class felt that their privileged position was more secure with the Tories. Unless Labour was able to recover the electoral support of wide sections of the new petit bourgeoisie and labour aristocracy it would never run the country again. It had to show that it could sustain the privileged material conditions of the labour aristocracy and new petit bourgeoisie by adequately defending the interests of British imperialism. Old Labour had to transform itself into New Labour.

6.1 *The background to Labour's 1945 electoral triumph*

The decisive factor in allowing Labour to obtain its huge parliamentary majority in 1945 was the vote of the middle class. In strongly working class constituencies like Glasgow or Liverpool, the swing to Labour was 2.5 to 6.5 per cent, but in some of the South East constituencies, it was as high as 20 per cent. 'Over two million middle class voters had voted Labour, many for the first time.'[1] Birmingham, which had failed to return a Labour MP in 1935, elected ten on an average swing of 23 per cent. In the counties, Labour took 110 seats as opposed to the Tories' 112, but polled more votes: 4.6 million against 4.4 million.[2] Twelve million people voted Labour; a substantial section of the middle class had rejected the Tories as its vote fell by 1.5 million.

This was in marked contrast with the previous election of 1935.

---

1. Morgan, *op cit*, p41.
2. A Sked and C Cook, *Post-War Britain, A Political History*, Harvester, 1979, p15.

Then, Labour had captured 8.3 million votes and 154 seats. This was an improvement on the 6.6 million votes it had gained in 1931 (with 52 seats), but still below its 1929 vote, when it had also won far more seats – 288. Overall, its 1935 electoral recovery had been limited, and was explained partly by the increase in the size of the overall electorate, and partly by increased support in the coalfield areas. Labour made no headway in the prosperous South and Midlands. In the South of England outside London the Conservatives won 156 seats, Labour 15; inside London the figures were 39 and 22 respectively. In the Midlands, the seats divided more than three to one in favour of the government, a figure nearly matched in the North West. Labour failed to gain the votes of workers employed in the new industries and the service sector who lived in the southern part of the country who had had little contact with the means test or the Public Assistance Committees. Pointing out that a redistribution of parliamentary seats would benefit the Tories rather than Labour, the Coles argued that

> 'As long as the suburbanites and the workers in the newer industries believe themselves to be tolerably secure in the conditions in which they are at present living, they will be in no mood for experiments which seem to them to threaten these conditions, however much the advocates of such experiments may hold out the prospect of a better society. They will vote predominantly for things as they are ...'[3]

They concluded that only a war could alter this state of affairs and bring about conditions in which Labour would become electable, because:

> 'What most deeply imperils the British standard of living is the threat of war ... Under present conditions international politics are in reality the key to the domestic situation, for the prospects of the British people depend on what happens in international

3. GDH and MI Cole, T*he Condition of Britain*, Left Book Club, 1937, p421.

> affairs. This is what the electors in the relatively comfortable areas must be made to see if they are to be detached from their present almost unreflective allegiance to things as they are.'[4]

The legacy of appeasement, the incompetence that led to Dunkirk, the free rein given to left social democratic intellectuals to broadcast and write to recruit working class support for the war against fascism, all had a significant impact on the middle class. On top of this came the Beveridge report on social security and its treatment in the House of Commons. When it was published at the end of 1942, the response of the government coalition (in which Labour participated) was indifference. During the parliamentary debate in February 1943, Labour backbenchers forced a division on an amendment demanding immediate legislation. All the Parliamentary Labour Party (PLP) outside the government joined the rebellion, while the Tories opposed it. Tainted already by their support for appeasement, the Tories were now seen to oppose Beveridge as well; for substantial sections of the middle class 'to believe in Beveridge was to have faith in a successful outcome to the war; more than that, it meant believing in a democratic distribution of the spoils of victory'.[5]

It took a world war to create an electoral constituency broad enough to return a majority Labour Government. This is important, because as the Coles had earlier pointed out, piling up the votes of the poor working class was never enough for a Labour victory: it had to win the votes of the privileged strata and a significant section of the middle class as well, a point that Ken Livingstone made much later in 1992: 'These bases of Labour's great success – led by Attlee in 1945 and Wilson in 1966 – came when we established a coalition between the highly-paid and skilled, and low-paid and unskilled sections of the working class electorate.'[6]

---

4. *ibid*, p423.
5. Sked and Cook, *op cit*, p20.
6. *Morning Star*, 28 April 1992.

6.2 *The post-war Labour Government*

The composition of Labour MPs reflected the new-found radicalism of the middle class. Chuter Ede, to become an extremely conservative, pro-hanging Home Secretary, spoke of the PLP teeming 'with bright, vivacious servicemen. The superannuated Trade Union official seems hardly to be noticeable in the ranks.'[7] Despite the extensive middle class influence and activism within the Fabians and the ILP, the first Labour MP who might be described as middle class was only elected in 1922. In 1945, of 393 MPs, 119 were trade union sponsored, as against 44 lawyers, 49 university lecturers, 25 journalists, 15 doctors and 18 company directors and businessmen.[8]

The Government set about its nationalisation proposals: the Bank of England – 'an essentially technical and institutional' change, and one which Churchill argued he could not oppose; Cable and Wireless – for 'the co-ordination of imperial cable and wireless services' – another one which the Tories could not oppose; the imperial factor enabled them to accede to the creation of British Overseas Airways Corporation and British European Airways without difficulty as well. These were followed by the creation of the Central Electricity Generating Board: 'Any opposition to the bill was mollified by the remarkably generous terms of compensation given to private stockholders, whether company or individuals',[9] the nationalisation of gas and coal: Government policy was to defuse opposition by making concessions 'over compensation paid to private stockholders in coal, gas and electricity (which, in retrospect, seem almost inconceivably generous, especially in relation to coal).'[10]

The compensation for coal was indeed extraordinarily generous, the Government paying £164 million, and £1 billion for the railways and canals; these were industries which in the words of one commentator 'were badly run down, or badly organised, or under-

7. Morgan, *op cit*, p59.
8. *ibid*, p60.
9. *ibid*, p103.
10. *ibid*, p109.

developed and in need of new investment.'[11] Such industries could no longer be run privately without severe rationalisation and consequent dislocation for the whole of British industry, as well as the creation of mass unemployment. Labour nationalised for the greater good of British capital as a whole, and to maintain full employment.

The Government also greatly extended the provision of state welfare, the 1946 National Insurance and National Health Service Acts and the 1948 National Assistance Act being particular landmarks. More than this, the Government was able to preside over conditions of near full employment. From 1948, when industrial recovery really got under way, Britain was the only significant European industrial power. As Ian Aitken put it, 'Most of Europe was still in ruins, there were no dollars to buy American goods, and Britain's clapped-out factories were therefore able to sell everything they could produce.'[12] The world shortage of dollars meant that for a short period, British industry met with little challenge, especially in its preferred Empire markets and within Europe itself. Unemployment in North East England, which had been 38 per cent in 1932, was 3 per cent in 1949; in industrial Scotland, the figures were 35 per cent and 4.5 per cent respectively, and in South Wales, 41 per cent and 5.5 per cent. In Scotland, for instance, 536 factories were built through the Scottish Development Agency providing employment for 150,000. By 1951, overall unemployment was 1.8 per cent.

Whether or not real wages for the working class rose slightly, fell slightly, or stayed the same, the fact remains that for large sections, real household income was much higher than prior to the war simply because they did not to have to support unemployed members of the family through the means test. The TUC therefore experienced little pressure when it co-operated with the Government in controlling wage rises. Where the union leadership failed, the Government had recourse to the 1920 Emergency Powers Act which it renewed in 1946, and proved perfectly willing to use troops – Aneurin Bevan as

11. Brady, *Crisis in Britain, 1950*, quoted in Coates, *op cit*, p53.
12. *The Guardian*, 1 June 1992.

well as any – to break strikes, most notoriously during the April 1950 dockers' dispute. The end of mass unemployment was the key factor in sustaining a reasonably stable standard of living for masses of workers, far more than state welfare itself. As Morgan notes:

> '... it was notorious that more affluent or middle class people received substantial help from universal welfare benefits. This especially applied to benefits in kind rather than cash, such as a free health service, free secondary school places, and food subsidies. The opportunities in health or education for the middle class (for instance, in the way they were able to benefit from the eleven plus examination through financial or cultural domestic advantage) enabled the gulf between them and manual workers to continue, if not grow even wider.'[13]

Despite these achievements, Labour's parliamentary majority over the Tories was slashed in the 1950 general election from 183 to 17, even though Labour polled 1.3 million more votes than it had in 1945. The South East had started to swing to the Conservatives, especially in the London suburbs, more than cancelling out a small swing to Labour in South Wales and Scotland. It was the 92 mainly middle class seats which had swung to the Conservatives by over 7 per cent that counted towards the result, rather than the 48 that had swung to Labour. It was not that the middle class had been frightened: more that it had returned to its natural home. The Tories had rid themselves of the stigma of appeasement, and had made clear their commitment to state welfare. In the new-found conditions of economic progress, there was a middle-class rejection of the continuation of consumer controls, through rationing in particular.

The trend was accentuated in the 1951 general election: with the Liberals fielding only a little over 100 candidates, nearly two million of their votes went to the other two parties, dividing 6 to 4 in favour of the Tories.[14] Eleven of the 21 Labour losses to the Tories were in

13. Morgan, *op cit*, p185.
14. Morgan, *op cit*, p486.

London and the Home Counties. Thus it was that Labour, with a larger vote than in 1950, and one which still exceeded that of the Tories, found itself out of government in the midst of a balance of payments crisis triggered by the Korean War and the consequent increase in arms spending. Never before, and never since, had the working class voted so solidly for Labour: the Party may have lost the two million middle class votes of 1945, but it had gained nearly four million votes from the working class. Subsequent elections merely confirmed the trend: Labour dominated in the big towns and cities, Scotland, the North of England and South Wales, while the Tories dominated in the South of England, the rural areas and the suburbs.

The 1945-51 Labour Government had laid the foundations of the post-war boom by firmly allying British imperialism with the might of US imperialism on the one hand, and making sure that the Empire paid for the costs of reconstruction on the other. As Ernest Bevin, echoing Churchill, had commented in 1946, 'I am not prepared to sacrifice the British Empire because I know that if the British Empire fell ... it would mean the standard of life of our constituents would fall considerably.'[15] Hence the living standards of the British working class did not suffer during this period of reconstruction: the fruits of Empire had been sufficient for British imperialism to make the necessary concessions domestically to ensure relative social peace. Even when in 1951 there was a massive increase in the balance of payment deficit as a result of the Korean War, the Government was able to allow the dollar surplus of the sterling area to take part of the strain: if the extra imports had to be paid for by extra exports, domestic consumption would have had to be cut by £350 million, not the £50 million proposed.[16] Labour had delivered, but on the backs of the oppressed colonial people.

15. Quoted in R Palme Dutt, *The Crisis of Britain*, *op cit*, p80.
16. Gupta, *op cit*, p337.

6.3 *Labour and the boom*

Despite the significant growth in industrial output under the Labour Government, and the relative increase in its contribution to the British imperialist economy, the tendency towards parasitism was never completely suppressed, and, as the first signs of crisis appeared, re-asserted itself ever more strongly. British imperialism had not liquidated all its overseas assets during Second World War and 'net indebtedness was estimated to be very small in those early post-war years and was very soon made up by further foreign investment at a level unprecedented in absolute terms in British history ... Britain made the transition from being a net debtor to being a net creditor in the early 1950s.'[17]

In 1948 Britain's share of world exports was more than twice that of France and Italy combined, at a time when the West German and Japanese economies were still scarcely functioning. Even as late as 1953, when the UK's share of world industrial output was 10 per cent, this compared favourably with the rest of the European Economic Community (EEC) countries at 16 per cent; Japan was a lowly 2 per cent. Yet within ten years, the EEC share had risen to three times that of the UK, and Japan almost matched it. By 1970, EEC output was over four times that of Britain, and Japanese output was double. Underlying this relative decline were low domestic investment rates, and low increases in productivity when compared with Britain's major competitors. This exposed the limits of reconstruction in the immediate post-war period: the temporary industrial ascendancy over its European rivals coupled with the protection provided by monopoly control of imperial markets, meant that there was no immediate pressure to carry out significant rationalisation. More profitable investment could be found abroad, and that was where it went. Side-by-side with boom conditions went relative industrial decline; with relative decline came balance of

17. G Phillips and R Maddock, *The Growth of the British Economy 1918-1968*, George Allen and Unwin, 1973, p139.

payment problems, augmented by the continuing export of capital. These could be resolved only by periods of deflation: hence the so-called 'stop-go' economic policies of the 1950s and 1960s.

Although British economic growth was slower than that of its major competitors, it was more than sufficient to provide full employment; indeed, such was the demand for labour that British imperialism had to turn to external sources of supply. The dislocation at the end of the war provided for the first wave of immigrant labour. Between 1945 and 1957, there was a net influx of 350,000 European nationals, together with a similar number of Irish workers. But as the European economies themselves expanded, this source dried up. Conveniently, another was at hand: the British colonies in Asia, Africa and the Caribbean, where imperialist under-development had created a huge reserve army of labour. Immigration from these countries started in earnest at the beginning of the 1950s, and continued throughout the decade.[18]

From the beginning, immigrant workers formed an oppressed section of the working class. They went into the lowest-paid jobs with the worst conditions, as white workers tended to move to better jobs, particularly in the service sector. Black workers were directed into NHS ancillary work and lower grade nursing jobs, and other menial public sector jobs, for instance in British Railways. The availability of this pool of labour helped maintain the viability of state welfare, and thus proved an indirect benefit for the middle class and the more privileged layers of the working class.

Black workers were also extensively employed in the more backward sections of British manufacturing in the small metal foundries of the Midlands and Sheffield, and in the textile mills of the North West where there was an extensive requirement for shift working. Such patterns of work directed them also into the clothing sweatshops and the hotel and catering industry of London. The existence

18. The material on racism in this section is drawn from M Williams, S Palmer and G Clapton, 'Racism, Imperialism and the Working Class', *Revolutionary Communist* No 9, 1979.

of this pool of labour enabled sections of British capital to extend the life-span of their assets, and therefore avoid the investment that would be needed to modernise the production process. In other words, immigrant labour was a substitute for fixed capital investment. Thus, between 1961 and 1971, whereas employment in manufacturing fell overall by 745,000, the number of people employed in this sector who had been born outside of the UK rose by no less than 272,000.

By 1971, 71 per cent of black workers were concentrated in four major urban areas (Greater London, West Midlands, South East Lancashire and West Yorkshire), compared with 28 per cent of all economically active persons. For the age group 30–44, 43 per cent of all married women worked full-time, whereas the figure for those born in the New Commonwealth (ie those countries which had obtained independence in the post-war period) was 74 per cent. 50.6 per cent of all economically active males were manual workers; the figure for Caribbean workers was 78.9 per cent, for Pakistanis 76.3 per cent, and for Indians 57.2 per cent. Shift working, which had greatly increased throughout the boom, was more prevalent among black workers: 15 per cent of white manual workers were on shifts, compared with 31 per cent of black workers. Immigrant labour was overwhelmingly working class, concentrated in the worst jobs with the worst pay.

6.4 *Labour in government 1964–70*

By the early 1960s, the extent of decline was making the successive balance of payment deficits ever more severe. It was clear that the Tories were incapable of overseeing the necessary changes to the industrial infrastructure, and that British capital needed a new approach. In 1964, Labour returned to office with a slender majority on a programme of state-sponsored technological and economic development, to turn around the conditions which had contributed to Britain's industrial decline. It was faced with the worst balance of payments deficit yet, £800 million. Labour met this by borrowing from the central banks and the IMF, together with a voluntary wage freeze and a mildly deflationary package in July 1965. Two months later it published its National Plan, which envisaged nearly trebling annual investment rates, and increasing output by 25 per cent between 1964 and 1970.

Labour had won the 1964 election not so much because it had gained support – in fact its total vote of 12.2 million was virtually the same as in 1959 – but because a section of the middle class and privileged working class defected from the Tories to the Liberals. In the March 1966 election, this section then moved to Labour, enabling it to obtain a parliamentary majority of over 100. British imperialism could still afford to support the Keynesian consensus which was based on guaranteeing the relatively privileged conditions of higher paid workers and the petit bourgeoisie whilst sustaining adequate living standards for the mass of the working class. In 1966, both the privileged and less privileged layers of the working class voted Labour in sufficient numbers to give it its second-largest majority up to that point. Yet these conditions were now drawing to a close and the response of Labour was to attack the working class which formed its electoral base.

The first evidence of this attack was Prime Minister Wilson's vitriolic attack on the striking seamen in summer 1966, claiming that their action was being orchestrated by Communists. In July, the government announced a deflationary budget which included a legally binding wage freeze for six months, with a subsequent period of 'severe restraint'. A year later, the underlying trends had not improved; following adverse trade figures in June 1967, a run on the pound began, and continued throughout the autumn. Much as in 1949, Labour, defending the interests of the City of London which required a strong pound, would not countenance devaluation until the last possible moment.

Attempts to defend the pound continued until 18 November, when the Government bowed to the inevitable and devalued it from $2.80 to $2.40. The Government secured credits of up to $3 billion, $1.4 billion of which was from the IMF. Claims by Roy Jenkins, then Chancellor of the Exchequer, that no strings were attached to the loans, and that there would be no need for a deflationary policy, proved to be lies. In January 1968, Labour responded to demands that it cut domestic consumption by £750 million with an emergency budget which deferred the raising of the school leaving age (from 15 to 16) from 1971 to 1973, reintroduced prescription charges that had been abolished in 1965, increased dental charges, and withdrew free school milk from secondary schools. That it also accelerated the withdrawal of British forces from East of Suez and cancelled an order for F-111 fighter bombers was further recognition of British imperialism's increasing inability to pursue an independent policing role.

A corollary of this process was a reduced requirement for immigrant labour. The first formal restrictions on immigration had been set out in the 1962 Commonwealth Immigrants Act, which was then supplemented by Labour's 1965 Immigration Act. The 1962 Act had introduced a voucher system to control the flow of immigrant labour: 'C' vouchers were for unskilled workers. The 1965 Act abolished 'C' vouchers and imposed a limit of 8,500 on 'A' and 'B' vouchers (for skilled and professional workers), halving the numbers who had been admitted in 1964. The purpose, in the words of the Bill, was 'to control the entry of immigrants so that it does not outrun Britain's capacity to absorb them.' As Roy Hattersley said at the time in defence of immigration controls, 'Without integration, limitation is inexcusable, without limitation, integration is impossible.'[19]

In 1968, as employment in manufacturing continued to decline and unemployment started to rise, a further Act was introduced: the Commonwealth Immigration Act, which set out the explicitly racist provision permitting entry only if the immigrant had a 'substantial connection' to Britain – that is, at least one grandparent. It also tore up the British passports of East African Asians and placed them within the same system of controls as other Commonwealth citizens. To this measure was added the 1969 Immigration Appeals Act. This shifted the vetting of dependants from the port of entry to the

19. Quoted in M Williams, S Palmer and G Clapton, op cit, *Revolutionary Communist* No 9, p28

country of departure, making the process of proving a link between the dependant and sponsor far more difficult, since it imposed a delay of many months and was far more costly. In practice, it removed the right of admission to Britain from the spouses and fiancés of immigrants.

With the increasing economic difficulties came the first signs of political instability. From 1964 to 1970 the annual number of strikes more than doubled from 1,456 to 3,906; the number of days lost rose from 2.8 million in 1967 to 6.8 million in 1970. Many of the strikes were against the so-called 'productivity deals', or speed-ups whereby British capital attempted to make existing assets more profitable rather than making new investments. In addition, there was the development of massive opposition to the Government's support for the US's war against Vietnam, to be followed by the emergence of the Civil Rights campaign in the north of Ireland. The unwillingness of the Government to take decisive action against the white settler state in Rhodesia, which had declared UDI in 1965, contributed further to its loss of political credibility. The final straw was the introduction of the White Paper *In Place of Strife* in 1969 which proposed to control unofficial strikes through statutory measures. The government now viewed such industrial action as the biggest obstacle to the rationalisation of British industry. The opposition to it from amongst the trade union leadership was too great, however, and it was withdrawn ignominiously.

It was evident by 1970 that Labour's strategy had failed. Far from there being an increase in the rate of domestic investment, it had continued to fall along with the rate of profit. British capital needed a new strategy, one which sought the rationalisation of industry through closure of the most inefficient sections ('lame ducks'). The Tories' 'no lame ducks' policy appeared to meet this requirement and in June 1970 they were elected with a substantial majority.

Yet Prime Minister Edward Heath's strategy was to prove a complete fiasco. The Conservatives' own Industrial Relations Act was introduced against a background of serious opposition; their 'no lame ducks' policy was blown off course by a prolonged 'work-in' at Upper

Clyde Shipbuilders. A national miners' strike in February 1972 was followed by a near-general strike in July when five dockers went to gaol in defiance of the Industrial Relations Act. In February 1974, as a second miners' strike plunged British industry into a three-day working week, a change of government was essential to prevent complete chaos.

6.5 *The deepening crisis: the 1974–79 Labour Government*

By the February 1974 election, the position of the British imperialist economy was very weak. An inflationary boom in 1972-73 had been followed by the Middle East war which drove up oil prices four-fold. A vast balance of payments deficit opened up, amounting to over £5 billion on visible trade, or over 6 per cent of GNP, which was only partially offset by an invisible surplus. Inflation was running at 16 per cent in 1973-74 and 24.1 per cent in 1974-75. The response was a strongly deflationary budget for 1975 to reduce the Public Sector Borrowing Requirement (PSBR) to 8 per cent in 1975-76 and to 6 per cent in the following year. In addition to budgetary control, Labour introduced a wages policy in agreement with the TUC. The first stage imposed a ceiling on wage increases of £6 per week – some 10 per cent of average earnings, much less than the inflation rate.

Although this wages policy was hardly breached, it did not resolve any problems. The visible balance of payments deficit was still running at 3 per cent of GNP in 1975 and into 1976. By January 1976, the pound had fallen to $2.04, and by the end of September to $1.64. Undaunted, the Government introduced the second stage of its income policy: from 1 August, increases were to be limited to 4.5 per cent, again in agreement with the TUC. The impact of this measure was later assessed by *The Economist*:

> '... the 7 per cent by which the past year's 10 per cent increase in earnings fell behind its 17 per cent increase in prices represents the biggest recorded fall in the average Briton's real disposable

> income for over a hundred years: worse than anything that happened in the 1930s.'[20]

In December 1975, the Government approached the IMF for its first loan to support the pound. With the PSBR still out of control, substantial cuts in public spending were announced in February 1976 (£2 billion, £600 million from education alone) and further cuts of £1 billion in July. The run on the pound continued: in the two months to April, the Government had used $2.75 billion supporting it, and had exhausted the IMF loan.

By autumn, with no fundamental change in the situation, and with the central banks refusing to bail it out, the Government turned once more to the IMF In return for a further loan of $3.9 billion, it agreed to impose cuts of £3 billion in public spending over a period of two years. In actual fact, state spending was to fall much further: from 49.35 per cent of GDP in 1975-76 to 43.25 per cent in 1977-78 before recovering slightly to 44 per cent in 1978-79. In real terms, it fell from £195.3 billion in 1975-76 to £181.1 billion in 1977-78, recovering to £190.1 billion in 1978-79; a feat 18 years of subsequent Tory rule could never achieve.

It was also during this period that the more parasitic features of British imperialism began to come to the fore, as the London Eurocurrency market became a central source of loan capital throughout the world. Between 1972 and 1979, Eurocurrency bank credits grew from $7 billion to $83 billion; of these, $2.5 billion and $48 billion respectively were to oppressed nations; 30 per cent of this was accounted for by the City of London. Direct investment, though on a much smaller scale, proved extremely profitable: between 1972 and 1977, the rate of profit on such investment in the oppressed nations averaged 18-20 per cent compared with 3.6-4.2 per cent for domestic industry. Overall, the private external assets of British imperialism grew from £61 billion in 1973 to £119 billion in 1977; in 1962, such assets had made up some 40 per cent of GNP; by 1977 they had

---

20. Quoted in Editorial, *Revolutionary Communist* No 7, 1977, p1.

risen to 93 per cent. The seeds of the debt crisis in the oppressed nations were sown in this period, as British imperialism utilised its pre-eminent position in the financial services market to shore up its domestic position. This was taking place at exactly the same time as Tony Benn was claiming that 'Britain had moved from Empire to colony status', arguing that Britain 'is a colony in which the IMF decides our monetary policy, the international and multinational companies decides our industrial policy, and the EEC decides our legislative and taxation policy.'[21]

A further stage in the wages policy was imposed in 1977, this time without TUC agreement, followed by a fourth stage in August 1978. But the strain for wide sections of the working class was too much, especially in the public sector where such policies could be more effectively imposed, and as unemployment rose by a million. The result was the Winter of Discontent, when low-paid council workers came out on strike in an attempt to restore their living standards. The post-war social-democratic consensus had broken down.

Although the mass of the working class suffered increasing hardship under the Labour Government, black and Asian workers experienced even greater oppression. Labour enforced the 1971 Immigration Act despite its earlier declarations of opposition. This Act essentially introduced a work permit system: there were to be no more immigrants, only 'guest workers'. As a corollary, there would be no secondary immigration associated with such migrant workers and the regime for such secondary immigration of dependants of black and Asian workers already settled in Britain as did take place was made brutally oppressive. The Act also greatly increased powers of deportation, to the extent that on average there were over 200 black people awaiting deportation each day. The Act facilitated the use of X-ray examinations to disprove children's age claims and the use of virginity testing. In 1977 it was tightened even further when a 12-month probation period was put on the marriages of immigrant husbands

21. Quoted in M Williams, S Palmer and G Clapton, *op cit*, *Revolutionary Communist* No 9, p3.

after extensive publicity about alleged 'marriages of convenience'.

This was not the end of its attacks on the black section of the working class. The Labour Government used thousands of police to defeat the Grunwicks strike of Asian women in 1976, and sanctioned a police attack on the Notting Hill Carnival in the same year. It tolerated the ever-extending use by the police of the 1824 Vagrancy Act – the 'sus' law – which enabled them to constantly harass black youth. Asylum seekers were not exempt from Labour's attentions: Cypriots fleeing the 1974-75 civil war were denied entry, as were Rhodesian draft-dodgers in 1976-77. The Prevention of Terrorism Act was introduced in December 1974 as an act of intimidation against the Irish community.

Given the presence of significant numbers of black and Irish workers in the state sector, the political consequences were to be significant. Irish people, traditionally Labour supporters when in Britain, had turned against it as a result of its policies of torture and criminalisation in the Six Counties. Black people started organising against racism: Asian Youth Movements emerged, as well as a variety of ad hoc committees to defend victims of state oppression. In November 1979, 20,000 Asian workers demonstrated against the immigration laws, cheering speakers who denounced Labour's racism, and booing Tony Benn when he attempted to defend Labour's record. A year earlier, a motion calling on the National Union of Public Employees, which organised low-paid public sector workers, to disaffiliate from the Labour Party had been debated at the union's annual conference. In defending their political interests, black and Irish workers were confronting the Labour Party. Labour's agreement during the 1979 general election campaign to use thousands of police to defend a National Front election rally in Southall merely drove the point home. 300 people were arrested, and Blair Peach was killed as the police fought a pitched battle with the youth. In the June 1979 election, thousands of black and Irish workers, once the most committed Labour voters, abstained from voting at all.

6.6 *Labour and the working class under the Tories.*

Although substantial numbers of poorer workers abstained in 1979, the principal factor in the Tories' victory was the defection of sections of the more privileged sections of the working class, especially in the South East. Labour's share of the votes of trade unionists fell from 66 per cent in 1970 to 55 per cent in 1974, and then to 51 per cent in 1979. In 1974, 49 per cent of the so-called C2 voters (skilled workers, foremen and the self-employed) voted Labour, enabling it to just scrape home. In 1979, the largest swing against Labour was from this sector – over 10 per cent. The division within the working class was now becoming evident at the electoral level.

Underlying this were fundamental changes in the structure of the working class, with a major shift in employment from the productive, manufacturing sector to the service sector (Table 9).

Within the manufacturing sector, the pattern of employment had also changed, as the number of white collar workers increased at the same time as the number of manual workers declined (Table 10).

Table 9 Employment changes 1948–79[22] (000s)

Employment Category	1948	1958	1964	1968	1972	1979
Coal Mining	802	785	596	446	330	300
Manufacturing	8035	8932	8796	8797	7613	7107
Railways	578	494	394	298	241	183
Distributive Trades	2033	2493	2962	2828	2587	3001
Banking, Finance & Insurance	434	501	627	674	983	1621
Professional Services (inc education and health)	1306	1786	2310	2702	3030	3432
Public Administration	1445	1283	1389	1507	1513	1668
Miscellaneous Services	1827	1598	2185	2148	2001	2037

22. Drawn from various issues of the *Ministry of Labour* and *Department of Employment Gazettes*.

Table 10: Employment in manufacturing 1948–79[23] (000s)

	1948	1958	1964	1973	1979
1 Total No Employees	8035	8932	8797	8048	7055
2 Manual Workers	6749	7038	6768	5876	5040
3 Admin, Technical and Clerical Staff	1286	1894	2029	2172	2015
(3) as percentage of (1)	16.0	21.2	23.1	27.0	28.6

The number of miners, railwaymen and manual workers in manufacturing – in other words, the core of traditional Labour voters – stood at 8.13 million in 1948, 7.76 million in 1964, and only 5.52 million in 1979. The number of those employed in banking, finance, insurance and professional services had risen from 1.74 million to 2.94 million and then 5.05 million over the same period. The rate of change in employment patterns had been far more rapid between 1964 and 1979, the years of deepening crisis, than it had been between 1948 and 1964. The privileged stratum of the working class still existed – it had however taken on a different form: skilled workers were now increasingly white collar employees, without the same commitment to Labour as their manual predecessors. The tendencies noted by the Coles in the 1930s were now a reality: to survive as a party, Labour would have to appeal to this new labour aristocracy or petit bourgeoisie.

The Tories had been elected in 1979 on the strength of their commitment to cut public sector expenditure, attack working class living standards and thereby halt Britain's economic decline on the one hand, while sustaining its role as a major imperialist power on the other. The first fruit of this shift in strategy was the slump of 1980-81, when unemployment rose beyond three million and employment in manufacturing fell from seven million to six million. Resistance was scant; a 14-week strike by steel-workers in the nationalised British

23. *ibid.*

Steel was defeated as steel continued to pour out of foundries in the private sector.

The response of Labour to losing the election was to adopt a series of radical policies. But the left's victories at successive Labour Party Conferences belied the increasing separation of the Party from the mass of the working class. At the 1980 Labour Conference, Tony Benn declared to enthusiastic applause that a Labour Government would grant powers to nationalise industries, control capital and implement industrial democracy 'within days', yet kept his mouth firmly shut during the conference debate on political status for Irish political prisoners.

The meaningless nature of Labour's move to the left became completely apparent in its response to uprisings by black and white youth during the summer of 1981 when they fought police oppression and racism in cities up and down the country. Labour, left or right, had no sympathy for the youth. Thus Michael Foot told the 1981 Labour Party Conference that 'what happened in Moss Side and Liverpool is what we in the Labour Party are dedicated to stop',[24] while Tony Benn was of the opinion that 'the Labour Party does not believe in rioting as a route to social progress nor are we prepared to see the police injured during the course of their duties.'[25]

This attack was reinforced by the left as it protected the open racists within the Labour Party. The SWP for instance, described black youth as a 'lumpen proletariat', a 'vulnerable underbelly of the working class'.[26] No matter how reactionary the Labour Party became, it would always have its defenders to the left, prepared to reconcile their support for Labour with anything and everything. In the absence of any movement which could represent their political interests, the youth were isolated. The same summer witnessed the hunger strike of Irish political prisoners, ending in the death of ten of them. Not one Labour MP publicly supported the prisoners, and Labour as a whole

---

24. Quoted in article by S Palmer, *Fight Racism! Fight Imperialism!* No 13, October 1981.
25. Quoted in Editorial, *Fight Racism! Fight Imperialism!* No 12, September 1981.
26. Quoted in Editorial, *Fight Racism! Fight Imperialism!* No 14, November 1981.

supported the Tories fully. Labour spokesperson on Northern Ireland Don Concannon visited Bobby Sands, who had just been elected MP for Fermanagh and South Tyrone, and who was now close to death, to tell him that the Labour Party did not support him.

The Fare's Fair dispute of 1982 showed the real limits of Labour Party resistance to the ruling class onslaught, when the Law Lords over-ruled any attempt to establish reasonable fares for London Transport, and Ken Livingstone's Greater London Council decided not to make a fight of it. It was not just Labour that was shown to be impotent in 1982: two industrial disputes showed that this was the case for the trade union movement as well. In the first, two railway worker unions, ASLEF and the NUR, first engaged in a slanging match, and then refused to co-ordinate any joint campaign over a pay claim against British Rail. Later in the year, a pay claim by nurses and ancillary workers was allowed to drag on without any resolution for seven months, with the TUC refusing to organise any support. The depth of the crisis was now such that the trade unionism of ten years earlier was no longer a viable way of defending the working class. In the early 1970s, there had still been some basis for unity between the privileged sections and the mass of the working class, the pre-condition for legal trade unionism. However, by 1982 British capitalism could only maintain conditions for the upper stratum of the working class, and this stratum became more and more willing to scab on the rest of the working class whenever the latter sought to defend itself in action. The 1984/85 miners' strike would drive this point home.

The widening division in the working class became further evident in election results during 1982 and 1983. In February 1982 Peter Tatchell was defeated in what had been Labour's sixth safest seat, Bermondsey, a clear result of organised anti-gay prejudice within the Labour Party. This was followed by the debacle of the 1983 general election, when Labour lost three million votes compared to its 1979 result, polling only 28 per cent of the votes cast. The election was marked by increasing levels of abstention in the poor, inner-city constituencies – a poll indicated that only 33 per cent of black people were going to vote – and the continued defection of the privileged strata of the working class: only 34 per cent of C2 voters supported Labour. The first rounds of privatisation, and the sale of council houses in particular, had started to give this section of the working class a substantial stake in the system. No less than 59 per cent of 1979 Labour voters who bought their council house between 1979 and 1983 switched their vote to the Tories at the second election. Since 1979, whereas the standard of living of skilled workers had remained stable, a council manual worker had suffered a fall in real wages of 4.6 per cent and semi-skilled workers 8 per cent.[27] The left resorted to incredible distortion to justify a vote for Labour; the SWP asking:

> 'Are you sick to death of rising unemployment? Are you bitter about the continual toll of factory closures? Are you opposed to the deployment of Cruise, Trident and other weapons of mass destruction? Do you think Thatcher's South Atlantic war was a futile and bloody venture? Do you want to resist anti-union laws? If so, you will vote Labour.'[28]

The self-satisfaction of the better-off stratum expressed itself in an increasing conservatism and an increased hostility to any action which might threaten their conditions. The TUC responded to this with the policy of New Realism, of avoiding struggle at all costs, whilst Labour responded with the election of Neil Kinnock as its leader as part of the 'dream ticket' with Roy Hattersley. During his leadership campaign, Kinnock made clear the constituency to which he would appeal:

> '…we can only protect the disadvantaged in our society if we appeal to those who relatively advantaged. The apparent over-concentration of our energies and resources on these groups like the poor, the unemployed and the minorities – does a disservice both to them and to ourselves...if we are to be of real use to the

27. Cited in *The revolutionary road to communism in Britain*, Larkin Publications, 1984, p125.
28. *ibid*, p136.

deprived and insecure we must have the support of those in more secure social circumstances – the home owners as well as the homeless, the stable family as well as the single parent, the confidently employed as well as the unemployed, the majority as well as the minorities.'[29]

In other words, a future Labour victory would depend on its ability to appeal to the privileged. This was a rebuttal of those like Livingstone who had argued that Labour had to appeal to precisely these groups 'like the poor, the unemployed and the minorities', in contrast to electricians and engineers whom he described as 'privileged "labour aristocrats",' and white collar workers who were 'middle class'. Once again, it was up to the left to come to the defence of privilege, Alex Callinicos from the SWP arguing:

> 'One wonders who is left in the working class according to Livingstone. The implication of this sort of analysis is that socialists must create a new popular base by linking up with groups which are not part of the working class. The examples most often given are those of such "minorities" as women [sic], blacks and gays.'[30]

Implicit in such a statement is the notion of the 'underclass': a view that the working class is equivalent to the trade union movement, and that any poor person who is not in a trade union is therefore outside of the working class. This notion would have been familiar to the old craft unionists, to Sidney Webb when he wrote his London Programme, and to those who opposed the unemployed workers' movement between the world wars. It is a view that stamps its protagonists as defenders of privilege, since they argue that it is the upper stratum of the working class that will be the agency of social change, much as the Webbs thought it would be the professional middle class. A report by Labour Party General Secretary Larry

29. Quoted in Editorial, *Fight Racism! Fight Imperialism!* No 33, October 1983.
30. Quoted *ibid.*

Whitty revealed just how privileged the average Party member was, even in 1987:

> '60 per cent of party members have a degree or equivalent higher educational qualification, compared to a national average of just 11 per cent. Labour Party members are twice as likely to be employed in the public sector as the private. 62 per cent of them read *The Guardian*, and only 25 per cent the *Daily Mirror*'.[31]

This was nearly ten years before the great influx of professionals and managers during Blair's membership campaign of the mid-1990s.

From 1983, Kinnock consistently pursued the interests of privileged sections of the working class and their middle class allies. The year after his election he was attacking councils which refused to set legal council rates: they 'would do best ... to stay in the positions to which they have been elected so that they can mitigate, protect and dilute the effect of central government planning',[32] an echo of George Lansbury's appeal 50 years earlier for Labour authorities to implement the means test. By 1985, any resistance to rate-capping – capping local council rates in order to receive central government funding – had collapsed.

But the decisive battle was the 1984/85 miners' strike, where the divisions evident in the strikes of the early 1980s came to the fore. The strike was a response to British Coal's secret plans to close more than 20 coalmines as the first step in a broader programme of pit closures. The relatively greater security and better conditions of the Nottinghamshire miners first made them indifferent to the plight of those communities that were under threat in Scotland, Yorkshire and Wales, then hostile, as they went through picket lines, and finally became willing tools in the effort by British Coal to break the strike. There were other differences, too. In Arthur Scargill, the National Union of Mineworkers (NUM) had a leader who probably came as close to a revolutionary trade unionist standpoint as was possible, and

31. Quoted in Cliff and Gluckstein, *op cit*, p351.
32. Quoted in article by R Clough, *Fight Racism! Fight Imperialism!* No 39, May 1984.

who was willing to stand by his members when they were attacked by the police and by the media. Miners were also ready to accept new methods of organisation: in particular, the support groups set up by miners' wives which harnessed support from within the communities. Yet the strike was defeated, not by the state, but by the trade union movement and the Labour Party leadership, who successfully isolated the miners and the section of the working class that supported them.

The process, which started with the refusal of Nottingham miners to support the strike call, continued when TUC General Secretary Len Murray declared one-day strikes in Yorkshire and Wales on 20 May 1984 'unconstitutional', and instructed union leaders to call them off. Tony Benn withdrew a motion to the Labour Party National Executive calling for national demonstrations in favour of a far vaguer one which committed Labour to nothing. Members of the steel workers' union, the ISTC, egged on by its General Secretary Bill Sirs, helped non-union labour unload a shipload of coal at Hunterston – enough to keep the Ravenscraig steel plant going for several weeks. As the nationalised British Steel Corporation stepped up imports of coal, there were attempts to get dock workers not to handle such cargoes. Yet whilst most dock labour scheme ports came out on strike, workers in unregistered docks did not. As a T&GWU branch secretary from Great Yarmouth, an unregistered port, said:

> 'We have helped the miners in the past with money but we draw a line at this. The talk about scab labour is just an excuse. We shall work and we shall cross picket lines if we have to.'[33]

The dockers' support petered out. The scabbing continued: Neil Kinnock denounced the miners for defending themselves at the September 1984 TUC Congress:

> '... violence, I do not have to tell this Congress ... disgusts union opinion and divides union attitudes ... and is alien to the

33. Quoted in D Reed and O Adamson, *The Miners' Strike 1984–85 – People versus State*, Larkin Publications, 1985, p45.

temperament and intelligence of the British trade union movement.'[34]

Power workers in the Electrical Engineers' and Plumbers Trade Union (EEPTU) voted by 84 per cent not to support the miners on 19 October. On 24 October, the colliery officials' union NACODS called off its strike after changes were made by the NCB to colliery review procedures. On 3 November, Kinnock announced that he was 'too busy' to attend any NUM rallies. Meanwhile, the TUC put intense pressure on the NUM to surrender. Yet the miners held out for a further four months in a desperate attempt to defend their communities before finally being forced back to work.

The trade union movement and the Labour Party had sided with the privileged section of the working class – the Nottingham miners, the colliery inspectors, the non-registered dockers. While police had besieged and terrorised mining communities, placed them under curfew, set up road blocks hundreds of miles away from any picket line, offered any amount of protection to scabs, arrested and beaten hundreds of miners, the official labour movement had denounced the miners when they attempted to defend themselves.

It was not just the leaders – it was their erstwhile left-wing critics as well. Hence *Socialist Worker* denounced miners' hit squads by saying 'such raids can give trade union officials an excuse not to deliver solidarity', and more generally argued 'we are opposed to individuals or groups using violence as a substitute for mass struggle. That's why we oppose planting bombs, assassinating politicians and criticise some of the miners' hit squads.'[35] NUM leaders, Scargill in particular, were made of different stuff from the SWP, and did not join in these cowardly attacks.

SWP leaders Cliff and Gluckstein went further in their attack on the conduct of the strike, and argued that compared to 1972, 'Rank and file activity was lower, and crucially, the miners showed less

34. *ibid*, p51.

35. *Socialist Worker*, 11 and 25 August 1984, quoted *ibid*, p45.

willingness to act independently of the bureaucracy'.[36] Defending the privileged section of the working class, they argued that the reason that sections such as power workers and engineers did not take action in support of the miners is that they 'lacked confidence'. Both here and over the issue of violence, the SWP, in common with the bulk of the left, put the interests of better-off sections of the working class before that of the majority. As after the 1981 uprisings, a section of the working class driven into action had found no political force to represent its interests.

6.7 *The impact of Thatcherism on the working class*

Throughout the 1980s, Thatcher was able to dramatically accelerate the changes in the social and political character of the British working class that had started with the onset of the crisis (Table 11).

Over the same period, the number of manual workers employed in manufacturing fell from 5,040,000 to 3,294,000. Adding in 206,000 railway workers and coal miners gives a total of 3,500,000: there had been 5,520,000 workers in these categories in June 1979 and

Table 11 Employment changes 1979–1991[37] (000s)

	1979	1991
Coal Mining	300	74
Manufacturing	7107	4642
Railways	183	132
Distributive Trades	300	3171
Banking, Finance, Insurance	1621	2616
Professional Services	3432	4124
Public Administration	1668	1571
Miscellaneous Services	2037	2096

36. Cliff and Gluckstein, *op cit*, p347.
37. Drawn from various issues of the *Employment Gazette*.

7,758,000 in 1964. In complete contrast, the numbers employed in Banking, Finance, Insurance and Professional Services rose from 3,699,000 to 5,053,000 in 1979 and 6,740,000 in 1991. This was not all: the number of self-employed also increased substantially: from 1,842,000 in 1979 to 3,222,000 in 1991. Finally, trade union membership fell from over 12 million to just over eight million during the same period; the fall was particularly sharp in the private sector as millions of manual workers lost their jobs.

Home ownership increased from roughly 53 per cent in 1979 to nearly 67 per cent in 1991 by which time 15.7 million people owned their own homes. Council housing stock fell from 6.5 million to about five million as more than a million tenants exercised their right to buy. The number of outstanding mortgages rose by 60 per cent, from 6.2 million in 1980 to 9.8 million in 1991. In 1990, one in four of the adult population was a shareholder compared with one in 13 in 1981.[38] Through privatisation, home ownership and so-called 'people's capitalism', Thatcher destroyed the old social base for the Labour Party and gave a substantial section of the working and lower middle class a material stake in the system.

At the same time the gap between rich and poor significantly widened. The real income of the poorest 20 per cent of the population fell from £3,442 per annum to £3,282 between 1979 and 1989 at constant prices. That of the top 20 per cent increased from £20,138 to £28,124: from six times the income of the poorest 20 per cent to nearly nine times. Income tax cuts worth nearly £29 billion were made between 1979 and 1991, the chief beneficiaries being the rich, the middle class and the better-off workers. In 1979, there were 7.8 million workers earning less than the Council of Europe's decency threshold. By 1992 the figure was 10 million – 47 per cent of all employees.[39] The gap between the highest and lowest paid male manual worker had become greater than in Victorian times. 10.3

38. Cited in Editorial: A conservative nation?, *Fight Racism! Fight Imperialism!* No 106, April/May 1992.
39. Cited *ibid*.

million people, including 2.6 million children, were living in poverty. By 1987, more than a third of the UK population were living in poverty or on its margins, up 50 per cent on 1979. Changes in the social security system were key factors in this rise.

However, it is the middle class and better-off sections of the working class who determine the outcome of elections, and if Labour was to recover their support, it had to adapt to their prejudices. The defeat of the miners removed any obstacle to this process. In 1986, Labour approved the sale of council properties, whilst in the following year, Kinnock's influential supporter Bryan Gould was able to argue that: 'The idea of owning shares is catching on, and as socialists, we should support it as one means of taking power from the hands of the few and spreading it more widely.'[40] Labour's official policy of unilateral nuclear disarmament was also under attack, even if indirectly: in 1984, Kinnock had visited the US to assure Britain's allies that Labour was 'neither cowardly, complacent nor pacifist': this position was overwhelmingly endorsed in 1986 when the Labour conference voted five to one to remain in NATO. In January 1985, when the *Secret Society* TV programme was banned because it would reveal the fact that a £500 million spy satellite project had been kept secret from Parliament, Kinnock stated 'I would have done the same. The Government are right to seek to take the action to prevent publication, wrong to fail to ensure all the angles were covered' – a reference to the fact that the details had got out in the *New Statesman* because of government incompetence.[41]

By this time, Labour had dropped any pretence at defending the poorer sections of the working class. It was left to charities or churches to express any concern, as the latter did with the publication of *Faith in the Inner Cities*. As if to underline this, Labour Chairperson Tom Sawyer urged the Party in the lead-up to the general election 'not to write off the white, heterosexual working class and replace

40. Quoted in article by Terry O'Halloran, *Fight Racism! Fight Imperialism!* No 72, October 1987.

41. Quoted in article by Terry O'Halloran, *Fight Racism! Fight Imperialism!* No 66, February 1987.

them with a coalition of the dispossessed.'[42] When the election came, however, the economy appeared to be booming: 1986 had seen Britain become the largest creditor nation with net overseas assets over £100 billion as the City of London remained the dominant financial centre of the world. Annual GNP growth was over 4 per cent; the government account was in surplus; unemployment was falling and house prices booming. In such circumstance, it was not surprising that the better-off sections of the working class continued to place their faith in the Tories and returned them with yet another large majority.

6.8 *To the 1992 general election*

In 1989, Labour became in its terms a 'fair tax party', when it agreed to set a maximum rate of 50 per cent income tax as official policy. It made clear it would oppose any campaign of non-payment of the Poll Tax. This position was passed overwhelmingly at a recall conference of the Scottish Labour Party in September 1988; the consequence was a heavy defeat in the Govan by-election in November 1988, when there was a 33 per cent swing to the Scottish Nationalist Party. Kinnock had earlier described such a campaign as a 'counsel of despair, fruitless'. Margaret Hodge, Labour leader of Islington Council in London, claimed a 'victory' in 'forcing' the Government to introduce the tax in one go in England rather than phase it in as was originally proposed. This, said Hodge, 'removes an unnecessary administrative burden' – but it also meant that the working class would have to pay more immediately. Administrative convenience assumed greater importance for Labour leaders than the poverty of the less well-off sections of the working class.

Whether it was led by the Militant or by the SWP, the campaign against the Poll Tax remained loyal to the Labour Party. In an echo of Labour's contempt for the poor, a leading member of the SWP, Chris

42. Quoted in article by Carol Brickley, *Fight Racism! Fight Imperialism!* No 68, May 1987.

Harman, argued at the 1988 Socialist Conference that it was not possible to build a community-based campaign against the tax because 'On council estates are drug peddlers, junkies and people claiming houses under false names. These people will complete the registration forms to avoid attention from the council',[43] and went on to argue that the central issue was the campaign for leadership of the Labour Party being waged at the time by Tony Benn and Eric Heffer. Sidney Webb would have approved.

Labour leaders never lost an opportunity to denounce those who fought back. The 1989 uprising by prisoners at Risley Remand Centre against appalling conditions caused Hattersley to exclaim 'No-one should defend the violence at Risley or react in a way which might incite similar action in other prisons'[44] – although a jury was later to accept that the actions of the prisoners were justifiable self-defence. Hattersley also called for forcible tactics to be used against the prisoners during the Strangeways uprising the following year, while local Labour MP Bob Litherland called on the Home Office 'to intervene and arrange for the SAS to take over.'[45] Hattersley was equally in his element in dealing with the London Poll Tax riot of 1 April 1990: 'I hope there have been a substantial number of arrests, and that the sentencing is severe ... exemplary.'[46] Strong stuff indeed, but essential if Labour were to win the allegiance of 'semi-detached' Britain.

Meanwhile Labour councils started to implement severe cuts in the wake of the Poll Tax. Newcastle Council cut 1,000 jobs as it reduced spending by £17.5 million; Coventry nearly 300 jobs; Manchester Council cut 10 per cent of its workforce over a four-year period and Lothian refused to fill 600 vacancies in social services. In London, Camden cut £30 million in its 1991/92 budget and raised council housing rents by £17 per week; Greenwich cut 450 jobs and New-

43. Quoted in article by D Reed and L Reid, *Fight Racism! Fight Imperialism!* No 79, July 1988.

44. Quoted in article by A Byrne, *Fight Racism! Fight Imperialism!* No 87, June 1989.

45. Quoted in article by L Reid, *Fight Racism! Fight Imperialism!* No 94, April 1990.

46. Quoted *ibid.*

ham 340 jobs in education and social services. Reductions in services were universal, as the poorer sections of the working class suffered doubly: having to pay more and getting far less in return.

Labour went into the 1992 election almost indistinguishable on major policy issues from the Tory Party it professed to oppose. It had not only renounced unilateral nuclear disarmament, but also refused to say whether it would cancel a fourth projected Trident submarine. It made no commitment to restore any of the under-funding of the state sector beyond spending an extra £1 billion on the NHS over a period of 22 months and £600 million on education, sufficient it felt to maintain the electoral support of the poorer sections of the working class. It was committed to the European Community and the Exchange Rate Mechanism, and strenuously opposed any devaluation of the pound. It would not revoke the fundamentals of the Tory anti-trade union laws, nor amend any immigration laws. It would increase state pensions – but only by £5 a week out of the £14 that had been lost since pension increases were no longer indexed to pay increases; it also promised to restore the cuts in child benefit. It emphasised that although it would raise the top level of taxation from 40 to 50 per cent, this would only affect those earning £38,000 or more. It also proposed to abolish the ceiling on National Insurance contributions, which stood at just over £20,000, to pay for its very modest increases in public spending which would hardly begin to address the poverty created by years of Tory rule.

In the end, even these small measures proved too much for wide sections of the middle class and better-off workers to accept. Where Labour gained support, it did so almost entirely at the expense of the Liberal Democrats, whose proposals for additional taxation were both more extensive and more frankly argued. Labour recovered support from skilled workers – just over 40 per cent voted for them in 1992, according to both Mori and NOP, as opposed to 35 per cent in 1987.[47] Yet this only took them back to the 1979 position and was far

47. Figures in this and the subsequent paragraph are drawn from *The Times*, 11 April 1992, and *The Independent on Sunday*, 12 April 1992.

short of the 49 per cent who had voted Labour in 1974. Amongst middle class trade unionists (a pollsters' term for better-off white collar trade unionists), it increased its support from 30 per cent to 36 per cent – but this just brought it up to the level of Conservative support. Overall, the middle class (C1) divided 52 per cent to 24 per cent in favour of the Tories. Labour's bare majority amongst working class trade unionists (51 per cent in 1987) was only slightly up, at 55 per cent. More significantly, it still had less support than the Tories amongst working class home owners – 39 per cent against 41 per cent.

In the South of England, the Tories still predominated, with 51 per cent of the vote outside of London as against 24 per cent for Labour. This gave the Tories 106 seats and just three for Labour. In inner London the gap, although smaller (12 per cent) than in 1987 (18 per cent), was still enough to give 46 per cent of the vote to the Tories, and with it, a substantial majority of the seats. The middle class and the more affluent sections of the working class felt that their interests were still safer with the Tories.

The inquest into the general election started immediately. Ken Livingstone argued the next day that 'We must be able to build socialism without taxing middle income families till it hurts', and continued:

> 'If you analyse the result I suspect that we just failed to win seats we should have because people on middle incomes were concerned. In London and the South East, £21,000 is average earnings and should not have been a target for higher tax. I have always argued the figure should have been £26,000.'[48]

All this was a far cry from his 1983 'coalition of the dispossessed'. Others on the left echoed his view. Militant thought that 'starting tax rises at £21,000 a year could give the Tories ammunition. The tax issue could still make the difference with better-paid skilled and

48. *Evening Standard*, 10 April 1992.

white-collar workers – vital votes Labour has to win back.'[49] According to its post-mortem, 'white-collar workers, middle ranking teachers and middle class voters who could be won to Labour' were not, because they 'got the impression Labour would tax them harder', referring editorially to the 'tax disaster'. This was in fact the only equitable proposal that Labour put forward during the election, and shows how much the left was prepared to concede to get Labour re-elected.

Another view was expressed by Labour MP Denis Skinner who complained of listening to the SDP and Liberal Democrats talk 'about how we should collaborate and accept their policies', arguing that instead 'it is time we represented our class. We don't need the Liberals and proportional representation to do that. What we need is class politics.'[50] But Labour had banned, proscribed, expelled, attacked and isolated anything that remotely smacked of working class politics throughout the Tory years, and Skinner did not suggest what forces existed to make Labour carry out such a *volte face*. The SWP also suggested that Labour had lost because it had 'turned its back on working class struggles'. However, this did not prevent it from urging support for Labour, or describing its defeat as a 'disaster'.[51]

The SWP was particularly determined to bury what it called 'the myth that it was the C2s, the better-paid skilled workers, especially in the South East, who cost Labour the election.'[52] But as we have seen, although Labour got 43 per cent of the C2 vote in 1992, it needed 49 per cent in 1974 in order to just scrape home. We have also shown the effect that purchasing a council house had on voting patterns in 1983.

---

49. *Militant*, 20 March 1992.
50. *The Independent*, 11 April 1992.
51. *Socialist Worker*, 18 April 1992. Luxemburg's description of German Social Democracy as a 'stinking corpse.' is pertinent here. There is no reason to suppose she thought any different of British social democracy, so it is somewhat surprising to be told by those who are so fond of the great revolutionary that the failure to elect this 'stinking corpse' is in fact a major 'disaster'. Unless of course they believe in re-incarnation...
52. *Socialist Worker*, 25 April 1992.

To attempt to bolster this position, the SWP argued that the C2 layer was made up of the self-employed and foremen as well as 'genuine' skilled workers, and that these 'genuine' skilled workers always voted Labour. But the collapse of manufacturing employment had made the foreman category far less significant, and the distinction the SWP drew between skilled workers as employees and skilled workers as the self-employed only disguised how this layer as a whole had benefited from the Tories' 'people's capitalism'. The number of self-employed rose by nearly 1.5 million during the Tory years; many of them were skilled workers investing their redundancy pay.

Although the opportunist left talked about class politics, its primary concern was with a minority section of the working class. It merely provided a radical interpretation of the standpoint of the Labour leadership. Thus John Smith, shortly to become Labour's leader, commenting on JK Galbraith's recently-published *The Culture of Contentment*, which argued that the basis for the post-war consensus had completely disappeared, said:

> 'I do not accept that his pessimism is warranted in Britain. Although we too have developed what has been described as the two thirds/one third society, I believe it well within the capabilities of Labour to develop policies for economic and social progress that can appeal to the contented majority.'[53]

Elsewhere Smith spoke of the need to 'target' benefits, a euphemism for means-testing. This was presumably one policy that would appeal to the 'contented majority'. Bryan Gould offered much of the same, referring to a 'time-warp' when Labour saw its role as '... offering help to a disadvantaged majority against a privileged minority', which meant that 'we had little to say to those on middle incomes whose votes decide elections ... Nor did we make much effort to match the potent appeal of Tory policies on privatisation and council house

53. *New Statesman*, 15 May 1992.

sales.'[54] He concluded 'We ended up alienating one group of potential Labour voters by appearing to cap their aspirations, while failing to appeal to another group who were not impressed by our attempt to offer them greater benefits.' Both Smith and Gould urged a reconsideration of the nature of the Labour Party's links with the trade unions, and embraced the idea of 'one member, one vote' at Labour conferences.

The growing pressure to modify or even break the links with the unions threw Labour's left supporters into something of a panic, since it was their last fig-leaf of justification for supporting Labour. However, the unions were now little different from what they had been at the beginning of the 20th century, organising only a minority of the working class, and mainly its privileged sections. The new huge amalgamations of this period – the AEU/EEPTU, Unison, the Civil Service Unions, the T&G or the G&MWU – had become private fiefdoms which depended on a secure income and an equally secure property portfolio running into hundreds of millions of pounds. They were now little more than friendly benefit societies, offering cheap holidays, insurance, anything that required the member to have a certain level of income. Provided the leaders could control the members – and these amalgamations had been structured with this in mind – then the fiefdoms would continue to accumulate even greater wealth. Because they could no longer unite the interests of all sections of the working class as they could in the 1960s and 1970s, they organised only the more privileged – the labour aristocracy and new petit bourgeoisie. Such unions could not represent the mass of the working class. The issue of the link was about which privileged stratum would direct Labour Party policy – the old labour aristocracy or the new petit bourgeoisie – and not whether Labour could represent working class interests.

54. *ibid.*

6.9 *From New Realism to New Labour*

The 1992 defeat showed that the Labour Party was still not sufficiently attractive to the new petit bourgeoisie and more affluent sections of the working class. To win power, Labour had to reassure them that it would defend their privileges, while convincing the ruling class that it would sustain the interests of British imperialism. To pay for this electoral alliance it was the working class who would have to suffer.

Neil Kinnock was despatched to a well-paid and superannuated job at the EU and was replaced as Labour leader by John Smith. Smith reassured business leaders that any future Labour Government would not be committed to a shorter working week as proposed by the 'socialist' group within the EU, this despite Britain having the longest working week in Europe for both men and women. At the 1993 Party conference Labour agreed to institute a policy of 'one member, one vote'. Although the Party had always been an alliance between the labour aristocracy and sections of the middle class, the former had always had the upper hand through the trade union block vote that they controlled. But the unions had been greatly enfeebled by anti-trade union laws, their constant capitulations and the loss of more than 40 per cent of their members since 1979. The Conference decision was able to force a decisive shift. The middle class – lawyers, journalists, lecturers, managers, professional politicians – were now in the driving seat. Tens of thousands of them joined the Party over the next few years.

When John Smith died suddenly in 1994 he was succeeded by Tony Blair. Blair, a comparatively young barrister with a private school and Oxford education, a wife who was also a barrister and two children, was the middle class epitome of Labour's so-called New Realism. The Labour PR machine under ex-Fleet Street journalist Alistair Campbell went into overdrive, using sophisticated polling and focus group techniques to tailor Labour's image to match middle class prejudices and ruthlessly stamp on anyone in the Labour camp who was not 'on message'.

Under Blair, New Realism became New Labour, matching economic liberalism with social authoritarianism. Labour's policies differed from those of the Tories only in detail and showed how far their interests were from those of the working class. Key points included:–

- No re-nationalisation of any of the industries privatised under the Tories.
- Acceptance of the purchaser-provider split that was the foundation of the market within the NHS.
- Retention and extension of virtually all the Tory elitist education reforms with a proposal to introduce student loans instead of grants.
- Implementation of all immigration laws. The only amendments Labour proposed to the Tory laws were to make them more oppressive.
- Retention of all the Tory anti-trade union legislation. Blair said that to do otherwise would be 'crazy'.
- Targeting of benefits to achieve cuts and force people into low-paid work or training.
- No commitment to an adequate minimum wage, or to the restoration of the link between the state pension and wage rises.
- Retention of increased powers for the police and attacks on civil rights that had begun under the Tories. Labour only abstained in the vote on the 1994 Criminal Justice Bill. Blair said Labour would become 'the party of law and order'.
- No new top rate of income tax. Blair said 'there are top-rate tax payers now who are hardly in the super-rich bracket and I think we have to be extremely sensitive to them'.

At this time 25 per cent of the British population were living in poverty, including almost a third of all children. A sixth of the population relied totally on income support. Over a million people were officially unemployed, the real total being nearer four million. Unemployment benefits and state pensions were lower in relation to living standards than in 1948. Yet even the timid recommendations of Labour's own Commission for Social Justice were considered too unpalatable for British capitalism and were brushed aside. Labour was saying loud and clear that the interests of the ruling class would be safe in their hands together with the privileged position of the middle class and better-off sections of the working class.

The Labour left and the trade unions, almost without exception, swung their support behind this lust for power and helped to prevent the working class from rocking the boat. When young people took to the streets of Blackburn in the autumn of 1992 to protest against poverty and racism, local Labour council leader Gail Barton promised 'we will do all we can to support the police'. In 1994 neither Southwark Labour Council nor UNISON took any action to defend black council employees when they were arrested as 'illegal' immigrants. In late 1992 the Tory Government announced plans to close 31 coalmines. This amounted to two-thirds of the remaining coal industry and would lead to 30,000 job losses. Miners' wives, united in Women Against Pit Closures mounted a determined and militant campaign. There was a widespread public outcry against the closure but there was no sustained opposition from the Labour Party or the TUC. When the TUC was forced to organise a token march, it included businessmen and Liberal-Democrat leader Paddy Ashdown on the platform. TUC leader Norman Willis called for the Government to 'bring people together – management and unions'. The following April the TUC chose to lobby the EU rather than join a day of action in support of the miners, while in the North West it wanted to cancel a day of action in favour of a convention with the CBI. The TUC told the NUR it would take a dim view of strike action in support of the miners and Bill Jordan, President of the AEEU, attacked striking workers at the Timex factory for inviting miners' leader Arthur Scargill to their picket line. Labour MPs on the Energy Select Committee eventually voted in favour of the pit closures.[55]

Wherever workers took action against poor pay and conditions or to defend their jobs they were either ignored or attacked by Labour

55. Cited in article by David Howarth, *Fight Racism! Fight Imperialism!* No 113, June/July 1993

and abandoned by their unions. Domestic workers at Hillingdon Hospital, Liverpool dockers and low-paid workers at JJ Foods in north London were all betrayed in the attempt to keep Labour's image acceptable to the middle class voters. The GMB unilaterally declared an end to a strike mainly by Asian women at a metal finishing factory at Burnsall near Birmingham. Darling of the Labour left Clare Short, whose constituency backed on to Burnsall, never once visited the picket line. UNISON quickly scuppered a strike and occupation at University College Hospital against hospital closures and teachers' unions NAS/UWT and ATU dropped their boycott of the National Curriculum following a few placebo words in the Dearing Report.

As the Labour Party cosied up to the middle class and polished its ruling class credentials, the British left became more concerned that its traditional stomping grounds in the public sector and the welfare state were under threat. Tony Benn wondered 'is the Labour Party dying?' and conceded that 'socialism has been explicitly repudiated'.[56] But the left refused to draw the obvious conclusion and call for opposition to Labour or indeed do anything that might spoil the chances of a Labour victory. Benn ended up with the very safe but empty conclusion that 'if we get things moving at the grass roots, the leadership might even start demanding the same things themselves'. The SWP produced a poster that read 'Do you hate the Tories?' and less prominently underneath 'Are you worried by Blair?' the implication being that Blair was not a class enemy to be hated in the same way as the Tories.

Nowhere was this hypocrisy more evident than on the question of Clause 4 of the Labour Party constitution. *Socialist Review*, the magazine of the SWP, quite rightly stated that 'Clause 4 never represented the triumph of the left in the Labour Party or the conversion of the Labour Party to socialism. The people responsible for Clause 4 saw it as a way of stifling not promoting socialism'. Yet the same

56. Quoted in article by Robert Clough, *Fight Racism! Fight Imperialism!* No 122, December 1994/January 1995.

article went on to proclaim 'we should resist with all our might' the attempt to get rid of what it had called an 'illusion' of socialism.[57] The Labour Party Special Conference in April 1995 sealed the political defeat of the Labour left and its radical petit bourgeois allies, voting to replace Clause 4 with an endorsement for 'the enterprise of the market and the rigour of competition' and a 'thriving private sector'. In a striking demonstration of their class origin, 90 per cent of constituency delegates voted in favour, along with 54 per cent of union delegates. The truth was that the SWP, like all the other British left organisations that participated in the fiasco to save Clause 4, would never make a decisive break with the Labour Party because it remained the main guarantor of the privileges enjoyed by the new petit bourgeoisie from which the British left recruited.

In October 1993 several of these left groups organised a march to 'Close down the BNP headquarters' in Welling, but when some of the 50,000 marchers attempted to do precisely that, SWP and Militant (now Socialist Party) stewards steered the march away from confrontation. When the TUC organised a Unite Against Racism march in Spring 1994 to polish the anti-racist credentials of the Labour Party before the May council elections, the SWP and Militant supported it rather than organise another like that at Welling. This was typical of the role consistently played by the British left, in particular the SWP; taking control of a movement in order to prevent anything radical from being built.

Following the abandonment of Clause 4, Arthur Scargill set up the Socialist Labour Party (SLP), initially with a clear determination to oppose Labour. However, the SLP still operated on the same class base as the SWP, believing that the chief arena for working class action was within the trade union movement. The reality was that the great majority of the working class was not to be found in the unions. By 1996 only about a third of all those in work were members of trade unions and of these a majority were, as the Labour Force Survey pointed out, 'educated, managerial, professional and associated

57. Quoted *ibid*.

workers'. The great mass of part-time, temporary, low-paid and unemployed workers created by the restructuring of capital in the 1980s and 1990s were not organised in unions. Even in unions with a substantial number of low-paid workers such as Unison, it was the better-off managerial staff who generally ran the branches and whose interests the union protected. In the 1997 general election the SLP did stand candidates against Labour but refused to stand candidates in left Labour constituencies or in marginal seats where Labour might lose to the Tories. The SLP became entangled in sectarianism and authoritarianism and failed to become the focus of a genuine working class organisation.

At the 1992 SWP conference Chris Bambery had said 'People who vote Labour are more important than people who don't vote'. Since a large proportion of those who don't vote come from the poorest sections of the working class, Bambery was making it clear where SWP priorities lay. Sure enough, come the 1997 general election the SWP called for a vote for Labour, albeit under the hypocritical slogan of 'Vote socialist or vote Labour'. The opportunist left, as ever, had to protect Labour's electability.

By 1997, Labour offered the ruling class a continued regime of privatisation and deregulation, a low-paid flexible work force and a more positive attitude towards Europe. Chancellor-in-waiting Gordon Brown promised low corporate taxes and a 'prudent' fiscal policy. This meant tight controls on public spending and government borrowing that would lead to low inflation and a stronger pound. At the same time foreign investors, in particular the United States, were reassured that investment in Britain would be encouraged, with few strings attached. Labour promised it would maintain the Trident nuclear programme and the European Fighter Aircraft project. David Clarke, the Labour defence spokesman, said that nuclear disarmament was 'a zany idea from the past' and that Britain must maintain its position as a great military power against (un-named) threats from 'dictators who can actually cause damage to our civilised West'. Ever greater numbers of businesses, multinationals and individual capitalists began to sponsor Labour events, contribute to the party or buy a seat at one of Labour's fundraising dinners. The seal was set on a Labour victory when in the summer of 1996 Blair visited Rupert Murdoch and received his endorsement.

6.10 *The 1997 general election*

Eighteen years of rampant parasitism under Tory rule had transformed the British economy. By 1997, Britain's total external assets stood at a massive £1,976.5 billion, 244 per cent of GDP. Direct investment amounted to £232.4 billion (28.7 per cent of GDP), portfolio investment at £651 billion (80.3 per cent of GDP) and other investment at £1,070.4 billion (132 per cent of GDP).[58] With two serious recessions, manufacturing output had hardly changed throughout the period. During the first, 1980-82, 25 per cent of manufacturing industry had been lost as high interest rates and an overvalued pound made much of it uncompetitive; by 1983, there was a net trade deficit in manufactured goods for the first time. By 1993, following the 1990-92 recession, British investment overseas (direct and portfolio) at £101.9 billion, was greater than the total capital investment in Britain at £94.2 billion, and more than eight times the investment in manufacturing industry. In 1996, even after the recovery in domestic investment and following a fall in portfolio investment abroad, British overseas investment was equivalent to 77.9 per cent of total capital investment in Britain, and nearly six times that invested in manufacturing industry.

Changes in the workforce continued to reflect these structural changes in British capital. Manufacturing employment stood at a mere 4.5 million, down from 7.1 million in 1979 (see Table 11 above). Jobs in finance and business services had risen to 5.0 million, a 67 per cent increase on 1979. Many of these jobs were highly paid: a new petit bourgeoisie had emerged whose increasingly affluent lifestyle depended directly on the success of British imperialism. On the

58. Cited in David Yaffe, 'Britain: Parasitic and decaying capitalism', *Fight Racism! Fight Imperialism!* No 194, December 2006/January 2007.

other hand there was also a growth in low-paid, casualised, part-time and temporary employment, especially in distribution, hotels and restaurants which rose overall from 5.5 million to 6.6 million: workers to serve the expanding consumption needs of this new petit bourgeoisie. Finally, and despite Conservative rhetoric, employment in the state sector also rose, from 5.7 million to 6.7 million. Again many of these were well-paid management jobs – for example, to run the internal market in the NHS.

With these changes there had been increasing poverty for the working class. The proportion of people living in poverty (ie below half average income after housing costs) rose to 24 per cent in 1995/7 or 14.1 million people, 9.1 million more than in 1979. By 1997, 34 per cent of all children, 4.6 million, lived below this poverty level, 3.2 million more than in 1979. 3.3 million households were workless, compared to 1.2 million in 1979. Only 35 per cent of the workforce was in full-time tenured work compared to 55 per cent 20 years earlier. Inequality had grown: in 1979 the richest 10 per cent had more than four times the income of the poorest 10 per cent. By 1995/97 it was nearly eight times, returning to Victorian levels.[59]

The Tories had taken the opportunity of the Poll Tax fiasco to dump Margaret Thatcher and her unrelenting hostility to the EU. But they went into the election still hopelessly divided over Europe, with one section of the party, representing small capital, effectively supporting complete withdrawal. This position was completely unacceptable to the City of London and the monopolies which understood that with British capitalism in decline and the economic power of the EU rising, British capitalism could not afford to remain aloof from Europe. In particular the City was in danger of losing its pre-eminent position to other financial centres such as Frankfurt. Thus, for the predominant section of the ruling class, another period of Tory Government was not a viable option.

The scale of Labour's victory, winning 419 MPs as against 165 for the Tories, was unexpected. Yet Labour polled fewer votes than the

59. Drawn from *Households below average income 1994/95–2007/08.*

Tories had in 1992 (13.5 million against 14.0 million), whilst turnout fell significantly, from 77.7 per cent to 71.3 per cent. Labour's vote rose by two million; that for the Tories fell by 4.4 million. By social group, the largest swings to Labour were amongst group C1 (professional, management and clerical) with 19 per cent, followed by group C2 (skilled manual workers, foremen and the self-employed) at 15 per cent. Amongst home owners the swing to Labour was 11 per cent and trade unionists 7 per cent.

Labour went into the election with a clear commitment not to increase taxation or national insurance rates and with none of the spending pledges it had made in 1992. The consequence was that it was able to assemble an electoral coalition of the mass of the working class, its privileged layers and the middle class, whilst assuring the ruling class that it would guarantee its interests. In 1987, Labour won only 35 per cent of the C2 vote, but could only increase it to 40 per cent in 1992. In 1997, it got 54 per cent whilst the Tories' share was a mere 25 per cent (40 per cent in 1992). In 1997, 47 per cent of the C1 vote went to Labour; in 1992 it was mere 28 per cent. The Tories' share fell from 48 per cent to 26 per cent. Labour's share of the home-owner vote was also greater than that of the Tories: 41 per cent as against 35 per cent. The swings among C1 and C2 voters were reflected in the increased number of seats that Labour won in London and the South East where there is a higher proportion of such voters: up from 37 to 88.

Overwhelmingly, the election was a media event mainly of interest to the middle class. In 17 inner-city constituencies, most of which had a substantial black population, turnout was less than 60 per cent; in Liverpool Riverside it was as low as 51.7 per cent. For nearly half the electorate in these poor working class constituencies, the election was an irrelevancy, and they showed it by not participating. *Socialist Worker* just before the election claimed that 'The Tories remain the party of big business and bosses', proving how out of touch with reality the SWP had become. Labour was now the preferred party of the ruling class.

PART SEVEN

Labour in government 1997–2010

Labour came to office with a completely reactionary programme. Its record over the next 13 years was to be one of unceasing war, racism and oppression. By the time it went down to a deserved defeat in the 2010 general election, it had been jointly responsible with the US for the deaths of tens of thousands of Afghan people and hundreds of thousands of Iraqis. Its neo-liberal economic programme had given full rein to the City of London, the banks and financial services and had combined it with relentless social authoritarianism. Reduced taxation on big business went hand-in-hand with a continuous programme of privatising state assets and services, especially in health and education. Alongside this Labour implemented a thoroughly punitive programme of state repression against black people, the working class and poor. Its legacy included seven Acts of Parliament on terrorism, six on asylum and immigration and seven on policing and crime, creating over 4,000 new criminal offences. Throughout, the opportunist left worked to prevent the development of any effective opposition, and to the very end called for a Labour vote despite its commitment to deepen its assault on the working class and cut public spending by £70 billion.

7.1 *Britain under Labour – parasitic and decaying capitalism*

On its arrival in office in 1997, Labour lost no time in demonstrating its commitment to British imperialism and its ruling class by handing control of the Bank of England to the City of London. Links with the multinationals were quickly forged at every level with leading industrialists and financiers appointed to serve in government and on advisory committees. In the first year corporation tax was cut to its lowest ever level. Average pay for top executives rose by 18 per cent. In less than three years under Labour the number of millionaires was to reach 74,000, more than double the 1995 figure. At the same time Labour launched its attack on the working class. Benefits were cut and plans laid to force unemployed workers into low-paid jobs. All the Tory repressive employment and anti-trade union legislation was retained. Public spending was cut even below Tory levels.

Labour's economic strategy was to consolidate and extend the City of London's position as the world's leading financial centre. Until the 2008 financial crisis, this was to be the foundation for British capitalism's stability and development and, with it, the material basis for the continued affluence of large sections of the middle class and labour aristocracy. Over a period of ten years, Britain's overseas assets grew from £1,976.5 billion in 1997 to a staggering £6,486.5 billion in 2007, 4.7 times its GDP, with 'other investments', predominantly bank loans and deposits by UK banks, 2.74 times GDP – a gigantic usury capital.[1] Two consequences followed. First, the Labour Government had to ensure that British imperialism maintained a close military alliance with the US in order to protect these expanding worldwide interests. Second, a steady increase in real earnings – an average of 10 per cent over this period for the mass of the working class and petit bourgeoisie, and more for higher earners – ensured social and political stability.

The parasitic features of British capitalism continued to drive changes in the make-up and structure of the British working class. The vast majority of workers are now employed in the services sector with financial and business services becoming more prominent. While not all service sector jobs are unproductive, there has been a massive

1. David Yaffe, 'Britain: Parasitic and decaying capitalism', *Fight Racism! Fight Imperialism!* No 194, December 2006/January 2007.

redistribution of labour from the productive to unproductive sectors. Between 1997 and 2010, the number of manufacturing jobs fell from 4.5 million to just over 2.8 million at the end of 2009, the lowest since records began in 1841. Jobs in finance and business services had increased from 5.0 million to 6.4 million, having peaked at 6.7 million at the end of 2007. By this time, manufacturing and industrial output was barely higher than it was when Labour came into power ten years earlier; business and financial services output measured in terms of gross value added had risen by 67 per cent.

Economic policy and public spending

Having handed over control of interest rates to the City, Labour during its first government catered further to the demands of the financial sector by putting in place policies to slash the public sector deficit and reduce the ratio of public debt to national income. Cuts in public spending were even more vicious than those that the Tories had planned. In the first three years of Labour Government this 'fiscal tightening' totalled £40 billion. By 1999/2000 Labour had a massive current budget surplus of £17 billion, which was augmented by a £20 billion windfall from the sale of licences to mobile phone companies. Rather than tackle the appalling state of public services, however, Labour chose to pay off £34 billion of the national debt and then cut corporate and capital gains taxes to the point where Chancellor Gordon Brown could boast in a speech to the British Chamber of Commerce on 5 April 2000 that: 'Britain now has both the lowest corporate tax rates for business ever and the lowest ever capital gains tax for long-term investors'.

For the middle classes Labour stuck to its promise not to raise income tax levels throughout its first term. Tax incentives worth £10 billion a year on pensions, savings and investment schemes were maintained and their limits extended. A new scheme to allow employees and managers to buy shares in their companies on very generous terms was introduced. The threshold for inheritance tax was repeatedly upgraded so that 97 per cent of estates became exempt.

By the end of Labour's first term in office in 2001 the decline in public services was threatening Labour's middle class supporters: those who expected decent health and education because they could not afford to pay privately. Millions of them failed to turn out in the 2001 election. Labour addressed this in the 2002 budget by promising an extra £40 billion per annum for health over five years; an average annual increase of 7.4 per cent. There was also to be a tiny increase in public investment. To pay for these, Labour made a 1 per cent rise in National Insurance contributions but refused to increase income tax – a move that once again proportionately favoured the rich at the expense of the poor.

Privatising Britain

Labour continued the privatisation of public assets and services initiated by the Tories. With most of the major British utilities already privatised by 1997, Labour found another way for private capital to exploit the public services: the massive expansion of the Private Finance Initiative (PFI) begun under the Tories. PFI enables private firms to construct public buildings such as schools, hospitals, clinics and prisons and then lease them back to the public sector. Leases typically last for 20 to 30 years at guaranteed high rates and with low risk because they are underwritten by the government. Such security gives construction firms the added bonus of low rates of finance. The public services concerned, however, face massive charges throughout the period of the lease. By September 2009 over 900 PFI projects worth £72 billion had been signed; nearly 150 of these were in the NHS where they accounted for almost 90 per cent of capital investment since 1997. In mid-2008 there were 107 PFI projects in education involving 845 schools and Labour's plan was to use PFI for half its *Building Schools for the Future* programme. Projected PFI fees for 2006/7 were £6.3 billion and set to rise every year until at least 2012/13.

Privatising health care

Labour's initial commitment to stick to Tory spending plans on the NHS effectively meant cuts in services as the health budget requires annual increases above inflation just to stand still due to such costs as new technology and drugs. By the end of 1999 hospital patients were waiting on trolleys for beds to become available, intensive care patients had to be transferred from hospital to hospital to find ITU space, elective surgery had all but come to a standstill and NHS Trusts were £500 million in debt. The NHS was in crisis. Even Labour peer and doctor Lord Winston was moved to say: 'We haven't been told the truth and I'm afraid there will come a time when it will be impossible to disguise the inequality of the health service from the general population'. An emergency bail-out of £1 billion at the beginning of 2000 staved off complete collapse, but Labour knew it would have to maintain an adequate free health service for those of its middle class and wealthier working class voters who could not afford private health care if it were to retain their electoral support.

Labour's response was to increase substantially NHS funding, but to ensure that it was accompanied by an accelerated privatisation programme, despite the fact that privatised health care is both inefficient and much more expensive because profits have to be added to the basic cost of a nationalised system. From 2001, there were real-term increases in NHS funding of between 5.3 per cent and 8.9 per cent each year for the following seven years. This raised health spending from 6.6 per cent of GDP to around the European average of 8.2 per cent in 2007/08. However, much of this increase went into paying the extra costs of PFI projects or supporting the extra bureaucracy required to manage the internal market that Labour developed under the 2000 NHS Plan. By 2008 the extra annual cost of private finance for these projects was estimated at £480 million, and had resulted in cuts of 25 per cent in clinical staff and a 30 per cent reduction in the number of beds. A study in *Public Money and Management* in April 2008 showed that the extra annual costs of the first 12 hospital PFI projects were £60 million, 25 per cent of the hospital trusts' income.[2] In London, 20 PFI hospital building schemes

2. Jean Shaoul, Anne Stafford and Pam Stapleton, *The Cost of Using Private Finance to Build, Finance and Operate Hospitals*, *Public Money & Management*, Vol 28, No 2, (April 2008), pp101–108.

costing £2.6 billion would require repayments of £16.7 billion, more than six times the basic cost; the annual cost of £250 million in 2009 will rise to more than £400 million in 2014.

Having maintained the division between service providers and purchasers established by the Tories, Labour set up Primary Care Trusts (PCTs) to become purchasers of hospital care and contractors of GP services and then in 2005 established the system of 'payment by results' which fixed tariffs for just about all non-emergency operations, enabling them to be bought from any hospital or clinic, public or private. Armies of managers and accountants have to run the system, and as a result administrative costs came to represent 12 per cent of the total NHS budget, compared to 6 per cent in 1991 before the introduction of the internal market.

A further step in privatisation involved the establishment of so-called Independent Sector Treatment Centres. By 2008 it was evident that the whole programme had been an expensive fiasco: there was little evidence that the contracts, worth a total of £5.6 billion, had delivered any extra capacity to the NHS as claimed by the Government; it was thought that in 2006 they contributed far fewer than the expected 170,000 procedures a year when the NHS was as a whole carrying out 5.6 million.[3]

In 2008 the Department of Health (DoH) accelerated the process of privatisation, extending the tariff system to community services and opening up a market to private providers worth £15 billion a year. PCTs had to 'divest' themselves of these services by April 2010. The DoH also established a review of the NHS property portfolio with the aim of selling off up to £20 billion worth of NHS premises and leasing them back from the private sector. It also established an appeals panel which would ensure that the private sector was not 'disadvantaged' in competing for NHS contracts and required any new or 'significantly changed' service to be put out to tender. In a sop to the middle class, a DoH review changed regulations on

3. Stewart Player and Colin Leys, *Confuse and conceal: The NHS and Independent Sector Treatment Centres*, Merlin Press, 2008.

co-payments to allow those who could afford it to purchase non-NHS approved drugs without losing their right to free NHS treatment.

Privatising education

Labour's elite education

Labour's education policy mirrored that for health. It wanted to provide space for private capital, yet had to try and ensure decent schooling for those of their supporters who could not afford private education. That concern did not extend to working class children.

Labour retained the full panoply of Britain's elite education system – the private schools, grammar schools where they still existed and church schools. Not only did it encourage the use of PFI, it allowed private businesses to take over educational and ancillary services such as exam boards, supply teacher and training agencies, careers offices, LEA administrative services, school cleaning and meals, etc. Labour introduced new means for private firms to be involved in the management of schools such as Educational Action Zones (EAZs). EAZs were pyramids of local schools, managed privately, that were exempt from national norms on pay and conditions and from having to teach the National Curriculum. They were run by companies such as Shell in Lambeth and the telecom company Comcast in Middlesborough.

No matter what means or methods Labour tried, educational standards, as measured by test results, refused to rise significantly above a plateau achieved shortly after Labour came to office. 'Naming and shaming', league tables, putting schools in special measures, parachuting in superheads, the Fresh Start programme, imprisoning parents of truanting children, threatening teachers, performance-related pay, EAZs, Beacon Schools etc, all failed to have a significant overall impact on standards in Britain's schools. After a short period of decline the number of pupil exclusions rose to record levels. Every day 50,000 children truanted from school. Of course, Labour would never admit that it was the very elitism they were defending, the class society, poverty and inequality they were maintaining, that sustained educational failure. When a report by Peter Robinson from the Centre for Economic Performance concluded that 'Over the long-run the most powerful "educational" policy is arguably one which tackles child poverty, rather than any modest interventions in schooling',[4] David Blunkett, then Secretary of State for Education, dismissed the whole report as 'claptrap'.

Education, education, selection

Alongside its doomed attempts to raise 'educational standards' across the board, Labour tried to find ways of differentiating within the system. It hoped some schools would escape from being what Labour ministers insultingly described as 'bog standard comprehensives'. It wanted centres of excellence that would provide more privileged places for the middle classes and ultimately prove attractive areas for private investment. Its first step was to set up specialist secondary schools that could select 15 per cent of pupils by ability in the specialism. Then it introduced City Academies, autonomous schools with their own budget independent of local authorities; in effect the same as the Tory direct grant schools that Labour had abandoned on coming to office. City Academies were able to select 15 per cent of their pupils by 'aptitude'; the euphemism used in the 1940s to justify 11-plus selection. City Academies could be potent targets for private take-over. Private industry, however, requires economies of scale if it is to get widely involved in school management. Sure enough, in 2005 Labour unveiled plans to greatly expand City Academies, creating the possibility of a major new source of privatisation while satisfying middle class educational demands at the same time. For an investment of £2 million, sponsors got a school with buildings worth anything up to £50 million. They contributed nothing to the school's annual running costs, yet they would manage the school's resources, choose its teachers, and decide its curriculum. Lord Harris of Harris carpeting owned six such academies by early 2008; one of his first

4. Quoted in Jim Craven, 'Labour's education fails the test', *Fight Racism! Fight Imperialism!* No 140, December 1997/January 1998.

steps had been to reduce paid maternity leave for teachers by half. Another sponsor, Sir Peter Vardy, owner of a second-hand car business who sponsored three academies, was a fundamentalist Christian and decided that his schools would teach creationism.

Pricing the working class out of higher education

Labour had fewer problems developing a market within the higher education sector. Universities were already used to getting much of their funding from the private sector through research services and joint projects with multinationals. The Government enabled them to make courses a commodity too by introducing student tuition fees. Initially set at £1,000, Labour later raised them to £3,000, allowing universities to adjust the price of courses according to popularity. The elite universities, where 50 per cent of students come from private schools, would be able to charge the highest fees. The Government also cut back student maintenance grants. The middle class of Blair's generation had enjoyed free university education but Labour's funding changes meant that students would complete their courses with debts of up to £25,000. For the middle class this was a debt deferred, to be repaid when future earnings reached a certain level. For the working class the new charges meant that even more would be deterred from going to university. The extension of higher education in the previous 10 years had already mainly benefited the middle classes. A smaller proportion of students came from working class backgrounds than in the 1960s.

Privatising housing

Labour's commitment to private provision spelled the end of decent and affordable housing for the working class. Under Labour the collapse in council house provision continued. Between 1981 and 1997 1.4 million council tenants bought their homes and under Labour they were joined by 500,000 more; Labour transferred a further million council homes to housing associations or 'arm's length management organisations'. There are now only just over two million council homes left. Labour built hardly any: in 2006 there were just

277 new council houses constructed nationally – with only four in London. The number on the council house waiting list soared to 1.6 million, up 60 per cent from 1997. The decline in social and, in particular, council housing affects the poorest sections of the population: in 2005/06 the average gross income for social tenants was £12,200 compared to £28,850 for households across all tenures; median household income was £368 per week or £18,813 per annum. With the poverty line at £11,280, more than half of social housing tenants had an annual income of less than £10,000.[5]

Labour's response was to punish the poorest section of the working class. In February 2008 Housing Minister Caroline Flint suggested in a *Guardian* interview that unemployed people in council housing could risk losing their homes if they did not prove that they were looking for work. Housing should be seen as a privilege: new council tenants should have to sign 'commitment contracts' agreeing to look for work in order to be eligible; if they failed to show their commitment to finding a job and to the principle of 'something for something', they could lose their council homes. This punitive approach contrasted with the indulgence of Labour MPs when it came to declaring allowances for their own second homes in London.[6]

Making the poor pay

Labour continued to tie rises in pensions and benefits to the retail price index rather than average earnings, which meant that recipients had to remain in poverty. It retained Tory plans to cut one-parent family benefits and the Jobseekers Allowance (JSA), extending the waiting time for new JSA payments to seven days and imposing 100 per cent benefit sanctions for those who didn't comply with JSA

---

5. From *2006/07 Survey of English housing preliminary results*, quoted in Louis Brehoney, 'Back to the workhouse', *Fight Racism! Fight Imperialism!* No 202, April/May 2008. The full report, *Housing in England 2006/07* is at www.communities.gov.uk/documents/corporate/pdf/971061.pdf.

6. Mark Moncada, 'Defend council housing', *Fight Racism! Fight Imperialism!* No 206, December 2008/January 2009.

requirements. Later, Labour also threatened unemployed pregnant women, lone parents and long-term disabled people with benefit cuts for non-compliance. It cut Council Tax benefits to the poor living in larger homes and cut the back payment period for all benefits from 12 months to four weeks. It then set about harassing those on disability benefit. Within nine months of the election 10 per cent of claimants had had their benefit reduced. By 1999 Labour had cut £750 million from incapacity benefits.

In January 1998 Labour's 'New Deal' forced 18–25-year-old workers who had been unemployed for six months or more to lose benefits or agree to one of four options: either work in the private sector for six months (the employer was subsidised), or do some voluntary work, or work on an environmental task force, or take a training course. The New Deal was later extended to long-term unemployed workers of all ages.

To justify this regime Labour sustained a vicious ideological attack to stigmatise sections of the working class as lazy, feckless scroungers. It variously described benefit fraud as anywhere between £4 billion and £7 billion – in reality it was about £1 billion – but never mentioned the far greater level of tax fraud. Young single mothers were a regular target, being accused of irresponsibly having babies just to claim benefits. Travellers, rough sleepers and those with mental health problems were all attacked. Even before the 1997 election Jack Straw had wanted 'winos and squeegee merchants swept off the streets'. It was clearly intimated that many of those claiming unemployment benefit, sick pay or disability allowance were cheating the system. Bad parents, noisy neighbours, truants and their parents, young people wearing hoodies were all part of the problem. The allusion was clear. Anyone likely to cost the state money or upset the sentiments of the middle class belonged to an undeserving poor underclass. The 'deserving poor' were those willing or forced to accept the low-paid, menial, temporary and mind-numbing work that increasingly became the norm under Labour's rule. The 'deserving poor' were not rewarded but merely suffered fewer attacks than the 'undeserving'.

In 2006 Labour announced plans to force 1.7 million people off incapacity benefit and back into work in order to save £8.5 billion a year. In July 2007, under the guise of 're-igniting the jobs campaign', the then Work and Pensions Secretary Peter Hain announced that those on 'inactive' benefits – lone parents with children over seven, those on incapacity benefit, unemployed 16–24 year olds not in education would be cajoled, bullied or starved into employment. In January 2008 Hain was forced to resign for not declaring £100,000 of the £200,000 he raised in his spectacularly unsuccessful campaign to become deputy Labour leader, and was replaced by James Purnell.

Purnell lost no time in getting to grips with the poor, trailing a range of punitive workfare proposals in summer 2008 before publishing them in a White Paper in December 2008. This stated that in the future 'virtually everyone' claiming benefits would have to do something in return for their money. Purnell said that most people on incapacity benefit would be required to attend job interviews and the unemployed would be expected to do four weeks' full-time activity after a year out of work. Pilot schemes would require them to work full time for their benefits after two years. The only exceptions would be carers, unemployed parents of very young children and severely disabled people. Claiming that the policies were consistent with the principles of the 1945 Government, Purnell said:

> 'Today, when the national effort is about a global downturn, we can no more afford to waste taxpayers' money on those who play the system than they could then ... Some people say that we should be slowing down the pace of welfare reform because of the downturn. The government believes we should do the opposite.'[7]

The White Paper proposed that drug users would get a treatment allowance instead of unemployment benefit, and would have to show

7. J Purnell, speech to House of Commons introducing White Paper: *Raising expectations and increasing support: reforming welfare for the future* 10 December 2008, www.guardian.co.uk/politics/2008/dec/10/jamespurnell-welfare.

they were addressing their addiction to receive it. It drew on a 2007 review of benefits by former investment banker Sir David Freud which argued that voluntary and private sector organisations should be involved in claimant reviews and that lone parents should be required to seek work earlier – according to the White Paper, once their children were over one year old. Freud defected to the Tories six weeks after the publication of the White Paper in February 2009 and subsequently as Lord Freud became the ConDem coalition's Welfare Minister. The Bill became law in November 2009.

Punishing the poor was not just about limiting eligibility for benefits: it also meant reducing their level in comparison to poverty thresholds. Income support for 18-24 year olds fell from 52 per cent to 40 per cent of the poverty threshold between 1997/98 and 2008/09, and for a couple without children from 60 per cent to 46 per cent.[8] By 2009, JSA at £64.30 a week (£50.95 for the under-25s) had fallen by 25 per cent against average earnings since 1997, and stood at 10.5 per cent of average earnings. This was half what unemployment benefit had been on average from its introduction in 1912 until 1979 when the Tories cut its link to average earnings and tied it to inflation.

A corollary was that inequality consistently increased during the years of the Labour Government. Between 1996/97 and 2007/08, the income share of the poorest 20 per cent fell from 5.9 per cent to 5.3 per cent whilst that for the richest 20 per cent rose from 43.2 per cent to 45.6 per cent. The ratio of the income share of the richest to the poorest 20 per cent rose from 7.3:1 to 8.7:1. While there were reductions in poverty, these were limited and had started to reverse by 2004/05. The number living in poverty (defined as below 60 per cent of median household income after housing costs) in 1979 was 7.9 million; by 1997, it had risen to 14 million. Although it fell in the

---

8. J Hills, T Sefton and K Stewart (eds), *Towards a more equal society?: Poverty, inequality and policy since 1997*, Policy Press 2009, p30 cited in Robert Clough, 'Labour presides over worsening poverty and inequality', *Fight Racism! Fight Imperialism!* No 209, June/July 2009.

early years of the Labour Government, by 2008 it was back up to 13.5 million and growing.[9]

Pensioners fared better: 29.1 per cent were living in poverty in 1996/97, and although this fell to 17.6 per cent in 2004/05, it then started to rise again, reaching 19 per cent in 2008. Improvements for children were far more limited: although the proportion living in poverty fell from 34.1 per cent in 1996/97 to 28.4 per cent in 2004/05, by 2007/08 it had returned to 31 per cent when there were 4.0 million children living in poverty compared to 2.1 million in 1979. Of those, nearly half lived in persistent poverty (defined as being below the poverty line in three out of four successive years). Labour failed to meet its initial target – reducing child poverty by 25 per cent by 2004/05 – by a considerable distance, and never came near its second target – halving child poverty by 2010.

Merging government and big business

Labour's economic programme involved welding together government and big business to provide optimum conditions for the ruling class, a process which started immediately after its 1997 victory. Lord Sainsbury became Science Minister, Lord Simon from BP advised on trade policies and Martin Taylor, Chief Executive of Barclays Bank, advised on tax and benefits, David Edwards from Nat West was appointed Director of Oftel, Sir Colin Marshall of BA became head of the taskforce on saving energy in industry and Sir Peter Davis of Prudential advised on 'Welfare to Work'. Altogether, business representatives filled 90 per cent of both the Department of Trade and Industry and Treasury taskforces. By 2004 over 35 per cent of the places on the 320 or so taskforces were filled by representatives of big business. Labour also seconded staff from the multinationals to work in government offices. Among companies with staff at the DTI were BP, Tarmac, Kvaerner, Shell and BT. Arms manufacturers British Aerospace, Rolls Royce and Vickers all had staff at the Ministry of

9. *ibid.*

Defence. BP paid for staff to work at the British Embassy in Washington and at the Foreign Office Middle East desk.

The credentials of such people seem farcical if you consider their role to be one of disinterested and balanced judgment, but perfectly logical when you understand that their real role was to help Labour run the country in the interests of the City of London and the multinationals. Chris Fay, Chair of Shell UK, a company with a dreadful environmental record, which destroyed the lands of the Ogoni people in Nigeria by crude oil pollution, became Chair of the Advisory Committee on Business and the Environment in 1999. In the same year, Stephanie Monk, Human Resources Director of Granada Group, which sacked workers who went on strike after their pay was cut from £140 a week to £100, became a member of the Low Pay Commission and New Deal Task Force. Ewan Cameron, President of the Country Landowners Association and owner of 3,000 acres of land in Somerset, who fought against the Right to Roam, became Chair of the Countryside Agency with responsibility for implementing Right to Roam and for tackling social exclusion in rural areas.

Representation was particularly strong among the banks. In October 2008, Gordon Brown established a National Economic Council to tackle the financial crisis. Key members included Baroness Vadera, Minister for Economic Competitiveness and Small Businesses, who was employed at investment bank UBS, and who advised the Government on public-private partnerships. There was Treasury Secretary Lord Myners as well, formerly of Rothschild investment bank and Gartmore fund managers, who remained on the board of hedge fund GLG Partners. GLG made huge profits from 'short selling' shares in Bradford and Bingley which the Government was then forced to nationalise in September 2008. Advisors to the Council included former BP boss Lord Browne, Marcus Agius, chairman of Barclays, and Sir Victor Blank, chairman of Lloyds TSB.

The alliance between Labour and big business worked both ways. For a period, the Labour Party was increasingly bankrolled by the rich. Major subscribers to Party funds included Lord Sainsbury, Lord

Hamlyn, venture capitalist Sir Ronald Cohen, property developer Sir David Gerard, curry emperor Sir Gulam Noon, Chair of Allied Domecq Sir Gerry Robinson, Sir Frank Lowe, Sir Sigmund Sternberg, Robert Earl owner of Planet Hollywood and publisher Christopher Ondaatje. In 2005, Labour's receipts from wealthy individuals were four times those of the Tories. In addition big business sponsored Labour Party events and took expensive stands at the party conferences. Such companies included BSkyB, Pfizer, Aventis, Novartis, TESCO, Nestlé, Virgin, British Aerospace and McDonalds.

Labour sleaze

Such a state of affairs always provides opportunities for sleaze and corruption to flourish and it certainly did under Labour. Ministers and MPs ate, slept and drank with the rich, shared or wanted to share the same greedy lifestyle and possessed the same arrogant intolerance of anything that stood in their way.

In 1997 Labour introduced a bill banning tobacco advertising and sponsorship in sport. Formula One motor racing was the one sport exempt from the ban. At the beginning of the year, Vice-President of the Formula One Association, Bernie Ecclestone, had donated £1 million to the Labour Party. In the same month Lord Gavron was made a peer, he donated £500,000 to the Labour Party. Labour donors Dr Chris Evans, David Brown of Motorola and Ronald Cohen of Apax Partners were all knighted. Lord Drayson gave Labour £500,000 after receiving a peerage and another £100,000 while his pharmaceuticals company was bidding for a £32 million government contract. In 2006 the police opened an inquiry into Labour's cash for honours scandals. A close aid to Tony Blair was arrested for her alleged role in the affairs and Blair himself was interviewed by the police.

Multi-millionaire Labour MP Geoffrey Robinson was appointed Paymaster-General with responsibility for advising on tax avoidance despite having his own offshore slush fund and ongoing investigations into his business dealings with the crook Robert Maxwell. In 1998 the press revealed that Robinson had made an undeclared low-interest loan of £373,000 to Labour Trade and Industry Secretary Peter Mandelson for his luxury London home. Mandelson had said he was 'very relaxed about people getting filthy rich'. Both Robinson and Mandelson had to resign. However, it was not long before Mandelson was back in government as Northern Ireland Secretary. Two years later, in January 2001, he was found lying again; this time trying to hide his role in helping the millionaire Hinduja brothers, under investigation for corruption in India, to gain British passports. Mandelson resigned again but then returned to the Cabinet for a third time in October 2008 as an ennobled Business Secretary.

In 2005, the vindictively self-righteous David Blunkett had to resign twice for lying and deception, the first time because, as Home Secretary, he tried to cover up his attempt to fast-track the immigration application of his partner's house-maid. Later, after being brought back into government, he 'failed to disclose' the lucrative business interests he had taken while out of office.

Yet it went on. In early 2009 came a succession of revelations about claims that senior Labour figures had made for second homes in London:

- Home Secretary Jacqui Smith claimed such an allowance whilst living with her sister in London; her main home was in her Redditch constituency. It also emerged that she had put in a claim for an 88p plug and the rental by her husband of two 'adult' films;
- Employment minister Tom McNulty claimed £60,000 for his parents' house in Hammersmith (nine miles from his Harrow constituency) even though he had moved out in 2002;
- Hazel Blears 'flipped' her home three times in a year, made £45,000 profit in selling one of her second homes without paying capital gains tax, and claimed two TVs in one year on expenses.

Former Labour ministers proved adept at finding lucrative jobs in the private sector. Amongst eleven of them at the beginning of 2008 were:

- David Blunkett, who earned £25-30,000 a year from A4e, a training firm bidding for contracts under Labour's new welfare reforms;

- Former Health Secretary Patricia Hewitt, who was on a similar amount as an advisor to Boots;
- Alan Milburn, another former Health Minister, was an advisor to Lloydspharmacy and to Pepsico;
- Richard Caborn, a non-executive director of Nuclear Management Partnerships;
- Tony Blair himself, who was advising US investment bank JP Morgan, for reportedly as much as $5 million (£2.5 million) a year and who is now worth an estimated £20 million.[10]

7.2 *Imperialist war without end*

As Foreign Secretary Robin Cook was to explain, 'nowhere in the world is so far away that it is not relevant to our security interests'.[11] The Labour Government rode on the back of US military power in order to defend the strategic interests of the British ruling class and the global financial role of the City of London, and to elevate its global status relative to that of France and Germany. Britain's arms industry was the second most powerful in the world, with British Aerospace three times the size of the nearest European competitor. The British ruling class uses this military strength to compensate for its relative economic decline. 'Punching above our weight' is how Tory Foreign Minister Douglas Hurd once put it. Blair said 'Britain must retain its role as a global player' and that he was ready to 'pull the trigger' on a limited nuclear strike.

At a press conference on becoming Labour's first Foreign Secretary, Robin Cook famously declared:

> 'Britain will once again be a force for good in the world. Our foreign policy must have an ethical dimension ... Ethics will be at the heart of our policy ... The Labour Government will put human rights at the heart of our foreign policy.'

10. BBC report, 21 January 2008, http://news.bbc.co.uk/1/hi/uk_politics/7196420.stm.
11. Quoted in *Fight Racism! Fight Imperialism!* No 199, October/November 2007.

Yet this was to be mere hypocritical spin as Labour almost immediately sanctioned the delivery of Hawk fighter aircraft and arms to Indonesian forces that were brutally repressing the people of East Timor, as well as rifles and other equipment to the fascist regime in Turkey. From the outset, Labour continued RAF bombing patrols over Iraq and reinforced the economic blockade which, according to the World Health Organisation, had killed an estimated 1.5 million people. This was not enough for Labour. In the winter of 1997/98 it sent warships to the Gulf, threatening to launch a wider attack. A year later it ordered British planes to join a four-day bombardment of Iraq in which schools, homes and hospitals were hit and 200 civilians killed. Within two years of Labour's election the RAF had dropped more bombs than in the previous 18 years of Tory rule.

On 24 March 1999 forces from the US and several European countries, including RAF fighter-bombers and Royal Navy warships, under the banner of NATO, launched a series of massive air strikes against Yugoslavia. Over the following two months, using Cruise missiles, carpet bombing, cluster bombs and depleted uranium weapons, they systematically destroyed the country's industry and infrastructure. Nothing was allowed to get in the way. Railways, buses, hospitals, markets, schools, libraries, theatres, museums, even monasteries, were destroyed. Rivers and water supplies were polluted with fatal toxins. Thousands of refugees and other civilians were killed and injured. The killers described their victims as 'collateral damage'.

Labour exposed itself as the most virulent and militaristic partner in the NATO alliance with Prime Minister Tony Blair saying 'We will redouble and intensify our campaign. We will carry on pounding day after day'. Labour was the first to extend the aims of the campaign, the first to propose a ground invasion and the first to talk of a protectorate in Kosovo. Without a hint of irony, Clare Short, then Secretary of State for International Development, described anyone who opposed the war as 'fascist sympathisers'. Labour tried to justify the assault as a 'humanitarian' mission to put an end to the ethnic cleansing of Albanians in the Serbian region of Kosovo. However, when half a million Kosovan refugees were displaced by the war the

Labour Government allowed a mere trickle to come to Britain for publicity purposes.

When it was politically difficult to use British troops directly the Labour Government relied on private mercenary groups such as Sandline and Executive Outcomes in Sierra Leone and Papua New Guinea. In the case of Sierra Leone, Labour did eventually send in around 1,000 British troops to secure the diamond mines for De Beers and Anglo-American in May 2000. The Sierra Leone police were put under a British commander.

In Ireland, Labour manipulated the so-called peace process, suspending the Northern Ireland Assembly and inventing pretexts such as a 'spy ring' at Stormont to demand ever greater concessions from the Republican movement. Sinn Fein became tied in to the parliamentary process. The IRA was disarmed and Sinn Fein accepted British policing in the north of Ireland. Other Republican groups were isolated and Republican prisoners who refused to give up the struggle against British occupation of the north of Ireland were kept in prison. The Republican working class was abandoned and had to defend itself against escalating Loyalist attacks. It remained an excluded minority, having gained nothing of substance from Labour's manoeuvres.

Labour – US attack dog

Within a week of the attacks on the World Trade Centre and the Pentagon on 11 September 2001, Labour had readied 20 Royal Navy vessels on exercise in the Gulf to support the invasion of Afghanistan and had authorised US bombers to use the airbase on Diego Garcia. Blair went on a worldwide diplomatic offensive during which he flew 50,000 miles to encourage support for the 'war on terror' and deflect criticism of the United States so they were free to wage the war more effectively. Labour's role led Noam Chomsky to describe it as 'the attack dog' of the United States.[12] Between October 2001 and

12. See www.chomsky.info/talks/19990404.htm.

April 2002 over 22,000 bombs and missiles were dropped on Afghanistan. Aid agencies estimated at least 8,000 civilians had been killed by explosives and a further 20,000 from starvation and cold. Clare 'Bomber' Short opposed any break in the bombing to allow in humanitarian supplies while Blair justified it as an opportunity to end opium production. Eventually, when imperialist forces occupied the country, British troops formed the largest part of the International Security Assistance Force (ISAF) in Kabul and, in total, outnumbered US forces in Afghanistan.

The invasion of Afghanistan provided Labour with the occasion to sanction the use of torture. A new official policy was drawn up by senior government lawyers and security service chiefs and sanctioned at the highest levels of government. As Tony Blair put it, 'the rules of the game have changed'. The new guidance stated that, while agents must not be seen to condone torture, if detainees 'are not within our custody or control, the law does not require you to intervene'. Thus terrorism suspects were 'outsourced' to countries such as Pakistan, Morocco, Egypt and the United Arab Emirates to be tortured on behalf of the British security services and convicted on testimony extracted through torture. In March 2009 the United Nations found that Britain:

- Co-operated with the US rendition programme to places where detainees were likely to be tortured;
- Sent British intelligence officers to interview detainees being held incommunicado and tortured in Pakistan;
- Sent interrogators to Guantanamo Bay torture camp in an example of what 'can reasonably be understood as implicitly condoning torture and ill treatment'.

In its last months, the Labour Government tried to have the cases of seven men, including Binyam Mohamed and former Guantanamo Bay detainee Moazzam Begg, who were seeking damages for their extraordinary rendition and torture facilitated by British security services, to be heard entirely in secret. Home Secretary Alan Johnson described accusations of torture as 'baseless, groundless'; however, both were later to receive substantial compensation for their experience.

Within Afghanistan, the Taliban regrouped, and by 2006 controlled much of the country. As Britain committed more troops, the then Labour Defence Secretary John Reid said 'We would be perfectly happy to leave in three years and without firing one shot because our job is to protect the reconstruction.'[13] British General David Richards was given command of the NATO forces. They were engaged in what one officer described as 'the most intensive fighting British forces had seen since the Korean War'. But the indiscriminate killing of Afghan civilians by NATO forces, together with the corruption and ineffectiveness of the Afghan puppet government and security forces, meant resistance continued to grow. By 2007 the total number of casualties among British forces was greater than that in Iraq; in mid-2010 the number of deaths had reached 300, and the ConDem coalition was forced to withdraw troops from Sangin where 100 had been killed in the four years since Labour had sent them there.

The war on Iraq

A decision to invade Iraq was made at least as early as 2001; it was delayed only because the US and British Governments were wary of international isolation. They pursued a programme of threats, lies and deceit, much of which only came to light after the invasion. However, on 20 March 2002, Defence Secretary Geoff Hoon said 'I am absolutely confident, in the right conditions, we would be willing to use nuclear weapons'. At the United Nations in November 2002 Britain brokered a resolution (Resolution 1441) which stated that Iraq was in breach of the ceasefire terms following the 1991 Gulf War in relation to weapons of mass destruction, the construction of prohibited missiles and the purchase and import of prohibited armaments. It also stated that '... false statements or omissions in the declarations submitted by Iraq pursuant to this resolution and failure by Iraq at any time to comply with, and cooperate fully in the imple-

13. Quoted in Jim Craven, 'Resistance in Afghanistan cannot be contained', *Fight Racism! Fight Imperialism!* No 204, August/September 2008.

mentation of, this resolution shall constitute a further material breach of Iraq's obligations.' This gained the support of France, Germany, Russia and China. Those countries, however, claimed that a second UN resolution would be needed before an invasion could be sanctioned. The British Attorney-General Lord Goldsmith evidently agreed with them but his legal advice was reversed under pressure from the British and US Governments. As demanded by the resolution Iraq allowed in UN weapons inspectors. By 27 January 2003 Hans Blix, the Chief Inspector, was reporting that the Iraqis had 'co-operated rather well so far'.

It was apparent, however, that Britain and the United States had no intention of allowing anything so trivial as the truth to halt their imperialist war mongering. US Defence Secretary Donald Rumsfeld said that if no weapons of mass destruction were found 'it would (only) prove that the inspection process had been successfully defeated by the Iraqis'. Labour Chancellor Gordon Brown had already designated a £1 billion war chest. When Iraq issued a massive 12,000 page dossier detailing its weapons programme it was seized and expurgated by the United States with British complicity. The dossier contained details of the 17 British firms that had been supplying the Iraqis. The British Government issued documents claiming that Iraq was producing weapons of mass destruction. One, the work of Jack Straw and Labour spin doctors, alleged Iraq was smuggling uranium to make nuclear weapons and that Iraq had the ability to launch an attack within 45 minutes. It was a pack of lies. Another report had been cobbled together from a 10-year-old PhD thesis filched from the internet and speculative material from *Jane's Weekly*. At that time Labour emphasised that its aim was the destruction of weapons of mass destruction in Iraq, not regime change. Two years later, when finally it had to admit that no such weapons existed, it switched emphasis to the removal of the Saddam Hussein regime.

The true reason for the invasion, in line with the global strategy of US and British imperialism, was to ensure military domination of the Middle East and control of its oil and oil transhipment routes. It had the added bonus that Iraqi oil would be directly at their mercy. As

Labour Foreign Minister Jack Straw admitted to British Ambassadors, the invasion was a strategic priority 'to bolster the security of British and global energy supplies'. At the time, British Petroleum and Anglo-Dutch Shell were the second and third biggest oil companies in the world.

So, without further reference to the United Nations, Britain and the United States launched their invasion of Iraq on 19 March 2003. Their tactics, boasted US Joint Chief of Staff General Tommy Franks, 'will be a campaign unlike any other in history' designed to 'shock and awe' the enemy into quick submission by overwhelmingly brutal aerial bombardment and ground attack. Though the imperialist forces had occupied the country effectively enough for President Bush to announce the war complete by 1 May, resistance quickly emerged to the subsequent occupation.

British troops in Iraq employed the divide and rule tactics that had been well practised in policing imperialist interests in Ireland and around the globe. In Basra, they allowed collaborationist death squads to terrorise anyone suspected of sympathising with the resistance. Prisoners were tortured, humiliated and in some cases murdered by both US and British forces.

Supporting Zionist terror

Strategic control of the Middle East also drove Labour's uncritical defence of Zionist terror against the Palestinian people. Within days of the start of the Intifada on 28 September 2000, US Secretary of State Madeleine Albright spoke of stone-throwing Palestinians as 'laying siege to Israel'. When the UN Security Council condemned the Zionists' excessive use of force, the US abstained, as did Britain. Already by 6 October Arab governments were reported as incensed by the Labour Government's attitude; Blair had made no public comment and both Foreign Secretary Robin Cook and his deputy Peter Hain had pointedly refused to offer any criticism of Israel.

This was to be an oft-repeated tale. On 14 July 2006 Britain and the US ignored a Lebanese call at the UN for a ceasefire following Zionist bombing of Beirut and southern Lebanon; at a joint press conference with President Bush, Tony Blair said that Iran and Syria were backing 'extremists' who wanted to derail efforts to strengthen democracy in Lebanon and 'end the process that could lead to the two-state solution' in Palestine and gave his approval to Israel's military action. In June 2007, following the failure of a Fatah-led coup against the Hamas Government in Gaza, Labour supported the imposition of a total blockade on the Gaza strip. Then at the end of 2008, as the Zionists launched Operation Cast Lead against Gaza, Britain openly blocked efforts in the UN to call for a ceasefire, claiming that the proposed resolution did not place sufficient blame on the Palestinians. Former British ambassador Craig Murray stated that British diplomats on the UN Security Council were under direct instructions to offer 'tacit support' to the US's efforts to block a ceasefire, even whilst Gordon Brown 'appeased domestic horror at the Israeli massacre in Gaza by calling for a ceasefire'.[14]

7.3 *Ratcheting up repression*

Labour reinforced its economic and ideological attacks on the working class with a succession of punitive legal measures; it was to create more than 1,000 new imprisonable offences and 4,000 new criminal offences overall. The aim was to criminalise any resistance should it materialise. Underlining this, Blair announced 'the end of the 1960s social-liberal consensus on law and order.' Early legislation included the 1998 Crime and Disorder Act, creating Anti-Social Behaviour Orders (ASBOs), parenting orders and the power to impose curfews on young people even though they had not been charged with any offence. The Anti-Social Behaviour Act of 2003 increased the powers of the police and local councils. The Criminal Justice Act of the same year completely overhauled sentencing. It introduced compulsory life sentences or minimum sentences for over 150 offences. It broadened the powers of the prosecution to bring into evidence a defendant's

14. Quoted in Thomas Vincent, 'Labour friends of Zionism', *Fight Racism! Fight Imperialism!* No 207, February/March 2009.

convictions for previous offences and other misconduct, whilst imposing statutory restrictions, for the first time, on the ability of defence lawyers to cross-examine prosecution witnesses about their own criminal records.

The consequences were inevitable: the number of people in prison reached record levels, rising from 61,500 in June 1997 to 83,000 in June 2009 with the numbers projected to rise to perhaps 95,000 by 2015. The number of women in prison nearly doubled over the decade to 2008 when it stood at more than 4,500. In September 2008 Barnardo's reported that the number of children aged 10–14 being imprisoned in England and Wales rose by 550 per cent between 1996 and 2006;[15] only 7 per cent of those incarcerated had been sentenced for 'grave' or 'serious' crimes. The figure was the third highest in Europe, behind Russia and Ukraine. Not that Labour was shamed by these appalling figures: in October 2008, Jack Straw as Justice Secretary said 'We should not shy from the fact that the sentences of the court are first and foremost for the punishment of those who have broken the law, broken society's rules.'

'Anti-terror' legislation

Labour started its 'war on terror' early. In 1998 the Criminal Justice (Terrorism and Conspiracy) Act was passed by Parliament in just one night when it was recalled after the Omagh bombing. For the first time it allowed the prosecution of anyone in Britain accused of conspiring to commit offences in another country. People could be convicted for membership of an 'illegal' organisation simply on the word of any police officer of superintendent rank or above. Two years later the government replaced the old Prevention of Terrorism Act (PTA), which officially was a temporary measure that had to be reviewed each year, with a new permanent Terrorism Act that extended the provisions of the PTA to domestic as well as Irish and international terrorism and to matters of ideology and religion as well

15. Barnardos press release, 22 September 2008, www.barnardos.org.uk/news_and_events/media_centre/press_releases.htm?ref=40745.

as politics. It introduced a new offence of 'inciting terrorist acts abroad from Britain'. Effectively, the state now had the power to arrest anyone they wished simply by categorising their beliefs as 'terrorist'.

At the beginning of 2001, using the new powers introduced in 2000, Labour Home Secretary Jack Straw proscribed a long list of organisations. They included the Kurdish Workers Party (PKK), the Tamil Tigers, the Basque organisation ETA, the Turkish communist group DHKP-C, the Lebanese Hezbollah and the Palestinian organisations Hamas and Islamic Jihad. Hamas remains banned despite it being the legitimate elected government of the Palestinian Authority. The Act's section 44 provisions allowed police to stop and search anyone in a designated area; the whole of London became such a designated area. In 2009 there were nearly 149,000 stop and searches, overwhelmingly against Muslims; in 2008 only one in a thousand such stops had resulted in a charge under any Terrorism Act.

Taking advantage of the attack on the World Trade Centre in September 2001, Labour rushed through the Anti-Terrorism Crime and Security Act in December 2001. This act reintroduced internment, allowing the state to detain without trial any foreign national it suspected might commit 'terrorist' acts in the future or even those who had 'links' to someone who was a member of a 'terrorist' organisation. A dozen such people were held under appalling conditions in top security prisons until the Law Lords finally agreed the measures had gone too far. Labour then simply used 'control orders' and house arrest in place of detention without effectively changing the nature of the legislation and extended its provisions so that they applied to British citizens as well.

In 2005 Labour introduced yet another Terrorism Bill that made it an offence to prepare or encourage terrorist acts; undertake or be present at terrorist training; disseminate terrorist publications or even 'glorify terrorism'. The Labour Government wanted suspects to be detained for up to 90 days without charge. It was forced to settle for 28 days in Labour's first parliamentary defeat, but this was still twice the previous limit. However, Labour was never content with the result: in 2008 it introduced a Counter-Terrorism Bill, its sixth piece of 'anti-terrorism' legislation since 2000, which sought to extend the maximum period of detention to 42 days. Although able to secure the proposed change through the House of Commons, the House of Lords defeated the measure, as well as a measure in the same Bill to allow the government to authorise the holding of inquests in secret.

Widening the net

Terror legislation was but one part of Labour's battery of repressive legislation. In its first two years in power Labour issued almost 70 per cent more gagging orders than the Tories had in the previous two years. A so-called Freedom of Information Act in 2000 was more restrictive than the previous conditions. It prevented the disclosure of information 'which would prejudice the effective government of public affairs' and 'commercially sensitive' information which together could be used to block just about anything the Government wished to hide.

Labour was also keen to extend the surveillance powers of the state, introducing the Regulation of Investigatory Powers Act in 2000. The Act allowed police and secret services to intercept anyone's e-mails or the details of their internet use. MI5 was given direct access to internet service providers. Local councils became enthusiastic users of its powers. In July 2002 Labour introduced its first plans for compulsory identification cards. A draft bill was introduced in 2005 that also included the provision for fingerprints to be included in passports and driving licences. In 2006, the Identity Cards Act was finally passed; independent estimates placed the cost of its implementation at £12–15 billion.

The Police Reform Act of 2002 gave the police even greater powers to co-ordinate information gathering including personal details from databases such as the NHS. It also allowed them to retain DNA samples. In 2006 the police admitted they were holding DNA samples from thousands of children who had never been charged or convicted of an offence. By the beginning of 2009, the national DNA database included five million entries, of which 1.1 million were children and over 850,000 of which had been taken from people subsequently found innocent. When in 2008 the European Court condemned the retention of samples from innocent people, Home Secretary Jacqui Smith simply ignored the three month deadline to comply with its ruling that such samples should be destroyed.

If all else failed, the 2005 Civil Contingencies Act gave the state unprecedented powers to control areas, deploy troops, ban gatherings and disregard the law. It was a blank cheque to define anything as an emergency in order to impose martial law.

Racism

With imperialism devastating the globe with bloody wars and economic exploitation, more and more displaced people from oppressed countries have been forced to seek refuge. At the beginning of Labour's period in office British capitalism had little need of their cheap labour since the Government was busy forcing the poorest sections of the British working class into low-paid work. Very quickly the new Labour Government set about cutting immigration and attacking asylum seekers. The 1999 Asylum and Immigration Act made it more difficult for people to enter the country, restricted their rights of appeal and made deportation easier. Immigration officers were given extended powers to arrest, detain, search and seize property and documents. Asylum seekers were cruelly dispersed around the country with no choice as to their destination. Food vouchers replaced state benefits.

Still people were so desperate to try and avoid poverty and persecution that they were willing to risk their lives to enter and work in Britain. In June 2000, 58 Chinese workers suffocated in a lorry carrying them to Dover. In February 2004, 21 Chinese cockle-pickers drowned in Morecambe Bay having braved bad weather conditions in order to avoid the racist attacks they were enduring daily. Immigrant workers and asylum seekers had to endure repeated vilification stirred up by Labour's hostile attitudes. Britain is the only European country to hold asylum seekers in criminal prisons. Others are held in detention centres that are no better than prisons.

For the rich, skilled and professional middle class migrants, however, the situation was very different. Labour welcomed and encouraged their immigration. British capitalism needed their money and their skills that had been achieved without expense for the British state. Another exception was made for workers from the former socialist countries which had joined the EU. Their willingness to take on all the worst and lowest paid jobs, often under illegal conditions and below the minimum wage, was a boon to industries such as agriculture, packaging and hotels. They were tolerated because they were white, likely to earn money and return home, whereas asylum seekers threatened to stay in Britain and possibly become a burden on the state.

Labour accompanied its attacks with racist rhetoric and scaremongering. In April 2002 Home Secretary David Blunkett spoke of asylum seekers 'swamping' local schools. Such ideological attacks on asylum seekers extended to other immigrant workers. Blunkett described young Asians who had defended themselves against police and fascist attacks in Bradford in 2001 as 'maniacs' and wrote that bilingualism was akin to schizophrenia. He attacked arranged marriages and immigrants who fail to adopt British 'norms of acceptability' and introduced an immigration snoopers' hotline while further restricting the right to appeal against the refusal of asylum.

In 2002 Blair promised to send gunships to stop migrants reaching Britain unless the EU agreed to threaten the withdrawal of aid to make countries such as Turkey and the former Yugoslavia prevent asylum seekers reaching the EU. When two 12 and 13 year old Afghan brothers escaped from a detention camp in July 2002 in Australia and walked 600 miles across the outback to seek refuge at the British consul in Melbourne, Labour Foreign Secretary Jack Straw ordered that they be returned to the Australian police.

The 2002 Nationality, Immigration and Asylum Act denied benefits to any refugee who didn't make a claim for asylum immediately on entering the country. It also introduced a test of knowledge and a 'patriotic' ceremony for those applying for British citizenship. In 2004 another Asylum and Immigration Act weakened still further the right to appeal and asylum seekers' rights to housing and benefits. Yet another Immigration and Asylum Bill published in 2005 proposed that asylum seekers should have just one chance to appeal, and that, if that appeal failed, all their benefits would be stopped and their children taken into care. Refugees who had lodged their initial claim for asylum in any so-called 'safe' country would be immediately returned there.

A further step in restricting immigration was the introduction of the points-based system for immigrant labour in February 2008. This was not the end of the stream of legislation: in January 2009 the Government introduced a Borders, Citizenship and Immigration Bill which merged customs and immigration, and which presented a series of hurdles for immigrants seeking British citizenship, and promised a further Bill later in the year.

Labour shed crocodile tears over such publicised racist events as the murder of black teenager Stephen Lawrence but racist attacks and the deaths of black people in police custody continued. In 2004 a series of reports demonstrated that there was no change to the racism within the police force, the armed services, prison service, the NHS, in education and in employment. A rising black and Asian middle class was conscripted within the Labour Party to help divert dissent among the radical youth into official channels. It was the poorest sections of the ethnic minorities that suffered the brunt of Labour's racist society. For instance, people of Caribbean, Bangladeshi and African origin are twice as likely to be out of work as white people. Black pupils are three times as likely as white pupils to be excluded from school. Young back adults are seven times as likely as their white counterparts to be in prison.

7.4 *Where was the opposition?*

Apart from a brief period in the lead-up to the war on Iraq, this most repressive and brutal of governments faced no significant opposition to its relentless onslaught on the poor and oppressed. The trade unions never had any intention of rocking the boat, playing a vital role in ensuring that there was no significant working class opposition. Unwilling to risk their financial position, they refused to confront the anti-trade union laws that Labour inherited from the Tories and kept in place. Time and again the trade unions undermined working class struggles: the Liverpool dockers, the Tameside care workers and SkyChef workers were early casualties of their commitment to Labour. In two successive years, 2003 and 2004, trade unions helped defeat motions at the Labour Party conference which opposed the occupation of Iraq.

Overall, the number of days lost through industrial action from 1997 reached historic lows, averaging 600,000 days per year during the life of the Labour Government. This was not surprising since the bulk of union membership was drawn from better-off public sector workers who benefited most from the increases in public spending after 2001. At the end of 2007, when the median wage for full-time workers was £457 per week, approximately 4.5 million or 60 per cent of all trade unionists were earning between £500 and£999 per week. This was nearly ten times the number of trade unionists in full-time employment who were earning less than £250 per week.[16] More than half of all trade unionists, 52.7 per cent, were either managers, professionals or associate professionals (41.9 per cent for all employees).

In conditions where trade union wealth had expanded significantly – at the end of 2008 the ten largest TUC affiliated unions had an annual income of £600 million and gross assets worth £614 million in property and shareholdings – and where they were paying their general secretaries six-figure salaries, there was no incentive for unions to act as fighting organisations of the working class or jeopardise their position by confronting the anti-trade union laws.

The opportunist left was equally ineffectual whether inside or outside the Labour Party. When it came to the war on Yugoslavia, only 13 Labour MPs out of 445 voted against the onslaught, of whom nine were drawn from the 44-strong Campaign group. Ken Livingstone, aspiring London mayor, voted in favour. The left variously

16. Robert Clough, 'The state of the unions' in *Fight Racism! Fight Imperialism!* No 208, April/May 2009.

described the war as NATO's or US imperialism's, never Labour's, and characterised Blair as a 'fellow traveller of US imperialism', Clinton's 'American factotum' or a 'cheer leader of US imperialism.' This enabled it to minimise the culpability of the Labour Government, the Labour Party or those who refused to break from the Labour Party when in fact Labour was the most virulent and militaristic partner in the NATO alliance. Hence *Socialist Worker* described the stand of MPs who voted against the war as 'courageous' when it was anything but.[17] Two years later, the Labour left could muster only 11 MPs to object to the Afghanistan campaign; from within the cabinet, Clare Short defended the use of carpet bombing.

Following the 2001 invasion of Afghanistan, the SWP established the Stop the War campaign (STW) in alliance with Labour lefts, consciously eschewing any anti-imperialist content. From early 2002, as young Muslims started to mobilise in significant numbers, STW demonstrations grew larger and more militant. When divisions opened up between the major imperialist powers over a war on Iraq, splits also appeared within the British ruling class. These created conditions for a huge demonstration on 15 February 2003 opposing the naked war preparation of the Labour Government. Having invited the pro-imperialist LibDem leader Charles Kennedy onto its platform, STW had nowhere to go once Parliament had voted in favour of the attack. The pass had been sold the previous year when STW luminaries appealed to Blair to commit to securing UN support.[18] Within Parliament, opposition to the war (supported by 140 MPs) was expressed in the most fawning terms: this House 'believes that the case for war against Iraq has not yet been established, especially given the absence of specific UN authorisation, but in the event hostilities do commence, pledges its total support for

---

17. Quoted in 'Labour: a party fit for imperialism' in *Fight Racism Fight Imperialism!* No 149, June/July 1999; in *Socialist Worker* 3 August 2002 Charlie Kimber was to refer again to Labour MPs 'courageously' voting against war, this time on Afghanistan.
18. Quoted in Bob Shepherd, 'Campaign to stop the war', *Fight Racism! Fight Imperialism!* No 172 April/May 2003.

the British forces engaged in the Middle East, expresses its admiration for their courage, skill and devotion to duty, and hopes that their tasks will be swiftly concluded with minimal casualties on all sides.'[19]

Although spontaneous actions took place as war broke out, most significantly those involving school children, the chance to create something lasting had gone. The SWP had squandered a historic opportunity. In November 2006 a mere 11 Labour MPs voted for an inquiry into the war; they were unable to force any vote after the parliamentary debate in January 2007, and in February 2009 Jack Straw refused to release any records of cabinet discussions on the lead-up to the war.

With little chance of building its forces through the trade unions, the opportunist left outside Labour adopted an electoral strategy, starting with the Socialist Alliance in 2001, moving on to the Respect Coalition in 2003 and then the Trade Unionist and Socialist Coalition (TUSC) in 2010. In Scotland there was the Scottish Socialist Party (SSP). Success was ephemeral: the election of six SSP candidates to the Scottish Parliament in 2003 depended on using second preference votes to avoid any direct challenge to Labour. By 2005 they had all lost their seats, and at the 2010 election both the SSP and its Solidarity split-off were consigned to electoral oblivion. It was much the same for the Socialist Alliance and Respect. Although George Galloway was elected as an MP in 2005, he lost his seat in the 2010 election, as did the majority of Respect councillors. TUSC candidates barely troubled the counters.

Where the opportunist left were not standing candidates they could be counted on to support Labour. In 2001, the SWP's mealy-mouthed slogan was 'Vote socialist where you can, vote Labour where you must.' The socialist candidates it supported came nowhere. In 2005 *Socialist Worker* told its readers 'to vote Respect and for those clearly opposed to the invasion and occupation of Iraq. Let's punish Blair and all those New Labour MPs who meekly trailed after him

19. *ibid.*
20. *Socialist Worker*, 30 April 2005.

into the lobby to vote for war and imperialism.'[20] In 2010 it campaigned through Unite Against Fascism in support of the reactionary and racist millionaire Margaret Hodge against BNP leader Nick Griffin and confirmed that it would once again 'vote Labour against the Tories where there is no serious left of Labour candidate.'[21]

7.5 *Conclusion*

Labour was defeated in the 2010 general election for two reasons: first, because the ruling class was not convinced that it would be able to contain possible trade union opposition to the spending cuts necessary to reduce the public deficit, and second, because it had lost the confidence of a large part of the skilled sections of the working class (the C2 social group, 1.5 million of whom deserted Labour) and sections of the C1 lower middle class. These social groups did not believe that Labour would be able to preserve their relatively privileged status in relation to poorer sections of the working class. Even though the Labour vote among AB voters – loosely, professionals and the better-off sections of the middle class often dependent on the state sector – held up, the electoral coalition that had given Labour victory in three successive general elections had broken down.

What drove C2 voters to abandon Labour was not actual proletarianisation, but the fear of it and the sense that Labour either would not or could not prevent it from happening because of its perceived policies on immigration. Post-election, therefore, Labour politicians explained their defeat by saying the Party had not been racist enough. Thus former immigration minister Liam Byrne said that Labour had nothing to offer 'aspirational families', adding that:

> 'When Gordon Brown and Tony Blair set out New Labour's principles, they put work, opportunity and aspiration centre-stage. We said: play by the rules and you'll get your reward. But today, too many families – working in retail, manufacturing, the

21. *Socialist Worker,* 13 February 2010.

> service sector, construction – feel they're working as hard as ever and just not getting on. They're not wrong. My research shows workers on between £20,000–30,000 a year have faced huge forces in our economy, squeezing pay packets and the cost of living for at least five years. That's why so many are so frustrated with welfare reform and immigration.'[22]

Another former immigration minister, Phil Woolas, complained that Labour did not sufficiently broadcast its policies of restricting immigrants' access to welfare benefits and social housing, or its withdrawal of welfare benefits from asylum seekers seeking indefinite leave to remain: in other words, Labour was adequately racist, just not sufficiently upfront about it. Meanwhile *The Guardian* reported that Ed Balls

> 'admits that on a host of issues – the minimum wage, tax credits, tuition fees, welfare eligibility, the education maintenance allowance – voters felt Labour appeared out of step ... Labour found itself on the wrong side of the immigration debate, and lost contact with a section of the semi-skilled working class. "We had people saying 'we work hard, and pay our taxes, but there are people who live near us, and are not working, and get more, where is the fairness in that?' ".'[23]

Similar views were expressed by other leadership contenders, David and Ed Miliband in particular. What an epitaph: this most reactionary of governments, in their view, had not been reactionary enough.

22. *The Guardian*, 14 May 2010.
23. *ibid*.

PART EIGHT

Towards the 2015 general election

Throughout this book, we have shown that the Labour Party is a racist, imperialist, anti-working class party, that it always has been, and always will be. Its purpose has been to defend the interests of the British ruling class, an entirely parasitic layer whose enormous wealth is obtained through the ruthless robbery of the rest of the world engineered by the City of London. Labour represents the interests not only of the ruling class but also of better-off sections of the working class – a labour aristocracy which at the turn of the 20th century was made up of skilled manual workers but now consists predominantly of university-educated public sector workers, as well as the trade union bureaucracy. A tiny proportion of the proceeds of the ruling class's global plunder is directed to providing this layer with material privileges to guarantee its allegiance to British imperialism. The labour aristocracy looks to the Labour Party to sustain this system of naked bribery.

We have argued that the primary purpose of every Labour government has been to serve the needs of British imperialism, and no one can seriously dispute that this was the case with the 1997-2010 Labour Government. Unending war, slavish adherence to the needs of the City of London, a legislative programme which introduced over 4,000 new criminal offences, the continuation of all the anti-trade union laws, persecution of asylum seekers; its record was one of unceasing brutality. This has not changed in the years of opposition since 2010. It has agreed with the ConDem coalition on the fundamentals of every major issue whether it is the attack on state welfare, privatisation of state services, immigration or foreign policy. With a general election looming in May 2015, however, its supporters are painting Labour in very different colours. Their concern is with their own self-interest, not with the mass of the working class who will be offered continued impoverishment and oppression.

This explains why Unite the Union general secretary Len McCluskey was prepared to stand reality on its head in telling the union's conference in June 2014: 'So let there be no doubt. Unite stands fully behind Labour and Ed Miliband in the increasingly radical agenda he has outlined. It is a people's agenda and this union will be proud to fight alongside Labour to secure it.' On the same day, Shadow Chancellor Ed Balls made any future Labour Government's position quite clear: 'I have said since 2012 there should be pay restraint in the public sector. We have to be committed to fiscal discipline.'[1] Who should we listen to, McCluskey or Balls? Only in April 2014 McCluskey had argued that if Labour supported a cautious 'austerity-lite' policy, it would lose at the general election and Unite might consider supporting a separate party 'representing the interests of ordinary people'. This was hot air: the trade unions have proved that they are not prepared to take on the ruling class. Cowering behind the anti-trade union laws, they are not prepared to sacrifice their positions of privilege and influence for the sake of the mass of the working class.

8.1 *A warmongering, imperialist party*

With the unravelling of the new world order that had been ushered in by the collapse of the Soviet Union, British imperialism has sought to defend its interests against potential rivals in alliance with the US. The ruling class will not tolerate for one moment a Labour government which was not equally committed to its worldwide aims.

1. *Daily Telegraph*, 30 June 2014.

However, it has never had reason for concern: from 1924 onwards, every Labour government enthusiastically defended the Empire, opposed colonial freedom, and waged countless wars against the oppressed. Nothing changed with decolonisation: Britain retained its global interests, and Labour governments continued to defend them. In their pursuit, the 1997 Labour Government was responsible for four wars – against Yugoslavia, Sierra Leone, Afghanistan and Iraq.

Although Labour leaders attempted to distance themselves from the Iraq war during the leadership election in 2010, their instinct is determinedly militaristic. In 2011, they supported the NATO onslaught on Libya, Ed Miliband telling Parliament 'it would be quite wrong given what is happening in Libya for us to stand by and do nothing.' The consequences have been disastrous for the Libyan people, with their country devastated by conflict between competing factions. In Parliament, Labour voted against unilateral intervention in Syria in August 2013 because the ruling class was split, and because there was massive opposition in the country. However, Miliband made it clear he would support military action against the Assad regime if it was endorsed by the UN.

Miliband stands full-square behind the ConDem coalition policy over Ukraine and sanctions against Russia. In Parliament on 1 September 2014 he unconditionally supported Prime Minister Cameron's aggressive stance:

> 'This continued Russian aggression must be met with a robust coordinated and united international response, which sends a clear signal to President Putin.'
>
> and asked
>
> 'Does the Prime Minister agree that now is the time for the EU to consider further sectoral sanctions, including in key areas such as defence, energy and financial services? Will he also tell us what plans will be put forward at the NATO summit [on 4/5 September] to provide support to Ukraine?'

Miliband also backed the July/August 2014 Zionist onslaught on

Gaza, telling the July 2014 Labour Party National Policy Forum:

> 'I have seen for myself the fear in Israel from the unjustified and appalling rocket attacks from Hamas in Gaza ... I defend Israel's right to defend itself against rocket attacks.'

There was of course no acknowledgement of the right of the Palestinian people to defend themselves against illegal occupation, blockade and terror. Telling Parliament that he 'deeply' regretted the loss of more than 2,000 Palestinian lives would only have had any meaning if he had demanded the immediate imposition of sanctions on the barbaric Zionist state. Israel is not Russia however: it remains a key player in imperialism's struggle to control the Middle East.

Miliband is even prepared to consider yet more repressive legislation than Cameron. During a parliamentary exchange in early September 2014 on measures to deal with what he called high risk terrorism cases 'where convictions in the courts cannot be achieved', he lamented the loss of powers to relocate suspects away from their communities that had been 'a central part of [Labour's] control orders'. He welcomed Cameron's recognition that the independent reviewer on terrorism regarded this as an inadequacy of their replacement, the Terrorism Prevention and Investigation Measures. For good measure he added that he supported proposals to seize passports from those suspected of involvement in the conflict in Syria, and proved willing to consider 'discretionary powers to exclude British nationals from the country'.

With the world made increasingly unstable by growing inter-imperialist rivalries, Labour is showing it continues to be a safe bet for a ruling class determined to preserve its global position. This was obvious in its opposition to Scottish independence. Labour's Alistair Darling as Chair of the Better Together Campaign led the opposition to independence: at stake was not just the imperialist Union, but 59 Scottish seats in Westminster, 40 of which are held by the Labour Paty. Losing these seats with an independent Scotland would make a Labour Westminster majority all but unattainable at a general election. When it seemed possible two weeks before the 18 September independence referendum that the Yes vote might win, the ruling class and Labour Party panicked. The pound and stock markets fell. Cameron cancelled Prime Minister's question time and rushed north to canvass for a No vote. He was joined by all the party leaders and 100 Labour MPs a week before the referendum. Banks threatened to transfer their headquarters south to London; the media, universally opposed to independence, spoke of massive price rises; 14 former defence chiefs declared that independence would lay Britain open to attack; Gordon Brown suggested that one million out of two million Scottish jobs would be lost. Whether the end result – rejection of independence by 55 per cent to 45 per cent – represents a real victory for Labour and the ruling class remains to be seen: there was evidence that for many young people and sections of the working class, a Yes vote also expressed rejection of austerity and the corruption of the ruling class and its Labour Party allies.

8.2 *Attacking the working class through austerity*

Ed Balls' commitment to 'fiscal discipline' is not new. Facing a worldwide crisis, the 1929-31 Labour Government attacked state spending by slashing civil service and teachers' pay as well as axing unemployment benefit, while the 1974-79 Labour cut state spending by 7.4% in a two-year period. Balls' position was always going to receive a ringing endorsement from Labour's Policy Forum: it defeated a proposal for Labour to drop its austerity policies by 125 votes to 14. The Party is committed to the ConDem coalition's spending plans for 2015/16. Balls' plans are not 'austerity-lite'. He told the Policy Forum that 'We will balance the books, deliver a surplus on the current budget and get the national debt falling as soon as possible in the next parliament.' This will be as devastating for the working class as it was in 1931: balancing the books means even deeper cuts. Throughout the life of the ConDem coalition Government, Labour councils have implemented swingeing cuts in jobs and services and willingly administered attacks on state welfare; not one has challenged the Government's austerity programme. Labour leaders could not bring themselves to support public sector workers when they took strike action on 10 July 2014 against an effective 20 per cent pay cut over the past four years.

The last Labour government acted first and foremost to protect the interests of the banks and the monopolies. If elected, Balls will continue this. Boasting that Labour 'started and supported successive cuts in corporation tax over the last 15 years', he is now against reducing it from 21 per cent to 20 per cent, but has pledged to keep it the lowest of all G7 countries. The drastic cuts in local government spending – 30 per cent since the ConDem coalition came to office, with the loss of 520,000 jobs – will not be reversed.

Balls' slavish devotion to the interests of the City of London is evident in his opposition to renationalising the railways. This was a swiftly-jettisoned pledge of the incoming Labour Government of 1997. Ed Balls has dismissed the proposal as 'ideological' when there is glaring evidence of the inefficiency and high cost of the current privatised and fragmented system. Since 1997 the government subsidy for the railway system has increased five-fold to £5.2 billion per annum, £136 per passenger, compared to £67 in France and £101 in Germany. Fares in the UK are 30 per cent higher than in France, Netherlands, Sweden and Switzerland. Operating costs are 40 per cent higher because of the fragmentation. Yet railway companies have still been able to extract £6.2 billion in profits and dividend payouts. Balls talks deceitfully of the need to develop a 'long-term investment policy' when the current franchise bidding system is anything but, as the Department of Transport shows in its current focus on seven-year deals. All that Labour will countenance is the possibility of the government participating in bids for franchises as and when they come up for renewal – the worst of all possible worlds but one which it hopes will keep the monopolies on side.

In 2009, Labour planned to slash £70 billion from state spending. In early 2010, Labour Chancellor Alistair Darling told the *Financial Times* that halving the public deficit in four years was 'non-negotiable'. Once the ConDem coalition announced its own accelerated programme of cuts, Shadow Secretary of State for Work and Pensions

Douglas Alexander proudly claimed that 'many of the government's current [welfare] reforms build on what [Labour] set in train.'[2] Labour, he said, would support cuts in housing benefit, reduced access to disability living allowance, temporary changes to the uprating of some benefits, and testing the availability for work of incapacity benefit claimants.

Attacking the ConDem Government's overall benefit cap of £26,000 per annum for being insufficiently stringent, Alexander's replacement Liam Byrne in July 2013 claimed that 'ministers have bodged the rules so the cap won't affect Britain's 4,000 largest families and it does nothing to stop people living a life on welfare.' 4,000 is a tiny proportion of all families receiving benefits, yet Byrne used them as a rod to beat all claimants. In his determination to be seen as hard on those he calls 'shirkers' he echoed the most vindictive and hate-filled attitudes of the tabloid press towards the poor. He was also repeating the prejudices that made the Labour Party oppose the movement of the unemployed in the 1930s.

Byrne's replacement, Rachel Reeves, prove to be no different. She explicitly agreed with the overall benefit cap. In October 2013, days after she became Shadow Secretary of State, she echoed the tabloid prejudice that being on benefits is a lifestyle choice:

> 'Nobody should be under any illusions that they are going to be able to live a life on benefits under a Labour government. If you can work you should be working, and under our compulsory jobs guarantee if you refuse that job you forgo your benefits, and that is really important ... We would be tougher [than the Conservatives]. If they don't take it [the offer of a job] they will forfeit their benefit ... we will not allow people to linger on benefits.'[3]

But Labour's solution – the Compulsory Jobs Guarantee – is no more than workfare under a different name. Under a future Labour Government, under-25s will be offered a job after one year of unem-

2. *The Guardian*, 9 November 2010.
3. *The Observer*, 12 October 2013.

ployment, over-25s after two years. It will require claimants to work a minimum of 25 hours a week for the minimum wage on pain of losing benefits. They will be worse off since they will have to pay for travel to work, and will lose Council Tax Support. In a further effort to show Labour as tougher than the Tories, Ed Miliband announced in June 2014 that a future Labour Government would stop JSA for 100,000 18-21 year olds and replace it with an allowance, means-tested according to parental income. However, a claimant would not be eligible for this allowance unless s/he had achieved a Level 3 qualification – thereby excluding 7 out of 10 in this age range. In addition, Labour will limit eligibility for the higher rate JSA of £71 a week by requiring claimants to have paid National Insurance for five years, instead of the current two.

As the 2015 general election approaches Labour will make much play about its intention to abolish the Bedroom Tax even though politically it is already a dead duck. However, on no other significant aspect of the ConDem coalition's attack on state welfare does Labour have any difference.

Labour is not to be trusted with the National Health Service. It has said that it will repeal the ConDem's Health and Social Care Act and stop the 'fast-track privatisation' of health services. Yet the last Labour Government prepared the ground for privatisation through the introduction of the internal market, its determined support for Private Finance Initiative funding of new hospitals, the establishment of Foundation Trusts and the introduction of Independent Sector Treatment Centres. Even as the Health and Social Care Bill wound its way through Parliament, Health Secretary Andrew Lansley constantly taunted his Labour opponents that he was only continuing along a path they had set. Labour had no answer: all it could argue was that Lansley was going too far, too fast.

The critical state of the NHS was revealed in a report by the Nuffield Trust in 2014. Into the red? A report on NHS finances which shows that 'One pound in every five spent by PCTs on community health services in 2012/13 was spent on care provided by independent sector providers, an increase of 34 per cent in one year alone.

Similarly, funding for independent sector mental health service providers increased by 15 per cent in real terms between 2011/12 and 2012/13 alone, while funding for NHS-provided mental health services decreased by 1 per cent.' These are contracts worth £3 billion a year which have to be added to the £1.6 billion being spent each year on privately-run hospital services. Labour will not give a commitment to terminate these contracts, or to stop new ones being agreed, or to put an end to PFI despite the huge burdens that they place on NHS finances, for fear of upsetting the multinational corporations or breaching EU laws on competitive tendering.

In September 2014, the King's Fund health service think tank warned that 'the next government will arrive in office with the NHS facing financial meltdown and social care in crisis.'[4] This situation is as much the outcome of the £20 billion savings plan imposed by the last Labour Government as it is a consequence of further privatisations. Annual NHS inflation runs at about 4 per cent – this is what is required to meet the cost of rising need, new drugs and treatment. Over the last three years NHS funding has stood still, further adding to the pressure on the service. Labour has refused to make any commitment to restore lost funding, has rejected income tax increases to cover the looming NHS deficit; Miliband's offer of £2.5 billion a year at the September 2014 Labour Party conference is a drop in the ocean compared to the loss of £20 billion.

Wherever we look, the story is the same. The 1997 Labour Government started the process of dismantling state education, marketising whatever service could be sold off. It set up the original academies programme which removed schools from the control of local education authorities and allowed them to set pay, terms and conditions for their employees. The programme has been massively expanded by the ConDem coalition, but Labour has reserved its criticism only for the lack of controls at some free schools. It is certainly not against the principle: Shadow Education Secretary Tristram Hunt has said 'I am in favour of parent-led academies which

4. *The Guardian*, 19 September 2014.

are going to be good parent-led academies. And we will keep the good free schools when we get into government.'[5]

Even Labour's much-vaunted promise to build 200,000 houses a year by 2020 turns out to be a damp squib. This is fewer than were built annually between 2004 and 2007, and nearly a third below the annual average achieved between 1931 and 1939 (see p131). There is no commitment for a minimum number of social housing properties, nor to end the so-called 'affordable rent' scheme whereby social landlords can charge up to 80 per cent of local market rents for new properties. In many places this pushes tenants on benefits through the overall benefit cap. As it is, social housing rents rose by 15 per cent between 2010 and 2013.[6] Labour's proposed rent controls policy for privately-rented accommodation allows a six-month probationary period on a tenancy during which landlords can evict tenants if they want to put up the rent. It certainly does not fit the Tory accusation that they would be akin to 'Venezuelan-type rent controls'.

8.3 *A racist party: playing the immigration card*

However, in order to win the general election, Labour also has to win back the support of better-off sections of the working class and middle class which it lost in 2010. It is these layers, ones which are facing proletarianisation as a result of the crisis, whom Labour leaders are addressing when they talk about the 'squeezed middle' or 'hard-working families'. It is to these layers that they are pitching their abject apologies about past immigration policy – not because of its brutal and ever-widening attacks on asylum seekers, but because too many migrant workers from Eastern Europe were let in to Britain. It was Gordon Brown who as prime minister spoke about 'British jobs for British workers' – allowing David Cameron to say that he had borrowed the slogan from the BNP. It was David Blunkett who accused children of asylum seekers of 'swamping' schools, and it was

5. *The Guardian* 13 October 2013.
6. *The Guardian* 18 March 2014.

Labour who locked them up in detention centres.

Now the constant refrain is that Labour was 'wrong when we dismissed people's concerns' on the subject; Shadow Home Secretary Yvette Cooper says the coalition Government 'is right to look at' so-called benefit tourism – although there is no evidence it exists. Tristram Hunt has blamed the failure of poor British white boys in school on uncontrolled immigration from Eastern Europe – again without a shred of evidence. Labour is prepared to pander to racist prejudice because unless it does this it will not win support from the most politically backward layers of the working class.

8.4 *No support for Labour*

Len McCluskey may be spearheading the campaign to promote Labour's election chances, but he will be joined by many others on the left. His ally in the People's Assembly, *Guardian* columnist and Labour Party member Owen Jones frets at Ed Balls' domination of Labour economic policy. When Balls said in 2012 that Labour would have to keep all the ConDem cuts, Jones wrote: 'Ed Balls' surrender is a political disaster. It offers vindication for the Tories' economic strategy, even as it is proven to fail'.[7]

Jones went on to argue that 'If a broad coalition of Labour activists and trade unions united around a coherent alternative and put concerted pressure on the leadership, this surrender can be stopped in its tracks.' Two and a half years later that has not happened, and it never could. The outcome of the Policy Forum shows the irrelevance of Jones' Labour activists for determining policy. The only thing to date that trade unions have stopped in its tracks is serious working class resistance. Where struggles have emerged, they have been small-scale and have had to fight Labour anyway: an example is the Focus E15 women's campaign for decent social housing in east London which has had to constantly battle the local Labour Newham council. McCluskey could not even bring himself to demand the repeal of the

7. *New Statesman* 15 January 2012.

anti-trade union laws in exchange for his support. It leaves Jones wishing pigs will fly: 'it will be a coherent and inspiring alternative that will deliver Labour electoral victory.'[8]

We cannot allow ourselves to be deceived by the wishful thinking of those determined to defend their privileges. Labour remains what it was when it was in government: a racist, imperialist anti-working class party. We have to oppose it.

8. *The Guardian* 30 June 2014.

APPENDIX

Lenin on 'the bourgeois labour party'

Theoretically, the left often attempts to justify its position on the Labour Party by referring to Lenin, particularly his speech on relations between the Communist Party and the Labour Party in 1920, when he argued that:

> 'Of course, for the most part the Labour Party consists of workers, but it does not logically follow from this that every workers' party which consists of workers is at the same time a "political workers' party"; that depends upon who leads it, upon the content of its activities and of its political tactics. Only the latter determines whether it is really a political proletarian party. From this point of view, which is the only correct point of view, the Labour Party is not a political workers' party but a thoroughly bourgeois party, because, although it consists of workers, it is led by reactionaries, and the worst reactionaries at that...'[1]

This is cited by the likes of Cliff and Gluckstein,[2] and Mark Harrison in *Permanent Revolution*,[3] to mention but two, who conclude that Lenin understood post-1918 social democratic parties such as Labour

1. VI Lenin, *British Labour and British Imperialism*, Lawrence and Wishart, 1969, p267. All page references in the appendix are to this volume).
2. Cliff and Gluckstein *op cit*, pp1-2).
3. M Harrison, *Permanent Revolution*, Autumn 1991, p6.

to be 'capitalist workers' parties' – parties with a working class base, but with a pro-capitalist leadership. Yet nowhere does Lenin ever refer to social democratic parties (let alone the Labour Party) as 'capitalist workers' parties'; in fact, he was at pains to point out how social democracy by definition was isolated from the mass of the working class, and the defection of these parties to the side of their own bourgeoisie on the outbreak of the First Imperialist War proved this. Lenin arrived at his definitive position in 1916, and expressed it most succinctly in his short pamphlet *Imperialism and the Split in Socialism*. He bases himself explicitly on Marx and Engels, developing their analysis to take account of the emergence of imperialism and inter-imperialist rivalries.

Hence he refers to Engels writing to Marx in 1881, where he states 'the worst type of British trade unions which allow themselves to be led by men who have been bought by the capitalists, or at least, are in their pay'. Engels also refers to Sorge in 1889 complaining that 'the most repulsive thing here is bourgeois "respectability" with which the workers have become thoroughly saturated', and later in March 1891, he refers to the skilled unions as 'rich and therefore cowardly'. Six months later, heralding the failure of the 1891 TUC to overturn the decision of Congress the previous year to campaign for an eight-hour day, he writes:

> 'The old unions, with the textile workers at their head, and the whole of the reactionary party among the workers, had exerted all their strength towards overthrowing the eight-hour decision of 1890. They came to grief ... and the bourgeois papers recognise the defeat of the bourgeois labour party.' (p144)

Lenin seizes on Engels' deliberate phrase 'bourgeois labour party', and uses it consistently from then on. Not 'capitalist workers' party' – which is a self-contradictory nonsense. When England's industrial monopoly and later its colonial monopoly came under challenge, conditions arose where every Great Power could 'bribe smaller strata of the "labour aristocracy."'

> 'Formerly a "bourgeois labour party", to use Engels' profound expression, could be formed only in one country, because it alone enjoyed a monopoly, and enjoyed it for a long period. Now the "bourgeois labour party" is inevitable and typical for all the imperialist countries.' (p146)

And, contrasting the opportunists to the increasingly oppressed masses, he continues

> 'the history of the labour movement will from now on inevitably develop as the history of the struggle between these two tendencies, for the first tendency [ie, of opportunism] is not accidental, it is "founded" on economics. The bourgeoisie has already begotten, nurtured, secured for itself "bourgeois labour parties" of social chauvinists in all countries ... The important thing is that the economic desertion of a stratum of the labour aristocracy to the side of the bourgeoisie has matured and become and accomplished fact.' (p146-7)

This split is irrevocable,

> 'The social chauvinist or (what is the same thing) the opportunist tendency can neither disappear nor "return" to the revolutionary proletariat.' (p148)

He concludes

> 'Engels draws a distinction between the "bourgeois labour party" of the old trade unions, a privileged minority, and the "great mass", the real majority. Engels appeals to the latter, which is not infected with "bourgeois respectability". This is the essence of Marxian tactics!' (p149)

and, driving the point home, states

> 'The fact is that "bourgeois labour parties", as a political phenomenon, have already been formed in all the advanced capitalist countries, and unless a determined ruthless struggle is conducted against these parties all along the line ... it is useless talking about

> the struggle against imperialism, about Marxism, or about the socialist labour movement.' (p148)

Lenin was absolutely insistent on the need to recognise the existence of the split within the working class, arguing, in some notes written in 1920, against those who spoke of the 'proletariat' as an undifferentiated whole, 'The new and material, the concrete is brushed aside, but they keep on talking about the "proletariat" in general', continuing:

> 'the proletariat, not in general, not in abstracto, but in the twentieth century, after the imperialist war, inevitably split from the upper stratum. Evasion of the concrete, deception by means of abstractions (dialectics versus eclecticism).' (p207)

In other words, to speak of the proletariat (or working class) in general is to use an empty abstraction since either term glosses over the existence of the split that imperialism has created in its ranks. But this is a closed book for the left.

The term 'capitalist workers' party' is an open concession to the view that Labour is (or was) in some way a working class political party. Hence Cliff and Gluckstein refer to the 'ultra-left insanity' of the CPGB when its 1928 Congress announced 'the Labour Party in 1928 has come out unmistakably as the third capitalist party'. Yet this is quite correct, Labour was the third capitalist party, and always had been. The CPGB argument was more fully developed in a pamphlet published prior to the 1929 general election entitled *Class against Class*. In it, they argued:

> 'The situation in 1929 is entirely different from that of the years prior to the General Strike and the Labour Government of 1924. In the years immediately after the war, the Labour Party, in spite of its anti-working class leaders, was forced by the pressure of the workers into action against the Tories and the Liberals, eg, threatened general strike against war on Russia, repudiation of the Versailles Treaty ... The Labour Party also had not yet become a closely-knit party with a single discipline. It was a federation ...

> offering facilities for criticism from within.'

However, the advent of the 1924 Labour Government had completely purged the Labour Party of any susceptibility to working class influence, and with it what remained of a federal structure. As the pamphlet concludes, the leadership had:

> 'tied the trade unions to the Tories and the Liberals under the banner of Mondism and transformed the Labour Party from a federal organisation to a single party with a capitalist programme under the banner of "Empire and Mondism".'[4]

Whatever the mistakes of the CPGB in this period, its characterisation of the Labour Party in the period of the 1929 general election was most certainly not one. It is in the same vein as Luxemburg's description of German Social-Democracy as 'a stinking corpse', which Lenin approvingly quoted.[5]

---

4. Quoted in N Branson and B Moore, *Labour-Communist Relations 1920-51*, Part 1, Our History Pamphlet, 1990 p50).
5. Quoted in VI Lenin, *The Proletarian Revolution and the Renegade Kautsky,* CW vol 28 Progress Publishers, 1965, p241)

Bibliography

General histories:

Ralph Miliband, *Parliamentary Socialism*, 2nd Edition, Merlin Press 1972.

David Coates, *The Labour Party and the Struggle for Socialism*, Cambridge University Press, 1975.

James Hinton, *Labour and Socialism, A history of the British Labour Movement 1867-1974*, Harvester Press, 1983.

Tony Cliff and Donny Gluckstein, *The Labour Party, A Marxist History*, Bookmarks, 1988.

John Callaghan, *Socialism in Britain*, Blackwell, 1990.

Francis Williams, *Fifty Years' March, A History of the Labour Party*, Odhams Press, 1948.

Herbert Tracey (ed), *The British Labour Party*, 3 vols, Caxton 1948. There is also a 1925 edition, *The Book of the Labour Party*.

Henry Pelling, *A Short History of the Labour Party*, 4th Edition, Macmillan, 1972.

GDH Cole and R Postgate, *The Common People*, Methuen, 1938.

AL Morton and G Tate, *The British Labour Movement*, Lawrence & Wishart, 1956.

Early history of the Labour Party and the economics of the period:

Philip Poirier, *The Advent of the Labour Party*, George Allen and Unwin, 1958.

Theodore Rothstein, *From Chartism to Labourism*, Lawrence and Wishart, 1983.

S Pierson, *Marxism and The Origins of British Socialism*, Cornell University, 1973.

Ross McKibbin, *The Evolution of the Labour Party 1910–1924*, Oxford University Press, 1974.

Bernard Porter, *Critics of Empire, British Radical Attitudes to Imperialism in Africa 1895-1914,* Macmillan, 1968.

VI Lenin, *British Labour and British Imperialism*, Lawrence and Wishart, 1969.

RM Fox, *The Class Struggle In Britain* (2 vols), Martin Lawrence, *ca* 1930.

EJ Hobsbawm, *Industry and Empire*, Pelican, 1969; also his *Age of Empire 1875–1914*, Sphere Books, 1989.

David Reed, 'Marx and Engels on The Labour Aristocracy, Opportunism and British Labour Movement', in *Fight Racism! Fight Imperialism!* No 27, March 1983.

Derek Aldcroft and Henry Richardson, *The British Economy 1870–1913*,

Macmillan, 1969.
Dan Nabudere, *The Political Economy of Imperialism*, Zed Press, 1978.
Jurgen Kuczynski, *Labour Conditions under Industrial Capitalism*, Frederick Muller, 1972.

On the Labour Party and British imperialism in particular:

David Reed, *Ireland, Key to the British Revolution*, Larkin Publications, 1984.
R Fox, *The Colonial Policy of British Imperialism*, Martin Lawrence, *ca* 1933.
R Palme Dutt, *India Today*, Left Book Club, 1940.
R Palme Dutt, *The Crisis of Britain and the British Empire*, Lawrence and Wishart, 1953.
Brian Lapping, *End of Empire*, Granada Publishing, 1985.
PS Gupta, *Imperialism and the British Labour Movement 1914-64*, Cambridge, 1975.
S McIntyre, I*mperialism and the British Labour Movement in the 1920s*, Communist Party 'Our History' Pamphlet 64, 1975.
George Padmore, *Africa, Britain's Third Empire*, Dennis Dobson, 1949.
USSR Academy of Sciences, *A History of Africa 1918-67*, Nauka Publishing House, Moscow, 1968.
Articles from *Fight Racism! Fight Imperialism!*:
No 29 (May 1983): The Labour Party and Zionism (Steve Palmer); No 30 (June 1983): The Labour Party and South Africa (Carol Brown); No 31 (August 1983): The Labour Party and Vietnam (Steve Palmer); No 32 (September 1983): The Labour Party and Kenya (Trevor Rayne and Eddie Abrahams); No 36 (February 1984): The Labour Party and Greece (Robert Clough); No 43 (October 1984): The Labour Party and South Yemen (Bill Hughes); No 99 (February/March 1991): The Labour Party and the Middle East (Robert Clough); No 103 (October/November 1991): The Labour Party and the Post-war Reconstruction of British Imperialism (Robert Clough)

On the economics of the post-war boom:

Paul Bullock and David Yaffe, Inflation, 'The Crisis and The Post War Boom', in *Revolutionary Communist* No 3/4, 1979.

On imperialism, racism and the split in the working class:

David Yaffe, (imperialism) 'National Oppression and the New Petit Bourgeoisie';
M Williams, S Palmer and G Clapton, (racism) 'Imperialism and the Working Class'; both in *Revolutionary Communist* No 9, 1979.
Manifesto of the Revolutionary Communist Group, Larkin Publications, 1984.

On the Labour Party and the working class from 1918:

Wal Hannington: *Unemployed Struggles*, Lawrence and Wishart 1977; *Ten Lean Years*, Left Book Club, 1940.

Richard Croucher, *We Refuse to Starve in Silence*, Lawrence and Wishart, 1987.
Noreen Branson and Margot Heinemann, *Britain in the 1930s*, Granada, 1973.
Kenneth Morgan, *Labour in Power 1945-51*, Oxford University Press, 1986.
Paul Foot, *The Politics of Harold Wilson*, Penguin, 1968.
DN Pritt, *The Labour Government 1945-51*, Lawrence and Wishart, 1963.
R Ovendale (ed), *The Foreign Policy of the Labour Governments 1945–51*, Leicester University Press, 1984.
David Reed and Olivia Adamson, *The Miners' Strike – People Versus State*, Larkin Publications, 1985.

On the imperialist crisis and war:

Eddie Abrahams (ed) *The new warlords: From the Gulf War to the recolonisation of the Middle East*, Larkin Publications 1994.
David Yaffe, 'The political economy of the middle class', review of Will Hutton *The State we're in*, *Fight Racism! Fight Imperialism!* No 124, April/May 1995.
David Yaffe, 'Globalisation: a redivision of the world by imperialism', *Fight Racism! Fight Imperialism!* No 131, June/July 1996.
Editorial, 'Yugoslavia: the shape of wars to come', *Fight Racism! Fight Imperialism!* No 148, April/May 1999.
Trevor Rayne, 'Imperialism out of Afghanistan', *Fight Racism! Fight Imperialism!* No 164, December 2001/January 2002.
Carol Brickley, 'Iraq: War for global domination', *Fight Racism! Fight Imperialism!* No 172, April/May 2003.
David Yaffe, 'Britain – parasitic and decaying capitalism', *Fight Racism! Fight Imperialism!* No 194, December 2006/January 2007.
David Yaffe, 'Desperate times – desperate measures', *Fight Racism! Fight Imperialism!* No 206, December 2008/January 2009.
David Yaffe, 'Capitalist crisis – no way out', *Fight Racism! Fight Imperialism!* No 208, April/May 2009.
Trevor Rayne, 'Imperialist hands off Libya', *Fight Racism! Fight Imperialism!* No 220, April/May 2011.

On the Labour Party and the trade unions:

Robert Clough, 'New Labour – old crap', *Fight Racism! Fight Imperialism!* No 125, June/July 1995.
Robert Clough, 'New Labour – Old Poor Law', *Fight Racism! Fight Imperialism!* No 128, August/September 1995.
Robert Clough, 'Labour – a rotten, racist history', a review of Mark Curtis: *The ambiguities of power – British foreign policy since 1945*, Zed Press, 1995, *Fight Racism! Fight Imperialism!* No 129 February/March 1996.
Robert Clough, 'Labour Party – 100 years of infamy', *Fight Racism! Fight Imperialism!* No 153, February/March 2000.
Robert Clough, 'The state of the unions', *Fight Racism! Fight Imperialism!* No

190, April/May 2006.
Robert Clough, 'The rise of New Labour', *Fight Racism! Fight Imperialism!* No 197, June/July 2007.
Robert Clough, 'Trade unions in Britain: unparalleled stagnation and decay', *Fight Racism! Fight Imperialism!* No 217, October/November 2010.

On Labour government policy:

Allyson Pollock, *NHS plc – the privatisation of our health care*, Verso, 2004.
Stewart Player and Colin Leys, *Confuse and conceal: The NHS and Independent Sector Treatment Centres*, Merlin Press 2008.
J Hills, T Sefton and K Stewart (eds) *Towards a more equal society? Poverty, inequality and policy since 1997*, Policy Press 2009.
Jim Craven, 'Labour's education fails the test', *Fight Racism! Fight Imperialism!* No 140, December 1997/January 2008.
Carol Brickley, 'Ten years of Labour – abuse of power', *Fight Racism! Fight Imperialism!* No 197, June/July 2007.
Hannah Caller and Robert Clough, 'New Labour – attacking our health', *Fight Racism! Fight Imperialism!* No 200, December 2007/January 2008.
Charles Chinweizu and Nicki Jameson, 'Immigration and the reserve army of labour', *Fight Racism! Fight Imperialism!* No 201, February/March 2008.
Robert Clough, 'Why is Labour privatising health?', *Fight Racism! Fight Imperialism!* No 182, December 2004/January 2005.
Louis Brehoney, 'Back to the workhouse', *Fight Racism! Fight Imperialism!* No 202, April/May 2008.
Robert Clough, 'Labour presides over worsening inequality', *Fight Racism! Fight Imperialism!* No 209, June/July 2009.
Nicki Jameson, 'Unequal Britain', *Fight Racism! Fight Imperialism!* No 218, December 2010/January 2011.

Other:

David Yaffe, 'The labour aristocracy and imperialism' in six parts from *Fight Racism! Fight Imperialism!* No 161, June/July 2001 to No 166, April/May 2002.
Robert Clough, 'General election – general fraud' *Fight Racism! Fight Imperialism!* No 214, April/May 2010.
David Yaffe, 'Coalition declares class war' *Fight Racism! Fight Imperialism!* No 216, August/September 2010.

All the cited *Fight Racism! Fight Imperialism!* articles are available on our website, www.revolutonarycommunist.org

Index